IRON ARM

Recent Titles in
Contributions in Military History
Series Editor: Thomas E. Griess

IRON ARM

The Mechanization of Mussolini's Army, 1920-1940

John Joseph Timothy Sweet

Contributions in Military History, Number 23

GREENWOOD PRESS
WESTPORT, CONNECTICUT • LONDON, ENGLAND

Library of Congress Cataloging in Publication Data

Sweet, John J. T.
    Iron arm.

    (Contributions in military history; no. 23
ISSN 0084-9251)
    Bibliography: p.
    Includes index.
    1. Italy. Esercito—History. 2. Mechanization,
Military. 3. Motorization, Military. 4. Tanks
(Military science)—Italy. I. Title. II. Series.
UA672.S93 355'.00945 79-6825
ISBN 0-313-22179-0 lib. bdg.

Library of Congress Catalog Card Number: 79-6825
ISBN: 0-313-22179-0
ISSN: 0084-9251

First published in 1980

Greenwood Press
A division of Congressional Information Service, Inc.
88 Post Road West, Westport, Connecticut 06881

Printed in the United States of America

10 9 8 7 6 5 4 3 2 1

BST
Cop.1

25.00

Contents

Illustrations

Figures

Maps

Maps

Preface

The most vigorously debated question of army policy during the interwar years has become one of the least considered in postwar military history. Throughout the period between the First and Second World Wars, the role of the tank on the battlefield was the subject of much discussion. Mechanization, the use of the tank as a decisive weapon in a war of maneuver, gradually displaced motorization, the integration of the tank into existing armies as a support weapon.

The successes of the German army in the early stages of the Second World War, coupled with its professed acceptance of mechanization, has dominated postwar historiography. Disregarding German superiority in equipment, planning, supply organization, and initiative, authors have advanced the acceptance of mechanization—in the form of the *blitzkrieg*—as the basis of German success. Following the lead of Liddell Hart and J.F.C. Fuller, who were radical advocates of mechanization in the interwar period, these authors have castigated those countries that did not accept mechanization as a policy. The idea of mechanization, in existence in varying forms since the early 1920s, had become the sine qua non of military thinking in the interwar period. Every nation should have accepted it.

This interpretation of the intellectual history of the most important military concept in the interwar period takes one idea completely out of the context of history and views it in the abstract. The social, political, and economic makeup of each society profoundly influenced the development of mechanization in its country. The acceptance of a very expensive and technical idea like mechanization required very specific support from the industrial and economic sectors.

By examining the development of mechanization in Italy against the background of the social, economic, and industrial realities, and comparing it with contemporary developments in other countries, I hope to demonstrate the importance of society in the acceptance of mechanization and its implementation. Additionally, the discussion of social influences on military development will, I hope, show the causes in Italian history of Italy's dolorous performance in the Second World War.

In preparing this study the lack of previous works on the subject required extensive archival research. As a result the assistance of the staffs of many archives was essential. In particular, I would like to thank Colonnello Rinaldo Cruccu, Capo Ufficio of the Ufficio Storico of the Italian Army General Staff, for the collaboration of his office. Colonnello Dottore Alberto Gennaro, Chief of the Third Section, and his assistant, Tenente Colonnello Guglielmo Manuguerra, head of the Archives Section, were of the utmost assistance in providing documents and working space during my stay in Rome. Tenente Alfredo Terrone and Tenente Ferdinando Frattolillo answered my every question and taught me a great deal about the Italian army that I could not have found elsewhere.

Also in Italy, Commendatore Augustino Constantino and Ragioniere Antonio Amabelli of the Centro Storico Fiat and Maggiore Adolfo di Leone of the Scuola Truppe Meccanizzate e Corazzate went to great lengths to assist me, as did Generale Manlio Timeus and his staff at the Museo Storico di Motorizzazione Militare. In England, Mr. P. H. Reed of the Imperial War Museum and Miss Mary Kendall, Librarian of St. Antony's College, Oxford, kindly assisted me with the Italian documents in their respective institutions.

In the United States, the list is much too long to mention everyone, but to single out only one of many, Professor Robin Higham's encouragement, assistance, and understanding ensured that this book would be completed. I can only hope that in some small way my study is worthy of their efforts.

J.J.T.S.

Manhattan, KS.
1 May 1976

John J. T. Sweet was killed on military duty, 12 March 1978.

Acknowledgments

Acknowledgment is gratefully given to the L'Ufficio Storico dello Stato Maggiore dell'Esercito, the Historical Office of the Italian Army General Staff for permission to reprint Figures 1 through 23 in this volume.

Note on Sources

Contemporary material on Italian armor policy—documents, official publications, and unofficial published material—all presented their own problems in research. Each of these sources felt the effects of the Second World War, but none so heavily as the documentary collections. The *Sezione Archivio* (Archives Section) of the *Ufficio Storico* (Historical Office) of the Italian army General Staff in Rome (referred to as U.S. in the notes) should be the repository of records of the army that are not at the originating unit, including the documents of the interwar period. However, the archives themselves were dispersed in the chaotic period after the Italian armistice in 1943. Much material still in the hands of units was destroyed by military action. As a result it is often impossible to identify the instigator or exact genesis of many actions.

Fortunately many documents have survived. In particular, the records of the various sections of the General Staff, reports on the annual maneuvers, and various miscellaneous collections provided substantial information. The *Ufficio Storico* contains the *Memorie Storiche,* the annual historical report that each unit in the army was required to prepare and submit annually. Although some reports have been lost, primarily during the war, the *Memorie Storiche* are the basic material for organizational history. The *Ufficio Storico* also contains an extensive collection of manuals and other published material. The *Biblioteca Centrale Militare,* under the Historical Office, also has extensive collections of military journals as well as information on books purchased in the interwar period, particularly the works of armor advocates.

There are two other collections of important documentary material. The collection of captured Italian documents (microfilm T-821) in the National Archives and Records Service at Washington (referred to as NA in the notes) has a most interesting history. After the Italian armistice, the Germans seized virtually all available records on the Second World War and related topics. Special teams sent railway carloads of Italian documents to an archive in Germany especially prepared for historical material on the war. The exact amount of material lost in this process is unknown, but at least one boxcarload definitely failed to survive the trip. This archive was then captured by the United States army and sent to Washington. It has now been microfilmed and the originals returned to the *Ufficio Storico*. This is an important collection for armor development since it includes the records of the *Armata Po* and the *Corpo d'Armata Corazzata,* and through them of the three armored divisions. Although nominally available in both Rome and Washington, the collection at the National Archives is easier to consult and without security restrictions.

The final important documentary collection I used is found in two locations. In 1945 and 1946, various British and American intelligence organizations established a unit in Rome to copy records of Mussolini's private office and other organizations, primarily the Ministry of Popular Culture. The material copied emphasized Italian intelligence and propaganda operations, especially agents and collaborators. The resultant copies were sent to the British Foreign Office and the United States State Department as well as being retained in Rome. The originals have disappeared.

The collection in the National Archives, on microfilm, contains some items not included in the British copy, at the Library of St. Antony's College, Oxford. However, the St. Antony's copy, on paper, is legible, while the American copy often is not. The collection (microfilm T-586) is important because it contains the Bitossi Papers, the collection of records, orders, and after-action reports assembled by Generale Gervasio Bitossi under the title *Frammenti di Una Esperienza Decennale di Guerra Motorizzata, 1933-1943.* Originally prepared in ten copies, this is the only known copy. It may have been sent to Mussolini although the actual provenance is unknown.

A final archival collection that proved useful was that of the United States Military Attaché at Rome. Located in the Navy and Old Army Branch of the National Archives, the attaché reports offer not so much factual information as indications of who and what were important. They paid particular attention to books and thinkers who were making an impression.

Italian industrial concerns proved a less fertile field. The heavy Allied bombing that disrupted tank production also destroyed the files at Fiat's Mirafiori plant. The *Centro Storico Fiat* does have a limited collection of records that illuminated the process of contracting for military production, but nothing specifically on tanks. Ansaldo, now a nuclear-engineering firm, had no remaining files.

Manuals of the period are difficult to track down. The *Ufficio Storico* has an extensive, but somewhat disorganized, collection, in which some armor manuals could not be found. However, the Library of Congress in Washington has a collection of captured manuals that contains the missing ones. Other official published material came from the library of the *Ufficio Storico.*

Unofficial published sources were collected from the attaché reports, notices of new books in various journals, and searching major professional journals. The *Rivista di Fanteria* proved most rewarding, since the tank units were part of the infantry branch. The *Rivista di Cavalleria* was disappointing because it was a veteran's journal. The majority of titles were found in the *Ufficio Storico* or the *Biblioteca Centrale.*

Among secondary sources, there is only one of any real importance, Angelo Pugnani, *Storia della Motorizzazione Militare Italiana,* published in 1951. Generale Pugnani had an unrivaled career in the Motor Transport Service, serving in key positions from the First World War to the Ethiopian war. His book, published fifteen years after his retirement, when the general was eighty-one, was based on his earlier *La Motorizzazione dell'Esercito e la Conquista dell'Etiopia.* Generale Pugnani, the leading advocate of motorization in the Italian army, viewed motorization as the ruling philosophy of the Italians.

All other specialist sources used *Motorizzazione Militare* as their base. There has been no one who went beyond Pugnani to look at the original materials. Those general English-language secondary works that are not based on Pugnani are often derived from Spanish Civil War material. Reporting on Italian armor in the Spanish Civil War and the early stages of World War II was often based on Republican propaganda of patent falsity. In consequence their view of Italian armor development tends to be overly pessimistic.

The most important general source on Italian military history in the

1920s and early 1930s is the *Enciclopedia Militare*. The encyclopedia is part of the Fascist era's renewed interest in the glory of Italian history, therefore the authors are often uncritical in their writing. However, it contains a very great deal of useful information and reflects army attitudes at a crucial time in the interwar period. Unfortunately, the articles are not signed.

The bibliography contains only those works consulted or cited in writing the text. A variety of other works discuss Italian tanks and armor operations but add nothing to understanding. There are no lists or bibliographies of books on this subject, although the *Ufficio Storico's Saggio Bibliographico sulla Seconda Guerra Mondiale* (Rome, 1955 to the present), essential to the study of Italian military history, covers many books on the topic.

The specific works consulted for this book are noted in the bibliography on page 199.

Glossary

Adowa (Adua): Italian defeat in Ethiopia, 1896

alpini: mountain troops of the Italian army

arditi: shock troops of the Italian army in World War I became a cult of popular heroes

Ariete: ram—traditional name of 132nd Armored Division

autarchia: autarky—Mussolini's campaign for economic independence in the 1930s

autoblindomitragliatrice: armored self-propelled machine gun, the Italian name for armored car

Badoglio, Maresciallo Pietro: Deputy Chief of Staff in World War I, Army Chief of Staff 1919-21, Chief of Defence Staff 1925-40

Baistrocchi, Generale Federico: Army Chief of Staff and Undersecretary Ministry of War, 1934-36

Bastico, Generale Ettore: general in Spain and first commander of Corpo d'Armata Corazzato, 1938-40

Berardi, Generale Paolo: artillery officer, writer on armor, later Army Chief of Staff 1943-45

bersaglieri: sharpshooters—light troops of the army, famous for their speed and courage

Bitossi, Gervasio: armor commander and author on armor topics. Commanded Reggimento Cavalleggeri Guide, 1° Reggimento Misto Motorizzato, and Divisione Corazzato *Littorio*

Cadorna, Generale Conte Luigi: Army Chief of Staff, 1914-17

Capo di Stato Maggiore dell'Esercito: army chief of staff, created 1882

Capo di Stato Maggiore Generale: chief of the defense staff, including all three services, created 1925

carri d'assalto: assault tanks—light tank in infantry tank unit, term used roughly 1920-37

carri di rottura: breakthrough tank—medium tank, term used roughly 1925-37

carristi: tankers—generic term for tank crewman, also used in singular to identify tank units (Fanteria Carrista)

carri veloci: fast tanks—light tank in cavalry unit, term used 1930-39

Carso: low limestone ridge forming major barrier along Italian-Yugoslav border

Cavallero, Generale Ugo: Undersecretary of War 1925-28, general manager, Ansaldo 1928-32, Chief of Defense Staff 1940-43

celeri: fast ones—the fast troops, cavalry and *bersaglieri,* especially when used together

Centauro: centaur—traditional name of the 131st Armored Division

ciclisti: cyclists—military cyclists in Italy, usually *bersaglieri*

circolari: circulars—changes in doctrine; normally published as circulars in the *Gazzetta Ufficiale* or *Giornale Militare Ufficiale*

Commissariato Generale Fabbricazioni di Guerra: General Commissariat for war production—controlling agency for raw materials and industrial production in wartime

Commissione Suprema di Difesa: Supreme Defense Commission—highest council on defense matters. Head of state and ministers with appropriate technical advisors

Corpo di Truppa Volontaria: Corps of Volunteer troops (CTV)—Italian force fighting for Nationalists in Spanish civil war, both Fascist militia and army troops were involved

Dall'Ora, Generale Fidenza: supply officer in Ethiopian war, first commander of Armored Army Corps after November 1938

Diaz, Armando, Duca della Vittoria: Army Chief of Staff 1917-19, Minister of War, 1922-24

direttive: directives—instructions establishing doctrine, normally published as a manual

Di Simone, Generale Carlo: armor commander, and author, commander Second Armored Brigade, 1937-38

divisione celere: fast division—division of cavalry and *bersaglieri* in equal parts between 1932-43, touted as an answer to the stalemate of World War I

Fabbriguerra: abbreviation for Commissariato Generale Fabbricazioni di Guerra

Gazzetta Ufficiale: official gazette—the official register of the Italian government, contained the most important military circulars

Giornale Militare Ufficiale: official military journal—the official register
of the army, in which circulars were published

Granatieri di Sardegna: Grenadiers of Sardinia—the elite guard infantry
of the Italian army

guerra di rapido corso: war of rapid course—the Italian version of the
blitzkrieg, a war of maneuver, announced in November 1938

ipotese: hypothesis—basic assumption on which Italian military planning
was based

Littorio: of the Lictor—traditional name of the 133rd Armored Division,
formerly the army infantry division in Spain

Maltese, Colonello Enrico: armor commander and author, commander,
Reparto Carri Armati, 1924-26

norme: norms or instructions on tactical doctrine, normally published as
a manual

ordinamento: ordinance or organization—the authorized strength of the
army, approved by the Parliament

Pariani, Generale Alberto: Army Chief of Staff, 1936-39, and Undersecretary of Ministry of War

piana di radunata: assembly plan—the assembly and operational plans of
the army, based on various *ipotese*

Pozzuolo del Friuli: greatest Italian cavalry battle of World War I, 1917

Pugnani, Generale Angelo: the foremost Italian armor writer, also Inspector
of Motorization, 1930-36

Quarra, Generale Edoardo: armor commander and author, commanded
Reggimento Carri Armati, 1933-36

reparti d'assalto: assault detachments—units of *arditi* or shock troops in
World War I

semovente: self-propelled gun on tank chassis

sottosegretario: undersecretary of an Italian government ministry. Under
Mussolini, the actual head and usually also chief of staff of each
service

Stato Maggiore: the general staff on any level of an armed service

Zoppi, Generale Ottavio: author, leading advocate of *celeri* concept. Also
Inspector of Alpine Troops, 1928-30; Inspector of Infantry, 1933-36

IRON ARM

1
Introduction

On the twenty-third of October, 1942, when the British 8th Army launched its decisive attack at El Alamein, four Axis armored divisions faced the onslaught. These veteran desert divisions, two German and two Italian, formed a mobile reserve on each flank of the Axis line. The German divisions have been much publicized. The Italians, given secondary roles by German commanders, have consequently often been ignored by historians. After the Germans had suffered substantial losses, the Italian units bore the brunt of the fighting and were virtually wiped out. While the destruction of two armored divisions was not a great loss for the Germans at this stage of the war, for Italy it meant the elimination of two-thirds of its armored force. And by the end of this battle the remaining Italian armored division, *Littorio*, was on its way from Albania to North Africa to reinforce the survivors.

The largest Axis armored forces in the North African campaign, both in number of vehicles and personnel, were these Italian armored divisions (*le divisioni corazzate Ariete, Centauro,* and *Littorio*). Although the German commanders often gave precedence to German divisions in operations, Italian units bore an equal share of the fighting. Even though equipped with inferior tanks, the *carristi* (tankers) fought the British and Americans until they were destroyed.[1]

At the same time, in Russia and the Balkans, three Italian cavalry divisions were contributing, in their own way, to Italian war efforts. These were the *divisioni celeri: Eugenio di Savoia, Emmanuele Filiberto Testa di Ferro,* and *Amadeo Duca D'Aosta.* The *celeri* (fast) divisions were a unique Italian military organization. They were integrated divisions of light troops with four cavalry battalions and three battalions of light infantry; there were also light tank battalions, but the majority of the mobile force was on horseback. This small number of tanks made the cavalry regiments little more effective than the horse-mechanized regiments the United States army maintained during this period, yet despite their antiquated organization the *celeri* divisions played a major part in the Italian campaigns in Russia and the Balkans.

In August 1942 the *Amadeo Duca d'Aosta* division fought a battle that stands in marked contrast to the massive armored might at El Alamein. On the morning of the twenty-fourth at the small Ukrainian village of Isbuschenskij, two horsed squadrons made *L'Ultima Carica,* the last cavalry charge, against a Russian infantry regiment.[2] The Italian cavalry, with sabers flashing, drove the machine-gun-equipped and entrenched Russians back and secured the objective, in total rejection of twentieth-century warfare.

These battles of the armored divisions and the *celeri* show the contrasts in the Italian army during World War II. The army attempted to modernize itself in the interwar period, but because of the problems of industrial and social development in Italy, failed. The army, through a process of logical development, attained an intellectual mastery of the concepts of modern war and the use of tanks, placing it on the level of that of Germany and Britain in the understanding of the nature of the next war. But modern war was total war in a new sense. No longer would the country with the most troops win, nor the country with the best general. Success in the Second World War, more than in any other, would depend on the economic and industrial capacity of the country. In this Italy failed. It was unable to provide the economic and industrial basis to build a modern mechanized army. The country fell short in the technological mastery of armored warfare, not in intellectual mastery, the understanding of the nature and concepts of armored warfare.

The development of armored warfare in Italy, as in any other country, consisted of a triad of factors. First was national policy: whether to have mechanization or motorization of the army. Mechanization was the restructuring of the army to use armored fighting vehicles as a major offensive weapon. Motorization was the use of motor vehicles to replace the horse or the man as a source of power but not substantially change the way of fighting. Second was doctrine, which in this context consists of the theoretical concept of the use of tanks, the organizational doctrine, and the training of tank units. The third factor was the equipment and manning of an effective force on the basis of the first two factors. In this crucial area technological mastery is essential. The determining factor is the ability of a society to provide not only the vehicles and equipment, but trained crews, support personnel, fuel, and continuous replacement of all these. A country's power in this area depends on whether or not the society as a whole is mechanized or motorized, whether the society has undergone the revolutionary changes produced by the motor vehicle or only used them to replace the more traditional means of transport without changing the patterns of life and labor. The mechanization of both an army and its society are founded on the basic nature of that society, the economic, social, political, and environmental factors that made it unique in the world.

The Italian army had, throughout the interwar period, an active program of research and development in armored policy. Consequently, Italy had created a large tank force by the mid-1930s. Mussolini's government used tanks extensively both in Ethiopia and in Spain. The General Staff established an armored corps in 1938, the first in the world. In the occupation of Albania during the spring of 1939 the *Centauro* Armored Division was the first such division in the world to be employed operationally.

At the time of the invasion of Albania, Italy was a major armored power. Britain had one active armored division, with two more planned for mobilization, and two independent brigades. France had two mechanized cavalry divisions. Germany was the leader with six divisions, the last three organized in 1938-39, at the same time as the Italian divisions. The United States, which would have the greatest armored force in the West at the end of the Second World War, had one mechanized cavalry brigade. Russia may have had as many as twenty-one brigades, but no divisions. The Russian brigades were controlled by seven mechanized corps, but they did not operate as integrated units like the Western armored divisions. Among her contemporaries, Italy was second only to a presumed friend, Germany. Italy by herself equaled her potential foes, Britain and France.[3]

The creation of Italian armored units and the factors that led to their ultimate failure present a microcosm of the history both of the Italian army in the twentieth century and of the history of technology and war. Beginning immediately after the First World War, the General Staff instituted a slow and careful program of development for tanks and tank units. Tanks were deployed to defensive positions within Italy by 1928. A program of tank construction begun in 1930 gave Italy the basis for much of its experimentation in the next ten years. Because of this program the army possessed a large number of vehicles, which while not effective, gave opportunity for large-unit maneuvers and observation of problems involved. In the Ethiopian war and later through Italian participation in the Spanish Civil War, the army acquired unequaled experience. This experience in the combat use of tanks was, in terms of the number of vehicles involved and their use with infantry troops of their own under their own commanders, something no other country had. The Italian army based its doctrine on an unrivaled familiarity with tank combat.

The Italians did, within the parameters of Italian defense and foreign policy, evolve a sophisticated armor program. This policy was founded on carefully evaluated experience and on standard assumptions about the character of any future war. The process by which this doctrine was achieved was slow and methodical. As a result a major armored force was developed in late 1938 and 1939. By 1939 the economy was badly strained by participation in the Spanish Civil War and by preparation for the impending Second World War, so improved vehicles could not be produced in sufficient time and numbers for modern warfare. Because of the weakness of Italian industry, Italy saw its substantial achievement in armored development swept away by the enormity of its defeat in World War II.

The development of armored policy in Italy was part of a worldwide movement. This radical new weapon, the tank, caused a major reappraisal of military doctrine. To understand the Italian situation, this universal trend must be understood. The struggle was between motorization, the conservative approach, and mechanization, the radical approach. Both sought to equip the preindustrial armies for the next war.

Preindustrial Armies

The story of the development of armored warfare in the period between the First and Second World Wars is that of the struggle to modernize the preindustrial armies of the nineteenth century. The tank, as a weapon, and the armored units had to create a place for themselves in the existing structure, which already had the battlefield divided into areas of responsibility. The older corps attempted to utilize the tank as an auxiliary to their action. More forward-looking soldiers wanted the tank as a distinct branch with its own role.

Prior to the First World War, armies were neatly divided into certain traditional branches or types of troops, the most notable of which were infantry, artillery, cavalry, and engineers.[4] There were also service and support troops, as well as specialties developing within the major branches, which would soon be important enough to demand autonomy. But on the field of battle the four basic types dominated, and their proportional size and representation among the general officers and staff of the army reflected this dominance.

Infantry was the main combat force. It consisted of the majority of the personnel before the proliferation of technical support. In the conscript armies of Europe, it was the arm through which a large number of young men passed in the course of a year, as they gained a semblance of military training.

From 1750 to 1850 the infantry spawned a number of offspring, such as grenadiers and riflemen; these speciality branches performed various subsidiary functions on the battlefield. The most notable were riflemen, or light infantry, first used in the middle of the eighteenth century.[5] They were select personnel, equipped with more precise arms than the average soldier, and trained in the utilization of terrain and rapid movement. Riflemen, in particular, used their rifles as accurate means of finding individual targets rather than as mass-fire weapons. The mobility and firepower of these units were their key features.

Mobility and firepower were also the characteristics of a late nineteenth-century innovation, the mounted infantry. Organized during the colonial wars, the mounted infantry gave increased mobility to ordinary foot soldiers.[6] Additional training, equipment, and so forth was required to increase the cavalry to adequate numbers for the mobile reaction forces required in many colonial situations. Mounted infantry produced these troops quickly by simply giving the infantry horses for mobility without the impedimenta of the cavalry. These colonial operations were to persist during the First World War. Mounted infantry continued to be used in a variety of formations and under many titles, as did the other specialized infantry, in name at least.

Despite the eighteenth- and nineteenth-century development of specialized infantry, by the end of the nineteenth century they had begun

to fade. The arrival of the machine gun and the abandonment of traditional tactics of line and column made the distinctions between types of
infantry solely those of tradition, uniform, ceremony, and music. The
tactical role was essentially the same for all infantry units: to fight its
opposite number in the enemy army. This required the lowest skill level
of any military duty and was ideal for the conscript armies of Europe.
A large infantry force could be trained in a limited time (in the year or
year and a half of the conscript's service). In theory, at least, a large pool
of men with the necessary skills could be on call for war mobilization to
fill cadre formations. The infantry used their relatively limited mobility
and firepower to maneuver against and defeat the enemy in close combat.
But the operational effectiveness and importance of the infantry was
mainly tactical. They had to defeat the enemy in a relatively small area
and the initial consequence of this victory would be tactical rather than
strategic.

On the western front in World War I this proved very much the case.
The firepower of automatic weapons, used on a wide scale for the first
time, made infantry tactics even more limited in scope and reduced all
combat to "set-piece" actions of precise planning and careful coordination. The only First World War innovation in infantry tactics was the
idea of shock or storm troops. This key feature, however, was a concept
rather than an organization.[7] Highly trained and motivated troops conducted audacious, small-unit operations designed to harass and interdict
enemy forces. In some ways this was a return to the light infantry of the
previous century. The new and rather uncharacteristic glorification of
individual initiative and prowess profoundly influenced some segments
of European society, particularly those who were to be involved in
fascism.[8] And it was the first recognition of the need for new troops to
break the stalemate of the trenches, the problem eventually solved by a
very different approach, the tank.

Basically the First World War was fought with the tactics of mass
infantry formations and combat between two similarly armed masses,
the traditional method of infantry combat. The great difference in the
First World War was the change in the roles of the two other battlefield
arms, the cavalry and the artillery. The cavalry had always been the
reconnaissance element. In the Napoleonic wars and earlier, the cavalry
had been divided according to battlefield roles; as a reconnaissance
force, as a counter to other cavalry units, or as a shock force against

infantry and artillery. When the increased firepower of infantry units in
the latter part of the nineteenth century reduced the possibility of successful cavalry attacks against defended locations, the reconnaissance and
exploitation role became the major tactical task.

There were secondary theaters in which the cavalry was able to play
a major role. In the Middle East large open areas and the weakness of
the opposing forces enabled it to operate without undue exposure to
intensive hostile fire. However, even in these areas, the cavalry role was
often little more than that of an elaborate mounted infantry. In the
principal western theaters of war, France and Italy, the cavalry had a
minor role. The Americans used only part of one cavalry regiment in the
entire war, and then as couriers. The only major employment of cavalry
was by the Italian army in the last portions of its operations against the
Austrians, when cavalry was used to exploit victories that had been gained
by the infantry.[9]

Cavalry, once the most prestigious of arms and the decider of battles,
had been downgraded, used only for reconnaissance and to exploit infantry success. In addition, the cavalry had suffered in the process of
universal conscription. It cost more in time, forage, and equipment to
train and maintain a cavalry trooper. As the bulk of the population moved
to the cities, fewer and fewer rural recruits proficient in horsemanship
entered from civilian life.[10] This combination of factors drove the cavalry
into a decline, aggravated by its performance in the First World War. The
cavalry dropped to third place in the military spectrum, behind infantry
and artillery.

Artillery, traditionally the most technical of arms, had greatly increased
in importance in the hundred years before the First World War. This en-
hancement was the result of technological advances that made the cannon
into a precision weapon capable of indirect fire. The ability to deliver
fire at a distance and with volume and effectiveness far superior to even
that of the American Civil War made artillery a decisive element. The
First World War, relying on heavy fortifications and set-piece frontal
attacks on these heavily defended positions, made artillery crucially
important. Britain and the United States converted a substantial part of
their cavalry to artillery, and artillery became second in importance to
infantry.[11]

The artillery had always been important and was generally regarded
as the intellectual branch, where much of the technical and scientific

knowledge in the army reposed. Most European armies had academies for the cadets of the different branches; that for artillery and engineers had a technical and generally highly regarded curriculum. The other taught infantry and cavalry cadets and was less technically demanding.[12] For example, Britain had Woolwich and Sandhurst, and Italy had Turin and Modena. This concept was often manifest in the type of student and the method of his recruitment. The sons of the new middle class competed for the positions at the technical academy, while the sons of the nobility were easily admitted to the infantry academy. This distinction in training and intelligence showed also in the promotion process.

Once royal favoritism began to decline in European armies, a long series of artillery officers, of whom Napoleon was the most outstanding, rose to high command. Their technical backgrounds and the increasing importance of the artillery tended to thrust them into the higher echelons of command.[13] The increasing importance of artillery, coupled with the increase in the sophistication, size, and amount of equipment needed in artillery units, led to a great increase in manpower in these units. This restructuring and shift in emphasis in European armies substantially reduced the mobile troops that could be used for maneuver. The struggle to fill this void pitted the resurgent cavalry against the new tank units. The debate over the policy that should be adopted on this question made up a major portion of the public controversy over the role of tanks.

In the years before the First World War, the other branches—engineers, transportation, supply, medical, and other corps—had undergone a general process of expansion. This was a result of the tremendous advances in the general level of knowledge, as well as in specific levels of military expertise, that occurred in the years before the war. But they all remained subordinate to the three main fighting branches. The only significant change that took place was the gradual and occasional introduction of motor vehicles. The use of automobiles often caused jurisdictional disputes, although the transportation branch of each army normally became the administrative organization for both vehicles and trained crews. The artillery ran a close second with their need for greater efficiency in moving their equipment. This was fundamentally the state of European armies in 1914. The tank would have to be integrated into this structure, or establish a new position for itself.

Motorization and Mechanization

The debate over policy in the interwar years centered on the competing concepts of mechanization and motorization. The more conservative approach, motorization, involved the use of motor vehicles in the traditional structure of preindustrial armies. The internal combustion engine was simply a source of power to replace horses and men. Mechanization was the radical reform of warfare. Motor vehicles, in particular the armored fighting vehicle, would be used to give greater mobility and firepower so that a war of maneuver could replace the wars of attrition. The adoption of mechanization would be a revolutionary change in military thinking.

As we have seen, previous changes had been minor. The introduction of light and mounted infantry and the shift in emphasis from the cavalry to artillery were limited in scope and impact on the army as a whole. But to deal with the machine gun required strong measures. The solution was the tank.

The machine gun was an understandable weapon. It was simply a crew-served, rifle-caliber, infantry arm that could be fitted into the established order of things without difficulty. There had been at various other times innovations in infantry, artillery, or cavalry tactics due to weaponry that produced major changes on the battlefield, but were easily assimilated.

The problems occurred when innovation was so radical that it could not be assimilated into the normal structure of the military. This was the case with the other new land weapon to make a major impression during the First World War, the tank.

Three aspects of the tank problem became the great points of contention in military strategy and organization in the 1920s and 1930s. First, who was to control the personnel? To what branch would they belong? The established branches struggled for additional manpower and for the promotional possibilities and budgetary advantages. The second problem was the tactical role of the new weapon. Each country's entire concept of the next war, and perception of its role in that war and in the postwar world in general influenced this decision. The third problem was technical; questions involving the various qualities that were desired, that is, what type of tank to produce and how many.[14]

Each of the three problem areas was interrelated, but a solution of each could be made independently. In many cases a choice was made without regard to a unified solution to the entire question. Such a solution would be either motorization or mechanization of the entire army. The climate of the period created or intensified many of the problems. Who would control the personnel may seem the easiest of questions, but it was to become one of the most difficult. The three combat arms had definite roles on the battlefield. The tank did not fit into any one of them. It had precision weapons that dealt with the enemy at long range like the artillery. It also had a petrol (gasoline) engine with which the artillery, of all the combat arms, was most familiar. But it moved and closed with the enemy, things that the artillery did not do. Many artillery men were involved in the early planning, and because of their technical expertise, continued to direct the technical development of the armored fighting vehicle. But the artillery was never a serious contender for complete control of the tank.

The infantry and the tank had a much closer affinity. The tank was designed for, used for, and successful in helping the infantry close with and destroy the enemy and his machine guns. The tank was employed in close coordination with the infantry in performing tasks assigned by the infantry under the overall command of the infantry commander. It engaged the enemy in the same manner as the infantry, at close range and with similar weapons.

But on the other hand, the tank possessed mobility far in excess of the normal infantry formation and required complex skills that the normal infantry officer did not have. Many visionary advocates of the tank suggested that it could be used in many different ways that would free it from being tied down (normally) to infantry or being used only in support of infantry operations.

On these grounds the cavalry was a possible claimant of the new weapon. The mobility of the tank and its potential for use as a breakthrough or exploitation vehicle seemed to make it a cavalry weapon. Its potential as a means of maneuver against machine guns made it a logical replacement for the horse. The horse and the cavalry, in the view of some observers, were finished on the battlefield.

Against this, the infantry could justly claim the tank as an infantry weapon, used primarily to perform the usual mission of infantry, after which the cavalry would be free to carry out its traditional mission. More importantly, the cavalry was not really interested in the tank as a new aspect of its mission. A combination of affection for the horse, disdain

for the new weapon, and general fear of innovation, coupled with the
fact that many of the younger and more innovative officers of the
cavalry had transferred either to the air force or to tanks, left the cavalry
with no real desire to compete for the new weapon.[15]

There was a fourth solution to the question that was, in general, advocated by officers who actually were in the tank units of the First
World War. They perceived the tank as a major new weapon capable of
being used as an independent means of attack. These officers believed it
could transform the conduct of war.[16] They proposed the establishment
of a completely new branch, to include all tanks and tank crews. The tank
corps could then develop to its fullest potential without interference
from nontank officers in command over tank units. This solution would
have further fragmented the army at a time when the air arm was also
demanding independence.[17] It was not a propitious time for the creation of new organizations. Other wartime branches worthy of similar
consideration, such as machine-gun units, chemical-warfare units, or
assault-troop units, were denied independent status at this time.[18]

The combat employment of the new weapon became the crucial question from which all others should have been determined, although the
considerations of manpower and control were more important in a peacetime army.[19] The problem could be better defined as the strategic versus
the tactical use of the tank. A vocal and determined group of relatively
junior officers, the majority of whom had been intimately involved in
tank operations in the First World War, advocated the tank as a solution
to the problems of modern war. The use of the tank, in mass and as a
strategic rather than a tactical weapon, would alleviate the suffering that
the trenches had caused. They suggested that the tanks be used in the
manner of naval forces, striking deep into enemy territory against supply
and command installations, with little support from, or concern for,
normal troops and traditional front lines and tactics.[20]

The advocates of the various solutions were very much creatures of
their environment. Their interest in the topic and their determination
to find a solution were the direct result of recent European history.

The First World War had profound impact on the European nations
and in particular on men who were the leading advocates of armored warfare. These men, deeply affected by the carnage of the war, were determined to do something to prevent its recurrence. Most European intellectuals were very concerned about probable future developments in the

interwar period. Some put their faith in the League of Nations, some in pacifism, some in the strategic bomber, and some in the tank. All of these visionaries encountered problems and, in most cases, disapproval. Those who were attempting reform in an institutional setting, such as the strategic airpower proponents and the strategic armor advocates, tended to push too hard and soon became rebels when their ideas were not accepted.[21]

The counterproposal to the tank advocates' position was the continued use of the tank as an infantry support weapon, accompanying the infantry assault while suppressing any machine-gun nests or other obstacles. This was essentially what the World War I mission of the tank had been. There were positions between these two extremes that were taken by a few.[22] These men, whose view was very close to what actually developed, generally became lost in the confusion of the vehement debate. Their realization that a compromise was essential only prevailed when proven in combat. The determination of the advocates of strategic armor on one extreme and of the military establishment on the other made their positions the two most loudly defended and widely publicized. The determined nature of the two groups and the vigor of their arguments tended to make the debate an either-or matter, without chance of compromise.

The technical questions were closely related. If the tank was to be used as a strategic weapon, the main requirements would be speed, efficiency, and firepower. If it was only to be used as an infantry support vehicle, it would need to be reliable, well protected, and armed with antipersonnel weapons. These questions were approached largely as adjuncts to the larger questions of tactics and organization. There were major technical problems in the improvement of armored fighting vehicles in this period and the major difficulty, at least into the 1930s, was development of the mechanically efficient vehicle.

A related problem was that of production. Beginning in the early 1920s, the supporters of a major role for the tank and of its use in the variety of possible situations, argued for the production of a large tank force. The advocacy continued until large tank forces were created in the late 1930s. They felt that the only way to prove the worth of the tank and to become proficient in its use was to have an adequate number. And if the tank and its efficiency in combat were to be a deterrent, it required a force in being.

The conservative forces refuted this on two grounds, finance and need. The most important was money. Throughout the 1920s and 1930s, few if any governments could afford to finance their large-scale production of

tanks. Those that did produced small, economical tanks with export
potential. The most notable examples were the British Carden-Loyd
tankettes (light tanks) and the Italian Fiat-Ansaldo copies. Together these
two tanks dominated commercial sales, leaving many countries with an
inventory of outdated tanks and little money to buy new ones in 1939,
when tank technology accelerated rapidly.[23]

The conservatives also questioned the need for numbers of new tanks.
Technology was changing quickly, no war was imminent, and many of the
theories were unproven. To produce a substantial number of tanks would
leave an army with rapidly outdated vehicles, possibly not designed for
contemporary tactical doctrine, and would perhaps tie up the budget for
several years. A temporizing approach was infinitely preferable to an
inventory of obsolete weapons. It is interesting to contrast this situation
with that in military aircraft procurement and production, where new
designs were appearing frequently. Several factors were at work. Aviation
technology was advancing at a much faster rate. Changes in aircraft were
more readily apparent than those in tanks, being easily expressed in
speed, climb rates, turn radius, and similar figures, while improvements
in much of tank technology were not.[24]

By the early 1930s a transition had occurred and the narrow question
of tanks and their role had been absorbed into a larger question, that of
mechanization versus motorization.[25] The transition from the narrower
view of motorization to the more sophisticated view of mechanization
in the late 1930s was gradual and in fact not recognized by many of the
participants. In Italy debate over mechanization did not begin until
1934. Before that motorization had been accepted without question. It
was not until 1938 that mechanization became official policy. It also
signaled a profound change taking place in society. Only as society became motorized and as the more sophisticated societies became mechanized, to transfer the analogy to civilian society, could the concept be
considered in the military.[26]

The military, being a microcosm of society, could force the kinds of
change that would produce a mechanized army. But it would only truly
be effective when the transition had occurred in society as a whole. For
example, although the United States—which was perhaps the closest to
a mechanized society—got a very late start in producing a mechanized army,
it was the most successful. The mechanized American society provided
skilled manpower and the essential production facilities and expertise re-

quired. Italy, with a substantial lead in doctrine, failed because its society was barely motorized.[27]

Problem Areas in Research

The Italian military defeat in the Second World War obscured the achievements of its army in mechanization. The attendant upheaval and destruction scattered much of the evidence of those accomplishments. Coupled with the Italian penchant for anonymity in preparing staff studies, this destruction has made it difficult to assign responsibility for many decisions made in this period.

Italy's withdrawal from the Second World War caused many of the problems. After the armistice of 1943, Italy became a cobelligerent. Its records were not captured documents but rather those of a friendly nation; therefore they were not treated like the German records, which were carefully preserved by the Allies. Political tampering in Italy has further reduced what survived. Many public figures wish to disguise their actions during the Fascist period. Unfortunately, few actual participants have survived. The Italian officer corps was relatively old in the interwar period. In the early 1930s, lieutenants with dates of rank in 1917 and 1918 were not uncommon. The colonels and generals who can be identified as influential were all middle-aged at best. All are dead, or in advanced old age. No one was available for an interview.

Industrial records have suffered in the same way as those of the army. Fiat's archives, stored in the headquarters of their production facilities, were destroyed in Allied bombing raids during November 1942. Other records, especially those relating to contracts and profits, are restricted.[28] Ansaldo claims no surviving records at all.[29]

The absence of detailed documentation in some periods has made it impossible to attribute actions to their initiators. Substantial material from the most crucial period, 1938 to 1940, still exists. However, sufficient documentary evidence remains from the entire period to construct a discussion of the major points in the development of Italian armored doctrine.

*   *   *   *   *

The history of military mechanization in the interwar period is that of the struggle between motorization and mechanization to dominate the modernization of armies. The problem was the same in all countries.

Mechanization, a true reform of the preindustrial armies, required the most effort. Motorization could be carried out slowly and with relatively limited resources. Only countries like Britain with small professional armies could have easily mechanized in the interwar years. Large conscript armies required much more effort. Indeed, mechanization might have had a national impact if carried out in a nonmechanized society. Most countries were unable, for a variety of reasons, to mechanize their armies. Italy, which tried, presents a good insight into the dynamics of this revolutionary change in military thinking.

Notes

1. The main driving track at the Armored and Mechanized Troops School, Caserta, is called "El Alamein." I was told this was to imbue the troops with the traditions of the branch (briefing, 27 January 1975). See Dino Campini, *Nei Giardini del Diavolo* (Milan: Longanesi, 1969) for the armored divisions in North Africa.

2. One of the cavalry-officer training companies at Caserta is named "Isbuschenskij." See Lucio Lami, *Isbuschenskij: L'Ultima Carica* (Milan: Mursia, 1971) for a detailed account of the battle.

3. Richard Ogorkiewicz, *Armored Forces* (New York: Arco, 1960, reprinted 1970), pt. 2.

4. For a broader background, see Theodore Ropp, *War in the Modern World* (New York: Collier Books, 1962), chaps. 6 and 7; David H. Zook, Jr. and Robin Higham, *A Short History of Warfare* (New York: Twayne Publishers, 1966), chaps. 14 and 20; Richard A. Preston, Sydney F. Wise, and Herman O. Werner, *Men in Arms* (New York: Praeger, 1964), chaps. 13 and 15.

5. See Arthur Bryant, *Jackets of Green* (London: Collins, 1972) for a discussion of the concept.

6. No work is known dealing especially with mounted infantry. There are a large number of regimental histories dealing with its use in British colonial wars.

7. *Enciclopedia Militare,* s.v., 6 vols. (Milan, 1927-33), "Arditi" is a good example of the concept and its attendant atmosphere.

8. Gabriele D'Annunzio is the outstanding example, although any of the heroes of the Fascist squads would qualify. See Denis Mack Smith, *Italy, A Modern History* (Ann Arbor: University of Michigan Press, 1959), p. 347; Ernst Nolte, *Three Faces of Fascism* (New York: Mentor Books, 1969), p. 256.

9. The most famous Italian cavalry action of the First World War in Italy was the battle of Pozzuolo del Friuli, during the Twelfth Battle of the Isonzo, better known to English-language readers as the Battle of Caporetto. Pozzuolo del Friuli was, in reality, a static defense of the village of that name south of Udine, enlivened by a charge by two squadrons of cavalry to halt a flanking movement. The most widespread English-language account, Cyril Falls, *The Battle of Caporetto* (New York: Lippincott, 1966), doesn't even mention the incident. For Italian accounts see *Enciclopedia Militare*, s.v. "Pozzuolo del Friuli," or Rodolfo Puletti, *Caricat* (Bologna: Edizioni Capitol, 1973), pp. 253-56.

10. In brief, there were problems in finding both sufficient horses and experienced riders.

11. See for example, *The Army List* (London: Her Majesty's Stationery Office, semiannually) for the British cavalry regiments amalgamated and the yeomanry (territorial cavalry) regiments converted. For the U.S., Mary Lee Stubbs and S. R. Connor, *Armor-Cavalry, Part II; Army National Guard* (Washington, D.C.: Office of the Chief of Military History, 1972) details the similar changes in the U.S. army. Italy had a reduction from thirty to seven regiments. Ufficio Storico dello Stato Maggiore dell'Esercito, *L'Esercito e I Suoi Corpi* (Rome: Tipografia Regionale, 1972), 2 vols., 2:pt. 2, p. 51.

12. G. J. Younghusband, *The Queen's Commission* (London: John Murray, 1891), p. 12 is an outstanding example of how the academies were viewed.

13. Besides Napoleon, Badoglio and Cadorna in Italy, Roberts in England, and Foch in France are examples.

14. Books on the subject of tanks, their development, and their advocates have proliferated in the last ten years. Good starting places are B. H. Liddell Hart, *The Tanks* (London: Cassell, 1959) and Ogorkiewicz, *Armoured Forces*. There is also an Italian edition of Ogorkiewicz: *I Corazzati* (Rome: Istituto per La Divulgazione della Storia Militare, 1964). Other books on this subject are cited in specific notes.

15. Liddell Hart, *The Tanks*, 1:234 for a British example of opposition.

16. The most notable of these are all British. Captain B. H. Liddell Hart, Major General J. F. C. Fuller, Colonel Charles Broad, Colonel Sir Fredrick Pile, Colonel P. C. S. Hobart, Colonel G. M. Lindsay, and Colonel G. Le Q. Martel were the leading British advocates; they were predominately from the Royal Artillery and Royal Engineers. Various books by the more prolific of them are cited in other notes. See Robin Higham, *The Military Intellectuals in Britain, 1918-1939* (New Brunswick, N.J.: Rutgers University Press, 1966) and Jay Luvaas, *The Education of an*

Army (Chicago: The University of Chicago Press, 1964) for overviews of the most prominent.

17. Robin Higham, *Air Power* (New York: St. Martin's Press, 1972), pp. 59-60 discusses this briefly and in more detail in his *Military Intellectuals in Britain,* chaps. 6 and 7.

18. Only in the United States army was a new branch created for a World War I weapon, the Chemical Warfare Service. Britain disbanded its Machine Gun Corps, although the Royal Tank Corps was created out of the MGC, on a rather tenuous basis. See Liddell Hart, *The Tanks,* pp. 201-2.

19. A variety of books cover this conflict. Ogorkiewicz is a good place to start.

20. B. H. Liddell Hart, *Paris or The Future of War* (New York: Dutton, 1925) is a good example.

21. The careers of Billy Mitchell, Douhet, Fuller and Liddell Hart are generally cited examples.

22. The best of these is V. W. Germains. He and his works are discussed in some detail in Higham, *The Military Intellectuals in Britain, 1918-1939,* p. 111.

23. Chamberlain and Ellis, *Tanks of the World,* section on Hungary, demonstrates the problem.

24. See Higham, *Air Power,* pp. 73-80 and especially pp. 78-79. An interesting contrast is between record-breaking sea planes and tanks. Between 1921 and 1931 plane speed doubled from 170 to 340 mph (Higham, p. 78). The Italian Fiat Model 21 tank of 1921 had a top speed of 15 mph. The U.S. Sherman tank, the most widely used tank in 1945, had a top speed of 24 mph. While there are obvious flaws in the comparison, it does indicate the lack of dramatic change in tank technology.

25. To the best of my knowledge the only place that this concept is developed in any detail is by the foremost Italian author on this subject, Generale Angelo Pugnani, a former head of the Motor Transport Branch of the Italian army (retired 1936, died 1956). See Angelo Pugnani, *Storia Della Motorizzazione Militare Italiana* (Turin: Roggero e Tortia, 1951). He first expressed these views in 1936 in a work on the Ethiopian War, *La Motorizzazione Dell'Esercito e la Conquista Dell'Etiopia* (Rome: Edizione Della "Rivista Transporti e Lavori Pubblici," 1936). See also *Enciclopedia Militare,* s.v. "Motorizzazione" and "Mechanizzazione."

26. Their interpretation of the reasons for German success tended to be based on purely military events, that is, strategic planning, tactics, and equipment, without regard for political and economic considerations. I don't deny the German achievement, only that the acceptance of the ideas

of Fuller and Liddell Hart were essential to its success. See Larry Addington, *The German General Staff and The Blitzkrieg Era* (New Brunswick,
N.J.: Rutgers University Press, 1971) for a detailed discussion of German
success.

27. See for example, B. H. Liddell Hart, *The Other Side of the Hill*
(London: Cassell, 1948), pp. 96-97; Heinz Guderian, *Panzer Leader*
(New York: Dutton, 1952), pp. 23-25; and F. W. von Mellenthin, *Panzer
Battles* (Norman: University of Oklahoma Press, 1956), pp. xv-xvi. That
the ideas of the armor advocates were known and tested in the 1930s is
undeniable, but that their acceptance or nonacceptance was a crucial
factor in the performance of armies in the Second World War is questionable.

28. Augusto Constantino, Direttore, Centro Storico Fiat, to the author,
20 February 1975.

29. Interview with Dottor Zoboli, Dirigente, Pubbliche Relazione,
Ansaldo Meccanica Nucleare, 18 March 1975.

2
A Short History of the Italian Army, 1860-1918

The development of policy in an army is a complex procedure. It comes not only from current trends in military affairs and the political system; the history and organization of an army determine the characteristics of the manner in which policy and doctrine decisions are made. In the case of armored warfare doctrine in the Italian army, the origins of that army, only fifty years earlier, and the structure of its high command were important. Together they removed the decision-making process from any public forum (as existed in Britain, for example). A group of well-established elite corps, supported by veterans' organizations, defended their own positions. The interest groups received special consideration when tanks were introduced and contributed to such anomalies as armored divisions in which the majority of combat personnel rode bicycles.

The recent army campaigns of the First World War and the colonial wars had exposed the officer corps to special situations that would influence later choices. In particular, the absence of a tank-equipped enemy was to have serious consequences. And the particular nature of Italian mobile operations in the First World War gave the cavalry an artificial aura of success that sustained it in the fight against tanks. Together these factors shaped the institutional influences on the development of Italian armored policy even though they did not determine it.

The Origins of the Italian Army

The manner in which the present Italian army was created had a profound effect on the relation between the people and the military. The estrangement caused by the creation contributed to the closed nature of military decision making. And this prevented the development of meaningful dialogue on policy, either in the professional journals or in the popular press.

Although the Sardinian army of the House of Savoy had an unbroken lineage from the seventeenth century, modern historians have chosen the Napoleonic wars as the beginning of the Italian army.[1] While there were Napoleonic armies in both northern and southern Italy, the northern one, the *Esercito Italico* (Italic army) is considered the predecessor of the modern army. Organized in 1799, it fought in Spain and Russia, just as its modern counterpart did.[2] With the defeat of Napoleon, Italy's armed forces again became fragmented, as its territory was. The Sardinian army was the only force in being. The remaining armed forces were satellites of other powers then holding sway in a disunited Italy.

As a result, the Sardinian army led the Italian Wars of Independence. The first campaign, of 1848-49 against the Austrians, was a failure largely attributable to weaknesses in the Sardinian army's equipment, leadership, and initiative. Nonetheless, the willingness of the Sardinians to fight for Italy gave them moral authority as the army of Italian liberation.

The years between the First War of Italian Independence and the Second saw a general increase in the armed forces of the Italian states as it became obvious that continued fighting would be the only way to unification and independence.[3] To gain more prestige and more of a voice in European affairs, Conte Camillo Cavour, prime minister of Sardinia, sent an expeditionary force to the Crimea.[4] There was substantial opposition to the use of the army in a foreign war when Austria still held Italian territory, but Cavour insisted.

Cavour astutely realized that Piedmont would require assistance in any future war against the Austrians. He allied Piedmont with the France of Napoleon III. The Second War of Independence in 1859 was brief but impressive in its effects. The Sardinian and French forces pushed the Austrians back easily, but, as in 1849, the task of defeating them was too much. Napoleon III had an alternative, however: he made peace, leaving the Italian allies without help and lacking one of their main objectives, Venetia.[5]

The victories that occurred had a decisive effect on Italy. First the small states of northern Italy rose and declared their independence. Then Garibaldi, with an army of volunteers, attacked the Kingdom of the Two

Sicilies. In a snowball effect, his army mushroomed with his victories, and he successfully defeated the Bourbons. Territorial union was followed by political union, ratified by plebiscites.

Unification created several problems for the military. The first and most important, even in the early stages of fighting, was manpower. The army needed to expand and the populace of newly freed states wanted to participate in the liberation of all Italy. The Sardinian General Staff chose to expand the Sardinian army to accommodate the new recruits rather than form a new army combining those of the independent states, as the Germans were to do on their unification later.[6] The Sardinians completed this unification in 1860-61.

This system quickly incorporated the manpower into the army, but it caused problems. The high command remained Sardinian, at least initially. The system definitely remained Sardinian. The south felt that the army, with its attendant conscription, was being imposed from the north by the foreign government of the House of Savoy rather than being a continuation of the traditional military service of the Kingdom of the Two Sicilies or the Papal States. The selection of personnel for the new regiments was by a panel dominated by Sardinians. Those discharged felt Sardinian prejudice turned them out. The release of numbers of trained soldiers without prospect of civilian employment led to brigandage. This period of brigandage, from 1860 to 1870, occupied much of the army in arduous and vicious campaigning. The final military excursion of this period was the capture of Rome in 1870. Italy now had its capital and territorial stability, though Austria still had to be dislodged from *Italia Irredenta,* the unredeemed lands of northeast Italy.

Thus from the very beginning the Italian army suffered from two problems that would interfere with the development of armored policy. These organizational and operational inadequacies of the wars of independence continued through the Second World War. And factionalism in the officer corps, whether based on Sardinian or Fascist loyalties, would also interfere with the development of armor.

With the conclusion of the fighting to unify Italy, the army slowly reorganized. Conscript service was gradually reduced to two years for most recruits. The government created a militia and other mobilization devices. The continual problem was money. In the newly created state, money was needed for everything, and there was not enough for all the demands. The military often suffered from lack of funds even though Italy was concerned about the danger of Austria and wished to maintain the military establishment of a major European power.

These events produced an army in Italy but not necessarily an Italian army. Both conscription and taxes had been introduced by the new government. The diverse populations that had just been united felt they had no voice in these foreign impositions; they endured both but supported neither. This problem continued throughout the period under discussion. The level of expenditure for the army was also too high for the economy to support. Italy simply was not wealthy enough to maintain the type of army political policy dictated. It was not really poor planning or poor financial management that kept the army underequipped in muzzle-loading cannon in the 1870s and in tanks in the 1930s. Nor was it military spending that burdened the population with heavy taxation. It was just that Italy attempted too much for her resources.

Structure of the Army

The structure of the Italian army contributed to many of the difficulties in deciding and implementing policy and doctrine in the 1930s. The origins of the army and its high command in the old Sardinian army have already been mentioned. Out of this tradition of loyalty to the House of Savoy grew many problems. The Ministry of War was politically involved, subordinate units trained under difficult conditions, and most conscripts received little training.

The organization of the army before the First World War was relatively simple. Between 1860 and 1914, the Minister of War, acting under the king and prime minister, was, with two exceptions, a serving soldier. He directed the army through the Ministry of War, which performed the administrative functions. A lack of continuity in the Ministry of War was a major problem; governments fell frequently and each minister had his own solution to the problems of the army, which entailed much wasted effort.[7] After 1882, when the position was created, all operational functions were under the jurisdiction of the Chief of the General Staff.[8] Under the General Staff were field units and commands, territorial commands, and military districts.

The military districts dealt with recruiting and with the military forces designed to reinforce the active army in time of war. Active army regiments, as a rule, were substantially under strength and required the addition of both individual replacements and often one or more full battalions from the militia to reach war strength. The regular regiments were training organizations for the large numbers of recruits that were supplied by the levy each year, and required some time for mobilization. The reserve and militia officers were generally trained on a fairly frequent basis but the enlisted personnel were not trained after their initial call-up. Finances again stood in the way. Similarly, equipment tended to be limited for the militia and for mobilization in general.

The Elites of the Italian Army

The Italian army, despite its recent creation, had a number of elite corps. These corps also had strong veterans' organizations behind them. Together the units and the veterans formed power blocs within the army, and within Italy in general, that enabled them to argue for special places in the structure of the modernized army of the 1930s. They included the *bersaglieri*, a light infantry corps; the *alpini*, mountain troops; the *Granatieri di Sardegna*, a royal guard; and the senior cavalry regiments. The *bersaglieri* and the *alpini* were special types of infantry with distinctive training and uniforms.

Bersaglieri, literally sharpshooters, were riflemen in the Sardinian army.[9] The Sardinian *bersaglieri* fought in all the wars of independence from 1849 to 1870 and were frequently in the forefront of the fighting. The real burst of popular enthusiasm for this type of troops was due to a group of volunteers. The Lombardians formed a volunteer unit equipped, uniformed, and trained like the Sardinian *bersaglieri*. These volunteers fought in Lombardy against the Austrians in 1848 and after the Sardinian defeat there they went to Rome.[10] They distinguished themselves in all the campaigns of independence and particularly in the assault on Rome in 1870. Due to these exploits the *bersaglieri* became the elite of the Italian infantry, exceeding even the royal guard regiment, the *Granatieri di Sardegna*. They also specialized in what was to become a distinctive Italian method of mobility, the bicycle.

The bicycle had arrived as a military item in the 1880s and 1890s. Britain had an Army Cyclist Corps and other armies used them to varying degrees, but the Italians raised the use of the military bicycle to its highest level. The bicycle troops were essentially a mounted infantry unit without a requirement for forage. They could also be used as couriers,

scouts, or in other traditional cavalry roles. The Italian army had introduced a cyclist company in one *bersaglieri* regiment in 1891. By the beginning of the First World War, one of the three battalions in each
bersaglieri regiment was cyclist.[11]

The cyclist units were used as ready reaction forces, mobile infantry,
and even in the Alps during the First World War. The Italians prided themselves on the speed with which *bersaglieri* could move on their bicycles.
In the interwar period, the *bersaglieri-ciclisti* became almost a cult.[12]
In the late 1930s and early 1940s the bicycle, on the basis of its World
War I record, was competing with armored vehicles as battlefield transportation.

Another innovation in the Italian army during the First World War
also involved the *bersaglieri*. The Italians found a need for specially
trained assault troops for the most dangerous missions. This was very
important in mountainous terrain, where a quiet approach often involved
extremely difficult climbing. These assaults required more skill and
motivation than could be found in draftees of the average regiment, so
units of volunteers had to be formed. In the Italian army these shock
troops were called *arditi* and belonged to units called *reparti d'assalto,*
or assault detachments.[13] (*Arditi* means fearless, daring, courageous.)
They were carefully selected from volunteers and specially trained in
assault tactics.

The assault troops added an element of danger and of great personal
courage to the earlier Italian fascination with the volunteer. This was to
become increasingly important as first D'Annunzio and then Mussolini
in their political activities began to emphasize the values and virtues of
the *arditi*. The Italian army was unspectacular and not overly successful.
So the individual courage of the Italian soldier was emphasized to give a
sense of national pride. This phenomenon often occurs in countries that
perceive themselves to be inferior in some way to potential enemies: they
emphasize some value or quality that makes their country superior.[14]
In the Italian version the individual Italian is a descendant of the Roman
legionary, unequaled in courage. It is immaterial that the army does not
do well, the individual is a hero. This concept was to have deep and lasting
effects on the development of armor in Italy.

Alpini were the mountain troops of the army. Under the Italian system
of conscription—where recruits were sent to a unit with some territorial

identification—the *alpini* were from the mountain regions of Italy, thus they were already adapted and trained for life in the Alpine regions. The army specially equipped and further trained them for mountain warfare. From their founding in 1872 to the First World War they had little chance to serve in their own mountains, but they did serve extensively in colonial campaigns, especially where there was mountainous terrain. They, like the *bersaglieri*, received a good deal of publicity about their operations and were popularly admired.[15]

The veterans' associations of these elite units were interesting phenomena that were very influential in Italy. Large numbers of Italians served their conscript duty. To keep them together for future mobilization, they were encouraged to join the branch association. The groups, such as the *Associazione Nazionale di Cavalleria,* published magazines and held annual meetings on a national level. On the local level, they often had a small social club, athletic teams, and bands. Under Mussolini the associations became very political.[16] The leaders were prominent Fascists and political education in the name of national defense became a main goal.

In the development of armor, these elites and their veterans' associations played an important role. Their political and propaganda power contributed materially to the creation of units like the *celeri,* who diverted needed assets from the armored units. And they supported the continuation of anachronisms like the cycle-mounted *bersaglieri* on the battlefields of the Second World War.

The First World War

The political and economic turmoil caused by the First World War and its aftermath had important effects on armored policy. Military planning before the Second World War was based on interpretations of the First World War; these interpretations limited the development of policy because of the narrow confines of conflict in the First World War.

The outbreak of World War I found the Italians still involved in Libya and barely able to make up the budgetary deficits from that war. The financial drain of even such a limited war was too much for the weak Italian economy. The political situation in Italy was also unfavorable for a new war. But the Austrians had been the traditional enemy of Italy for a very long time. They were still in possession of the unredeemed lands of Trentino, Alto Adige, and Istria (*Italia Irredenta*). Italian honor demanded participation against the occupiers of Italian territory.

In the year between the beginning of the First World War and Italy's entry into it, in May 1915, little was done to prepare the army. The entry into the war was based on popular sentiment, at least among a vocal minority of society, rather than increased military preparedness. This clamor for Italian participation was based on a number of factors, including the idea that Italy, a great nation, had to fight or lose face. Irredentist claims, Austrian intransigence over the Italian lands in the Austro-Hungarian Empire, and the secret treaty of London with the Allies also played their part. Italy entered the First World War on the side of Britain and France.

For Italy the war was largely confined to a small area along the northeastern border, where it joined the Austro-Hungarian Empire. The battleground ran roughly from Lake Garda on the west, along the line of the boundary between the Alps and the Venetian plain, to the Carso, a low ridge that effectively ends the plain on the east. The geography of the area meant, except in the region of the Carso, an uphill battle. The Austrians occupied the hills and mountains. The Italians attempted to capture them from the plain and the valleys. Because of this, most of the fighting on the western flank of the front was limited to the area around the two major rivers that pierced the mountains, the Adige and the Brenta. Both rivers lead toward the city of Trento. The road through Trento then leads to Bolzano, the Brenner Pass, and into the Austrian heartland.

On the eastern front, the terrain was easier, although broken by a number of rivers flowing parallel to the front line from the Alps to the sea. These rivers, the major natural barriers in Venetia Julia and Friuli, were the key features in the battles on the eastern section. It was there that the war of movement occurred on the Italian front.

Italians fought on other fronts in the First World War: in France, Albania, and Greece.[17] However, these were relatively minor theaters of operation. As a demonstration of Allied solidarity, an Italian corps of fifty thousand men was sent to France, where they fought as part of the French army.[18] These Italian troops experienced a rather different type of warfare than those who remained in Italy; especially important was their experience with tanks, the first that Italians had ever seen in action.

The main focus of the war was on the troops in Italy, some two million, or ninety-one percent of the army.[19] In addition, the most important figures of the army, both generals and heroes, were involved on this front. The front was close to the centers of population in northern Italy (only Turin was any appreciable distance from the front). Venice, Verona, and even Milan were close enough to the fighting to be in serious danger should a major breakthrough occur.

The first battles were inconclusive as the Italians struggled to mobilize and equip their army and the Austrians tried to fight a two-front war. Later the collapse of Russia freed substantial numbers of troops from the Austro-Russian Front. This led to a new phase in which major battles involved substantial movement of the front line in Venetia.

Before the arrival of more Austrian troops, the battles were limited in size and location. The major fighting had been in the eleven battles of the Isonzo, named after a river flowing north to south from the Alps to the Adriatic Sea parallel to the ridge line of the Carso. In the Twelfth Battle of the Isonzo, the Battle of Caporetto, the Italian line quickly broke, and the Italians only managed to regroup along the Piave, another north-south river, well to the west.

The defeat at Caporetto led to massive changes in the army high command, attempts at reorganization, and the arrival of British, French, and American reinforcements on the Italian front. One of the most publicized changes was in the chief of staff of the Italian army. Up until this time, November 1917, Generale Conte Luigi Cadorna had been Supreme Commander. He was replaced by Generale Armando Diaz. Diaz brought with him as Deputy Chief of Staff a young officer with whom he had served in Libya in the Italo-Turkish war, Pietro Badoglio.[20] Badoglio later held the highest positions in the Italian army for the next twenty-five years. Diaz and Badoglio, with British artillery, Italian, French, British, and American troops, and a renewed war spirit in Italy, were able to launch a new offensive. The offensive, named after the ultimate objective, the town of Vittorio Veneto, at the foot of the Alps, coincided with the crumbling and ultimate collapse of the Austrian army and the Austro-Hungarian Empire.[21] The collapse of the opposition meant that there was little fighting in the Alps.

The occupation of Trento and similar towns located in alpine valleys was without major opposition. Italian popular accounts nevertheless often emphasized the mountains and the difficulties of fighting in this terrain. And, of course, a good deal of fighting, particularly on the western flank of the Italian front, was in the mountains. This involved very difficult terrain and all the skill that the *alpini* had. Nonetheless, the decisive battles in the First World War, and for that matter in all Italian wars, were fought on relatively flat land. The mountains may have influenced the course of events, since they funneled movement and had to be occupied to prevent their use by the enemy. Still, the battles that decided the wars were fought on the plains.

The political changes at the end of the war altered this situation. The political boundary was moved from, roughly, the line between the Alps and the plain to a line along the crest of the Alps. Only on the eastern flank was the new frontier one that would allow for open warfare. This lack of good tank terrain on the Italian frontier reduced the attractiveness of the tank as a strategic weapon against her potential enemies. The General Staff, viewing their new borders, forgot the lessons of World War I. Virtually all postwar planning emphasized mountain combat. Disregard of these lessons delayed Italian armor development several years.

Mobile Operations in the First World War

The tank was introduced as a weapon of mobility. Much of the debate on the tank versus cavalry in the interwar years centered on this mobility. Could the cavalry conduct mobile warfare on the modern battlefield? Would the tank restore mobility that the machine gun had taken away? In consequence, each country's perception of its mobile operations in the First World War became very important. Britain and France had similar experiences. Only with tanks had their armies been able to conduct anything approaching mobile operations. In Italy the situation appeared to be very different. For most of the war the cavalry had been unsuccessful. Still, the major cavalry operations at the end of the war, against a collapsing enemy, had been very successful. This final campaign was the one that influenced Italian planners.

Four divisions of Italian cavalry were employed in the early stages of the fighting, enabling the Italians to take advantage of the Austrian unpreparedness to occupy enemy territory. By February 1916, after little more than nine months of war, the situation had changed dramatically. The four cavalry divisions, which had formed a cavalry corps, dismounted. This "hard sacrifice" converted the divisions into infantry, in which role they fought in some of the major battles.[22] The divisions, however, retained their horses so that they could be used as cavalry or mounted infantry as the situation demanded.

In addition to the use of cavalry personnel for the medium-gun units, many individual cavalry officers served in noncavalry positions. Most notable among these were the pilots, such as Francesco Baracca and Gabriele D'Annunzio, the two most famous Italian aviation figures of the First World War. D'Annunzio managed to serve as an infantryman with a dismounted cavalry unit, as a bomber pilot, and as the leader of a motor torpedo boat raid on the Dalmatian coast, all as a cavalry officer.[23]

Despite the reassignment of so many officers, the Italian cavalry still managed to distinguish itself. Often, however, the glory that the cavalry received was the reflected glory of a great victory. In the early stages of the war there were a number of heroic charges to secure bridges or similar objectives, but these were usually squadron (small-unit) operations.[24] The great cavalry battle was Pozzuolo del Friuli, during the retreat after Caporetto. The small town of Pozzuolo was held by an infantry brigade and the Second Cavalry Brigade, which was technically a divisional brigade, but was being employed as a screening element during the retreat.[25] When the town was in danger of being outflanked by the Austrians, a cavalry charge by one regiment of the brigade halted the flanking movement and enabled the force to retreat intact. This protection of the infantry was the high point of Italian cavalry operations in the war.

Although the cavalry played a larger part in the operations after Caporetto, these final stages of the war consisted of victories over a defeated and collapsing enemy, in which the cavalry role was a glorious achievement simply because it was part of the victory. The cavalry led the way into Vittorio Veneto, Trento, Trieste, and most of the other cities captured by the Italians after four years of hard fighting. However, there was little fighting in these final cavalry operations. The publicity and the glory given the cavalry because of these operations was the result of the victories gained by the armed forces in the final liberation of *Italia Irredenta*. After four years of war the victories that signaled the end of the fighting were scenes of rejoicing and adulation for the victors, without regard for their contribution to the victory.

There had been no real war of mobility on the Italian front. Cavalry units could not operate in any terrain against entrenched, machine-gun equipped troops. This crucial lesson of the First World War was amply demonstrated on the Italian front, but the successes of the last month of the war obscured it. Italian planning took virtually no account of the true nature of cavalry operations in World War I. Instead, defense policy at the beginning of the Second World War placed a heavy emphasis on horsed cavalry, wasting valuable resources that could have helped the armor program.

The Colonial Experience

The only combat Italian troops saw between the wars of independence and the First World War was in colonial operations. The army received little praise for its years in Africa. Much of the budget was used for these operations instead of for needed modernization. Colonial operations and their expense also alienated much of the population. These Italian colonial adventures—Ethiopia, Libya, and Eritrea—never paid for themselves. Many individual Italians made money, but the Italian government had to pay continually for this social and political achievement. The bulk of the population gave their sons and money, and received nothing in return. Contrary to the Fascist slogan of later years—"Many Enemies, Much Honor"—the colonial campaigns of the 1890s and during the Libyan war gave the Italian army little honor and more enemies at home than it defeated abroad.[26]

Nevertheless the colonial wars had a major impact on the Italian army. Beginning in the 1880s Italian troops were in more or less constant combat until they lost their African possessions in the 1940s. While there were only a few major campaigns, there were always minor operations against bandits or to prevent tribal incursions. This imperial warfare was a constant financial drain. It involved, as well, large numbers of Italian soldiers, primarily officers for the large colonial force that was created. Italy first took Eritrea and Italian Somaliland in 1886 without great difficulty. The army then formed units of indigenous personnel that were used in later campaigns. Substantial numbers of Italian troops were also used. For example, in the campaign against Ethiopia, which ended in the Italian defeat at Adowa in 1896, the force involved consisted of three Italian brigades and one native brigade.[27]

However, the events that directly affected the majority of soldiers occurred at home. Social unrest in Italy increased with industrialization and with the real or apparent discrepancies in treatment and conditions between northern and southern Italy and between rich and poor. In the

1890s, in addition to the operations in Eritrea, the army was employed against insurrections by farmers in Sicily and by marble workers in the north, and against industrial violence throughout the country.[28]

While all of these skirmishes were going on, the army was torn by a number of influences. The economic difficulties of Italy led to constant demands for economy and reorganizations of the army to cut expenses. These cuts often involved expediency, for example, combining recruiting districts and remount districts, or disbanding headquarters one year to save money then establishing new headquarters the next year to manage funds more efficiently.[29] The poor performance of the army at Adowa was a great blow. The right wing said it was because not enough was spent; the left said too much was being spent and Italy should not even have been involved.

In the context of this turmoil Italy embarked on the next war. Because of French acquisition of Tunisia, Italy felt its traditional interest in North Africa and, in particular, in the area directly across from Sicily and the Italian sea lanes was endangered. Consequently Italy went to war with Turkey for the possession of Libya. The war with Turkey was decided by Italian naval power in the Aegean and the Mediterranean, but the undermanned and poorly equipped army bore the brunt of the fighting. Lack of adequate manpower, coupled with indecision both on the scene and in Rome, failed to subdue the unexpected resistance of the native population. The opening of the First World War, two years after the supposed end of the Italo-Turkish war, found Italian forces, often largely Eritrean colonial forces, still in combat in Libya.[30]

* * * * *

A key feature of Italian military history is that Italy has been a passive participant in most wars. Italy has been, since Roman times, the invaded country rather than an invader. The First World War supported this defensive mentality. Italian planning heavily emphasized defending invasion routes rather than aggressive operations. In the interwar period tank units were deployed to block the routes. The newly created air force was also planned to give Italy a means of striking at the enemy while the army blocked the land routes.[31] This passive attitude to land operations explains much about the development of armored policy. The tank could only reach its full potential in offensive warfare. Armored operations required grand maneuvers and open territory. The Italian emphasis on the defense did not consider these factors. The destruction of an enemy in a limited area of mountainous northern Italy needed a weapon with very different characteristics than those of a tank. The tank suffered under this concept of Italian operations until 1938.

Many authors mention other factors that are less definite. Generale Alberto Pariani, the *Sottosegretario per la Guerra,* the undersecretary who was the effective head of the army from 1936 to 1939, stated that Italians are a naturally cautious people. The army would have to work hard to keep up with other armies because it would take the Italians longer to adopt a new idea.[32]

Cautiousness is only one of the somewhat questionable explanations advanced. The mountains of northern Italy are frequently cited as a reason for Italy's weakness in tanks. The authors who advanced this idea never explained why all three armored divisions were deployed along the Alpine frontier. An Italian belief in individual heroism is also blamed for deemphasizing the mechanical approach to warfare, but the numbers of tanks in Italy contradict this idea.

The historical events mentioned did not determine the exact course of development of armor in Italy. Badoglio's Piedmontese background and longevity or the power of the *Associazione Nazionale Alpini d'Italia* did not send the *Littorio* division into the Western Desert inadequately prepared. But taken together, the events of fifty years of Italian military history had created an army that did things in certain ways. The army was not really at home in its own country. Much of the population disliked what it stood for and the burdens it imposed. The army had no real winning tradition, from the French and Prussian victories of 1859 and 1866 to Allied aid after Caporetto. Much of its experience was against aborigines and striking workers. Finance was a continual problem, heavily influenced by politics, as was the higher direction of the Ministry of War. The army was always short of equipment, and money for training and maneuvers was limited. The peacetime army trained vast numbers of conscripts but seldom had time for advanced training. The combination of these factors handicapped the Italian army in all its activities. The army had too many problems to focus on any individual problem. In the 1920s and 1930s, when armored warfare should have been a major topic, these traditions and problems distracted the army and prevented it from focusing on modernization.

Notes

1. The area ruled by the House of Savoy is normally referred to as Piedmont, Piedmont-Sardinia, or Sardinia. The normal Italian phrases are *Esercito Piemontese,* Piedmontese Army, or *Esercito Sardo,* Sardinian Army.

2. Ufficio Storico, Stato Maggiore Dell'Esercito, *L'Esercito e I Suoi Corpi,* 2 vols. (Rome: Ministry of Defense, 1971), 1:23-34.

3. Amedeo Tosti, *Storia dell'Esercito Italiano* (n.p.: Istituto per Gli Studi di Politica Internazionale, 1936), pp. 35-40.

4. *L'Esercito e I Suoi Corpi,* 0:19; Tosti, *Storia,* p. 8.

5. *L'Esercito e I Suoi Corpi,* 0:19; Tosti, *Storia,* p. 8.

6. *L'Esercito e I Suoi Corpi,* Vol. 2, 1 for infantry regiments, and Vol. 2, 2 for cavalry regiments. A more detailed account of the cavalry regiments is in Rodolfo Puletti, *Caricat* (Bologna: Edizioni Capitol, 1973), pp. 11-17.

7. Tosti, *Storia,* p. 125.

8. *L'Esercito e I Suoi Corpi,* 1:8.

9. See Fermo Roggiani, *Storia dei Bersaglieri d'Italia* (Milan: Cavalotti Editore, 1973) for a detailed history.

10. Roggiani, *Bersaglieri,* pp. 37-38.

11. *Enciclopedia Militare,* s.v. *"Ciclisti";* Roggiani, *Bersaglieri,* pp. 90-91.

12. Roggiani, *Bersaglieri,* chap. 8.

13. *Enciclopedia Militare,* s.v. "Arditi."

14. For example, the use by Pakistan of the concept of "martial races" in propaganda against India.

15. Emilio Faldella, ed., *Storia Delle Truppe Alpine, 1872-1972* (Milan: Cavalotti Editore, 1973) is a good history done by the National Association of Alpini, the most powerful veterans' organization in Italy. Ezio Mosna, *Storia Delle Truppe Alpine D'Italia* (Trento: Il Museo Storico Nazionale Degli Alpini, n.d.) is a good brief history with the important facts and figures.

16. The head of the Associazione Nationale di Cavalleria from 1936 to 1939 was Alessandro Lessona, formerly Minister of Italian Africa, a senior Fascist propagandist, and leader of postwar Neo-Fascists.

17. Ufficio Storico, *L'Esercito tra La 1ª e La 2ª Guerra Mondiale* (Rome: Ministero della Difesa, 1954), p. 8.

18. *L'Esercito tra la Guerra,* p. 7.

19. *L'Esercito tra la Guerra,* p. 8.

20. *Enciclopedia Militare*, s.v. "Cadorna, Conte Liugi"; "Diaz, Armando"; and "Badoglio, Pietro." Piero Pieri and Giorgio Rochat, *Pietro Badoglio* (Turin: Unione Tipografico-Editrice Torinese, 1974), pp. 19-20.

21. *Enciclopedia Militare*, s.v. "Vittorio Veneto."

22. Puletti, *Caricat*, p. 241.

23. Puletti, *Caricat*, p. 242; *Enciclopedia Militare*, s.v. "D'Annunzio, Gabriele."

24. Puletti, *Caricat*, pp. 253-54.

25. Puletti, *Caricat*, pp. 260-61; J. F. C. Fuller, *A Military History of the Western World* (n.p.: Minerva Press, 1956), 3 vols., pp. 315-18.

26. *Molti Nemici, Molto Onore*, motto on the medal for Meritorious Service in Ethiopia, 1935-36. Also a frequent Fascist motto.

27. *L'Esercito e I Suoi Corpi*, 1:112. See pp. 107-13 for an account of the entire campaign. Also see *Enciclopedia Militare*, s.v. "Adua" (Adua is the Italian spelling).

28. Denis Mack Smith, *Italy, A Modern History* (Ann Arbor: University of Michigan Press, 1959), pp. 71-75. Also see Puletti, *Caricat*, pp. 186-89 for details of cavalry operations, and *L'Esercito e I Suoi Corpi*, Vol. 2, 2, Specchi Riepilogativi (summary tables) for battle honors.

29. Tosti, *Storia*, pp. 124-25.

30. On the Italo-Turkish War, good books are hard to find. John Wright, *Libya* (New York: Praeger, 1969), chaps. 12-14 is the best account in English. Paolo Maltese, *La Terra Promessa* (Milan: Sugar Editore, 1968) is a good recent, if somewhat revisionist, Italian account. The only book that emphasizes the important naval aspects is Commander W. H. Beehler, *The History of the Italian-Turkish War* (Annapolis, Md.: privately printed, 1913). It, like most other books in English, is badly out of date.

31. Higham, *Air Power*, p. 61.

32. Generale Alberto Pariani to All Italian Military Attachés, 11 February 1937, Raccoltore 231, U.S.

3
The Italian Economy

The mechanization of an army depends on the mechanization of the society that supports it. This mechanization of society has two facets. One, industrialization, can be judged in the most concrete of terms. Manufacturing capacity, steel production, tons of ore mined—all contribute hard facts. But the other facet consists of intangibles. The exposure of recruits to motor vehicles determines their acceptance and understanding of mechanization. Even the supply and maintenance systems can depend on the experience and understanding of the personnel who operate them. An army can be forcibly mechanized, by imported technology, without a mechanized society, but that army will never be as efficient as an army supported by a mechanized society.

Italy did not have a mechanized society in the years between the First and Second World Wars. This prevented military reality from catching up with policy and doctrine. The army's policy of mechanization was implemented only on a very small scale because the society could not support a larger scale. The lack of mineral deposits meant that virtually all raw materials had to be imported. The cost of raw materials and the small market in Italy prevented the development of a strong industrial base. This, with other factors, kept the Italian economy on a marginal basis, and, in turn, kept the country poor, which prevented governmental intervention in support of any of the weak economic areas.

Governmental policy aggravated the natural weakness of the Italian economy. Prior to the Risorgimento, the division of Italy into small states prevented national economic development. In the years after unification, parliamentary conflicts hindered the development of effective economic planning. After the advent of fascism, policy failed to overcome the inertia of centuries. Indeed, dogmatic implementation of some ideas did more harm than good.

With the weaknesses of the Italian economy and industrialization, the army could only further its policy of mechanization on a very limited scale. Industry could not provide more tanks, nor sufficient trucks to completely motorize the army. Italy's choice of allies and lack of resources meant petroleum products would be in short supply. The Italian army in World War II failed not because of lack of will or knowledge, but because of these weaknesses that were present at the founding of the country.

The *Risorgimento* and Before

The resurgence of Italian nationalism that led to the unification of Italy in the 1860s had much of its origin in the economic situation. The liberal reformers wanted an economic unification as well as a political one. They believed it essential to the development of a strong Italy. The new government passed legislation to eliminate economic problems immediately.

The legislative attempts to stabilize and develop the economy failed. Political differences and indecision over the best course of action prevented a consensus. The inherent weakness of Italian resources provided no foundation for growth. Long inactivity had weakened Italian banking so that little venture capital was forthcoming. And the lack of manufacturing meant that few if any trained managers were available. The origins of these problems lay in the history of the Italian peninsula.

The prominence of Italy in the world economy prior to the nineteenth century had always been based on trade. Her position in the center of the Mediterranean made Italy, or rather a few enterprising cities, the hubs of trade between the East and Europe. This trade in material objects produced capital that allowed some banks to establish a trade in money. But these trading activities influenced only a small part of the land area that would become Italy; the remainder of the country was agricultural.

Trade declined in the fifteenth and sixteenth centuries. New shipping routes, by water rather than land, avoided Italy. The discovery of the New World shifted the focus of trade to the Atlantic. The Protestant

Reformation and its attendant wars reduced the influence, wealth, and territory of Rome. Italy slipped into a state of economic inactivity from which it did not emerge until the Risorgimento.

This inactivity meant that the Industrial Revolution passed Italy by. When Britain underwent its revolution, no activity took place in Italy. The vast majority of the land was purely agricultural and only a few of the larger business centers had any contact at all with the major economic trends in the rest of Europe. When industrialization began in Italy in the 1830s and 1840s it was limited to these areas. Industrialism was brought to Italy; virtually all the techniques, equipment and management personnel came from the advanced countries of Western Europe.

Consequently, at the end of the Risorgimento conditions in Italy varied greatly. For the majority of the population agriculture was the main activity. Southern Italy was exclusively agricultural, as were the lands of the Church. Industry existed only in the north and on the western coast.

This industrial activity centered on shipbuilding, railways, and agricultural equipment, all goods that Italy required. Most of the manufacturers came from abroad; those that were Italian often had either government or foreign backing. Because it was located in limited areas—the triangle of Turin, Genoa, and Milan; in the Bay of Naples area; and at Livorno— industry affected only a small part of the population. In these areas, workers learned about cash economies and through their purchases stimulated the development of other manufacturing businesses. But this affected only the limited industrial areas.

To increase manufacturing, the government of unified Italy had a philosophy of extensive financial intervention in the economy.[1] The government subsidized most industries to some degree and directed the development of those that it felt important. The constant problem was financing. In the twenty years after 1860, military expenditures and the national debt consumed an average of sixty percent of the national budget, while only ten to fifteen percent went to general development.[2] In addition foreign concerns held one-third of the debt. This meant that Italy had a large nonproductive expenditure, much of it involving foreign exchange, at a time when it needed money to industrialize. This problem continued throughout the period this work covers.

Italy had a relatively limited number of major industries on which growth had to be based. They all had in common the need for foreign materials, foreign markets to some extent, and often the need for a favorable geographic situation. The textile industry was both the oldest and one of the best examples.

Textiles were the largest sector of the manufacturing economy from unification to 1910.[3] For the most part the cloth industry used natural power sources, primarily the fast-flowing streams of the Alps. They introduced machinery fairly early. But much, if not all, of the raw material had to be imported, and many products were not competitive in the export market. The textile industry thus produced a net outflow of capital.

Another industry with raw-material problems was the steel and iron industry. Italy required a variety of ferrous-metal products for its railway, shipbuilding, and tool industries. But the Italian metals industry was never equal to the demand. Lack of raw materials prevented extensive development. Both iron ore and coal or coke had to be imported. The coal situation had many ramifications. In an attempt to reduce costs, primitive charcoal smelting survived until the turn of the nineteenth century. Even with the most modern furnaces, the cost of iron and steel production was high. The government had constantly to subsidize the steel industry and still it produced little profit. In consequence there was little impetus to expand and the percentage of Italian steel requirements produced in Italy remained much less than that in any other major European nation. After 1914 the metals and machine segment of the economy became the largest industry. Still, Italian prices remained thirty-five percent above the world average.[4]

Because of the financial difficulties the metals industry, like many Italian industries, turned to protectionism. One of the major companies, ILVA (Ilva Alti Forni e Acciaierie d'Italia), first attempted to establish a monopoly by controlling the major producers and rationalizing their production to reduce competition. Although this failed, the major companies did form a cartel to control prices. But agreements with the German steel cartel prevented the introduction of cheaper supplies, which made the cost of producing military equipment in Italy high and limited the availability of cheap steel that might have formed stockpiles.

The steel-using industries—railroads and shipbuilding—depended heavily on government support. Cavour, prime minister at the time of the Risorgimento, had seen the importance of communications and pushed the construction of railways. Prior to unification, limited trackage existed in the various states. With the Risorgimento the government attempted, through a variety of private and semiprivate companies, to construct a major network of railways that would tie the country together economically and politically. Through mismanagement and the weakness of the economy, the railroad companies frequently failed. In 1905, after reorganizations and periods of governmental or quasi-governmental management, the government took the major rail lines under its control and created the State Railways.[5] This produced another drain on the government, since much of the equipment was obsolete. This pattern, of an overburdened government taking on more responsibilities, is continuous in Italy and is one of the most disruptive features of the economy. When a major crisis occurred, such as rearmament in 1939, the government could not respond because it was already overextended.

The introduction of railroads on such a large scale required the production of great quantities of equipment. The majority of Italian heavy machinery construction companies originated with this need. Ansaldo, Orlando, Terni, and Breda all started during the railway boom from 1845 to 1870.[6] The same companies dominated shipbuilding, which required similar expertise, and they controlled some steel-producing firms. Because of the emphasis on defense spending, a large part of their business consisted of orders for military equipment from the government. This special relation of the major industrial concerns and the government has lasted down to the present.

Another feature of Italian heavy industry has been its foreign connections: many of the companies had foreign origins. Genoa, which always had strong ties to Britain, had several steel works run by Englishmen. One became Ansaldo, while several other firms were founded by Italians trained in these English-run companies. Later Ansaldo allied itself with Armstrong, as Ansaldo, Armstrong and Company, and then with the French manufacturer Schneider-Creusot.[7] Terni, more a light-weapons producer, allied with Vickers. This continuing relation with foreign companies meant that in later years the Italian manufacturers produced large numbers of licensed items, to the detriment of their own designers and sales. Italy did not produce a native tank design in quantity until the very eve of World War II. In the interim, the Italians used a French World War I design and then a British machine-gun carrier (the original design was from Vickers Armstrong, Italian production was by Ansaldo).

The government, in addition to direct subsidies, aided the Italian economy by imposing a number of tariffs. Sardinia, under Cavour, had had a system of very low tariffs to stimulate trade. Like the military system, the new government extended these low tariffs to all of Italy after unification. But many other areas of the peninsula could not compete as well as Piedmont had against foreign trade. Agriculture, as well as some of the manufacturing industries, produced limited amounts at high prices. A long worldwide depression of prices, beginning in 1874, especially affected the Italian market and brought an overwhelming call for protection.

As a result, in 1878 Italy introduced the first series of tariffs, which had a disastrous effect. Protection enabled marginal Italian producers to remain in business and prevented the development of an export trade in any goods. Those industries that could compete were the victims of countertariffs in retaliation. The net result was that Italian industry was hampered in its development.

The Italian economy on the eve of the First World War was the product of all these factors. The historic dominance of Italy in trade had disappeared some three hundred years before. The economy had only emerged from the ensuing dark age within the last fifty years. In that period, industrialism had been introduced but Italy had not undergone an industrial revolution. Agriculture remained the base of the economy.

The industries that had developed tended to depend heavily on the government for support. The government supplied, at various times, direct subsidies, tariff protection, and large orders. These produced industries whose manufactured goods could not compete in international trade.

Although industry could not compete, international trade played an important role in the Italian economy. A large proportion of the raw materials required by manufacturers came from overseas. In particular, the steel industry, essential for military production, imported iron ore and coal in large quantities. This dependence on foreign supplies was initially endangered by the First World War.

Italian Industry in the First World War

Italian participation in the First World War reinforced many of the trends in the economy. Major industries became more dependent on government orders and less able to compete. Foreign trade suffered as Italy was cut off from traditional markets. Imports increased as the war demanded both raw material and finished goods. The national debt increased dramatically. Together these factors aggravated the weaknesses that already existed.

The major heavy-construction companies, flooded with orders, increased their capital and their capacity greatly. The demand for war production and the profits to be made attracted capital.[8] With the capital, whether from profits or investors, Fiat, Ansaldo, and the other great companies expanded their plants. They made impressive contributions to the war effort, producing tremendous numbers of motor vehicles, aircraft, and weapons. War losses, however, especially in the battle of Caporetto, placed additional strains on industry, and virtually all plants worked at capacity.

As a result, Italy imported substantial quantities of war material. The United States provided thirteen thousand railway cars.[9] Britain and France sent artillery pieces. Ammunition came from as far away as Kansas City. Even then many troops were ill equipped. Uniforms, shoes, and food headed the list of things the soldier and civilian noticed in short supply.

The artificial protection of the economy prior to the war caused many of the supply problems. The exception was the new and expanding automobile industry, which produced not only sufficient vehicles to fill the needs of Italy, but exported substantial numbers. Some industries, on the other hand, artificially protected for years and with little competition, could not produce sufficient equipment, which had to be imported instead.

The war stopped much of the normal foreign trade in consumer items. Italy had traditionally exported north through the Brenner Pass and east into the Balkans. Allied economic blockades and the front line cut off these markets, so nonmilitary production fell badly. This further injured the civilian sector of the economy.

The national debt increased enormously during this period. As much as fifty percent of the national income went for military expenses during the war. The Italian tax system could not cope. Like so much else, taxation was based on the old Sardinian system and had only been haltingly modified to deal with the changes in society since 1860. The government could not effectively tax the real sources of wealth in wartime Italy. Despite several new taxes on war profits and increased salaries, land and consumer sales remained the basis of taxation. Without adequate income, the government borrowed more and more. Until a moratorium on government debts, reparations, and so forth—proposed by U.S. President Hoover on 20 June 1931—payment on the debt remained a major drain on the economy.

The First World War showed the weakness of the economy in a mobilization: the industrial sector could not cope with the demands of a major war. Both raw materials and finished goods would have to be imported. More importantly, the majority of these requirements came from the Anglo-French world or from the United States. American grain and Iraqi oil required an open Mediterranean. Mussolini and the Fascists forgot these lessons in the interwar years.

The Fascist Epoch

Mussolini and his Fascist followers claimed to have an economic system that would improve the efficiency of the economy while satisfying owners and workers. The Fascists slowly introduced this system, called corporatism. They also found it necessary to resort to protectionism and government intervention in their attempts to stabilize and develop the Italian economy.

These measures, however, failed to improve the economic situation. Protectionism provoked countertariffs, which hurt export sales. Part of Mussolini's protectionism was the discouragement of foreign ownership. This reduced the number of firms in some fields, cutting capacity. Government intervention supported companies without regard to their efficiency. And the government never had enough funds for aid to completely renovate or reorganize an industry, only to support it.

The Fascists based their entire economic system on corporatism.[10] Workers and owners were organized into unions. These unions, or corporations, represented various business fields. The National Confederation of Industry, for example, represented companies like Fiat, while the workers in Fiat and Ansaldo belonged to another confederation or union. In theory the government was the third member of this system. It arbitrated between the two sides, management and labor. The government would work for the best interests of the nation; its decisions would be those that were best for both confederations. In this way business and labor could work together harmoniously.

The actual result was to unleash management.[11] Under the Fascist police state, the workers had little opportunity to influence or oppose government decisions handed down through the corporations. The com-

panies themselves, however, now had a public role. As part of the corporations each company had a part in the determination of public policy
and a duty in the development of the Italian economy. The major
companies turned this public role to private advantage.

Through their confederation and the Ministry of Corporations, the
grand industries influenced policy to their benefit. The government
changed labor laws, import quotas, and taxation for them. The companies used their position to demand exemptions from many of the labor
and tariff laws. Despite the attempts of the Fascist government throughout the 1930s, the major companies avoided all efforts to harness them
for national rather than individual interests.

While industry sought to avoid government regulation, agriculture
suffered under major controls.[12] Mussolini wished to make Italy self-
sufficient in all things. Two related policies resulted. In the "battle of
grain" the government directed the growing of wheat. This attempt to
eliminate imports meant that much land was replanted to grain. Other
crops with better export potential were neglected. Marginal land received much effort in attempts to produce more grain.

The other policy, *autarchia* (autarky, or self-sufficiency), involved pro-
tective tariffs for all products. Mussolini wished Italy to be independent
of all foreign imports. The tariffs began with the battle of grain but
rapidly expanded. When Italy protected grain, other countries retaliated
and by a rapid escalation many Italian exports soon lost any edge they
had in foreign markets. At the same time Italy still required many essential imports, particularly in raw materials. Mussolini's struggle for autarky
had worsened the situation rather than improved it. Italy was still dependent on imports and many items, imported or locally manufactured,
now cost more.

Another aspect of autarky involved discouraging foreign ownership.
While this policy was motivated by a desire to have the means of production in Italian hands, most foreign-owned companies left the country,
and no local companies took over, so there was an absolute reduction in
capacity. In the automotive industry, for example, French concerns closed
down and no Italian manufacturer took over equivalent production.

Mussolini's policy produced an economy less able to respond quickly
to the demands of war. The consolidation of control in industry from
both corporatism and autarky reduced the potential manufacturers of
equipment. The tariff wars made the cost of both raw materials and

finished products rise. This made the cost of rearmament higher, in a country that already had little to spend for military procurement.

The Direction of the War Economy

One of the great weaknesses of the Italian economy was its lack of direction. This manifested itself particularly in wartime. It was difficult to get the various industries working effectively. Each had its own interests and would, if it could, work toward its own ends. In the First World War, the government coordinated the production of war material through a commission. But in the interwar period and at the beginning of the Second World War, Mussolini's government failed to establish an effective system for any future war.

The original World War I *Sottosegretario per le armi e munzioni* (undersecretary for arms and munitions) directed mobilization.[13] An army officer, Generale Alfredo Dallolio, filled the position and, despite a late start, successfully coordinated the majority of industries. He could requisition plants, grant draft exemptions for skilled laborers and allot resources. His office, later raised to the level of a ministry, had to approve new projects, such as the Renault tanks in 1918.

In the interwar period, the *Commissione Suprema di Difesa* had economic planning and management responsibilities.[14] This commission consisted of the ministers and undersecretaries of most ministries in the government. It lay dormant until the late 1930s, when Mussolini activated it for defense planning. While the commission established priorities and directed allocations of raw materials, it operated on too high a level to coordinate industries effectively.

In 1935 Mussolini created an agency just for stockpiling. This *Commissariato Generale Fabbricazioni di Guerra* failed in large part.[15] The tariff wars of autarky had destroyed Italy's foreign trade. Many industries retained control of their essential materials, such as coal, rubber, and petroleum. The three services also had independent procurement systems that competed. As a result, the commissariat accomplished little.

No central direction of the industrial war effort existed until the beginning of the Second World War, when Dallolio returned to arms and munitions procurement. He quickly resigned when he discovered that he would have less control than he had in the First World War.

Italy failed throughout the interwar period to organize sufficiently what limited resources were available. Companies competed for material, and even manufactured competing machine-gun designs using different cartridges. Italian industry produced even less of Italy's requirements in the Second World War, and Italy was now allied with countries that could not supply what she needed.

Fiat and Ansaldo

Two names dominated tank production, Fiat and Ansaldo. Fiat, the great automobile company, produced engines and suspensions for all tanks manufactured after 1930. It also built the first two Italian tank prototypes, the Fiat 2000 and the 3000 (or Model 1921). Ansaldo, a shipbuilding and heavy construction company, did design work and built the chassis of all post-1930 tanks. Both the companies had prospered in the First World War. And they both had special relations with the government.

Ansaldo, founded in 1854, had been a major defense contractor since its beginning.[16] It built ships and guns for the military as well as merchant ships, trains, and heavy equipment. During the First World War it prospered, increasing its capital from thirty million lire to five hundred million. But in the immediate post-World War I period Ansaldo had difficulty converting to peacetime production. It had overextended in its wartime expansion and could not find new capital. The firm tried to get the government to buy its products at artificially high prices; when this failed the company collapsed.

Reorganized in 1922, Ansaldo recovered. It remained dependent on government contracts, building many of the ships for Mussolini's new navy in addition to the new tanks of the 1930s. The appointment of Generale Ugo Cavallero, a former undersecretary of the Ministry of War, as general manager in 1928 emphasized the close relationship with the government.

Fiat emerged from the same war in much better shape.[17] Founded in 1899, Fiat had rapidly expanded in the years before the war. Dominated by Giovanni Agnelli, one of the founders, the company began producing passenger cars with an emphasis on performance on the mountain roads near its factory at Turin. In World War I the company rapidly expanded to produce aircraft, trucks, cannon and machine guns in addition to cars.

The company had no difficulty in converting this production to the civilian market at the end of the war. It used the capital accumulated during the war to buy smaller firms and established a preeminent position in the Italian automotive industry.

Even with its insurmountable lead Fiat used the corporative state and Mussolini's other policies to its own ends. It took advantage of autarky to eliminate foreign competitors while it demanded special consideration in the application of laws. Fiat used its position to bypass labor laws and import quotas, and to get the government to finance capital improvements. The company did this by, among other methods, refusing contracts unless its conditions were met.

Fiat and Ansaldo had achieved, despite some temporary setbacks, positions of great importance in the Italian economy. By far the largest companies in their fields, they dominated such a large sector of the economy that they were virtually beyond government control. They could demand and receive special treatment even in the production of military necessities in wartime. There were virtually no other companies to challenge them.

The Automobile in Italy

Despite the prominence of Fiat, the automobile played a limited role in Italian life in the interwar years. The cost of the vehicle, and of gasoline, limited ownership and usage. The government developed road networks, but they were primarily for military and commercial purposes rather than civilian traffic. A few prominent race drivers and the success of Italian race cars presented a different image to much of the world, but Ferrari did not build tanks.

The average Italian read of these racing exploits but did not drive a car himself. In 1939 Italy had 290,000 cars registered;[18] one car for each 112 people. The number of cars had tripled since 1929, yet even if each vehicle may have had several drivers, relatively few Italians drove in the interwar years. Mussolini directed that the majority of car production be exported to bolster foreign trade, but the tariff war prevented this. In the late 1920s, Italy exported seventy percent of her car production, but by the late 1930s the percentage dropped below thirty.[19] In consequence the automobile industry had little opportunity for expansion.

Even if an Italian had a car, he could not afford much gasoline. Italy had no oil fields of her own, thus all crude oil had to be imported at great expense. Mussolini started a massive campaign to change this, but with little success. He formed a state oil company, which purchased Rumanian oil fields, built refineries in Italy,[20] and searched for either oil or an acceptable substitute in Italy.

Despite the effort expended, especially on the search for a synthetic motor fuel, Italy remained dependent on foreign supplies. These supplies, even when refined in Italy, cost a great deal. Gasoline cost four times more in Italy than in Great Britain in the 1930s. The cost and the foreign exchange involved prevented the stockpiling of petroleum products.

The cost of cars and gasoline kept Italy from becoming more of a motorized state in the interwar years. The life-style of the individual Italian was little changed by the car. Transportation depended on the train much more than the car and many Italians had no experience driving a car. This limited the number of mechanics and other trained automobile service personnel.

*   *   *   *   *

Mussolini failed to reform the Italian economy. In 1939 it still suffered from the weaknesses built up over the last three hundred years. Since the decline of its trading economy Italy had not established a viable new economic system. The peninsula did not contain the raw materials to become a great manufacturing nation. Nor could agriculture provide a sufficient foreign trade balance so that imported material could be used.

The First World War increased the problems. Those companies with the capital and expertise dominated defense production, limiting the number of possible manufacturers. Fascist reform attempts in the interwar years served only to reinforce the hold of the major companies and caused foreign trade problems that prevented the buildup of stockpiles.

The increased strength of the major companies also prevented the effective control of industry in support of the war effort. Attempts to institute the system used in the First World War failed because of company opposition, government indecision, and lack of planning.

While industry struggled, the individual Italian did little better. The cost of everything in Italy was high in the interwar years. In particular the price of automobiles and gas prevented their widespread use. Combined with the limited development of industry, the lack of cars meant that the average person had limited experience with mechanization.

Italy did not have a mechanized society in 1938 and 1939 when the Italian army adopted mechanization. The industrial base of the country could not support such a society. Nor did Italy have the resources, in money, material, or people to mechanize itself in a short period of time.

Notes

1. Denis Mack Smith, *Italy, A Modern History* (Ann Arbor: University of Michigan Press, 1959), chap. 7 discusses this policy in detail.

2. Shepard B. Clough, *The Economic History of Modern Italy* (New York: Columbia University Press, 1964), p. 51.

3. Clough, *History,* pp. 61-66.

4. Clough, *History,* p. 88.

5. P. M. Kalla-Bishop, *Italian Railroads* (New York: Drake, 1972), chap. 2.

6. Kalla-Bishop, *Railroads,* chap. 1; Clough, *History,* pp. 69-71.

7. Clough, *History,* p. 65; Emanuele Gazzo, *I Cento Anni dell Ansaldo, 1853-1953* (Genoa: Ansaldo, 1953), chap. 1.

8. Rodolfo Morandi, *Storia della Grande Industria in Italia* (1931; Torino: Einaudi, reprint ed. 1959), pp. 145-50.

9. Clough, *History,* p. 191.

10. Clough, *History,* chap. 7 is the best English source.

11. Roland Sarti, *Fascism and the Industrial Leadership in Italy* (Berkeley: University of California Press, 1971), an excellent interpretation of the period, advances this idea.

12. See Clough, *History,* chap. 7. Franco Calatano, *L'Economia italiana di guerra* (Milan: Istituto Nazionale per la storia del movimento di liberazione, 1969) is an anti-Fascist discussion of the philosophy behind policy in this period.

13. Clough, *History,* p. 179.

14. Ministero delle Comunicazioni, *Ordinamento e compiti della Commissione Suprema di difesa* (Rome: Istituto Poligrafico dello Stato, 1940).

15. Clough, *History,* p. 260.

16. Gazzo, *I Cento Anni dell Ansaldo,* is the only history.

17. Valerio Castronovo, *Agnelli* (Turin: UTET, 1971) is the best Italian history. *"Fiat" A Fifty Years' Record* (Verona: Arnoldo Mondadori Editore, 1951) is the English history.

18. Michael Shepard, *Cars of the 1930's* (London: Batsford, 1970), p. 223.

19. Ibid.

20. Clough, *History,* p. 257.

4
Reggimento
Carri Armati

Italian industry first produced tanks, the basis of military mechanization, in 1918. They immediately ran afoul of the fundamental facts of Italian industrialization. Financial difficulties hindered production. Attempts to have the vehicles produced in France were unsuccessful. The General Staff, struggling under the burdens of conducting the war, neglected tank development for long periods. Nevertheless, Italy did embark on a program of armor development.

The development of armor in Italy in the interwar years falls into three phases. The first phase, of experimentation and gradual development under a policy of motorization, lasted from the end of the First World War to 1930. A second phase, one of transition, lasted through the beginning of the Ethiopian war; the final period, mechanization, was based on the Italian experiences in Ethiopia and in the Spanish Civil War. In the first period, the debate on mechanization versus motorization had not developed. The General Staff followed the single policy of motorization. Tanks were infantry-support vehicles and nothing more. Tank units were organized as support units, designed to reinforce infantry units in the attack.

The sterility of concept during the 1920s is reflected in literature. There were only four major works on tanks published in this period. Varying little from official manuals, they discuss the tank only as an auxiliary to the established branches. Doctrine presented in official publications was equally sterile. Tank units were trained only for the limited role assigned by policy with little encouragement to think of greater roles in combat. The lack of innovative ideas was matched by a lack of advocates of armor use, such as existed in Britain and France. Giulio Douhet, the famed airpower advocate, was the only innovative military thinker in Italy at this time. Despite these handicaps, Italy moved slowly ahead from the introduction of tanks in 1918 to the deployment of the first battalions ten years later.

Armor was introduced in Italy during the First World War. The tank in Italy followed closely the development of its predecessors in military mechanization, the truck and the armored car. The Italian army first used trucks in the Italo-Turkish war of 1911-12. From that time an independent motor service slowly developed. The Italians adopted the truck for most military roles and quickly saw the possibilities of the use of armored vehicles. Fiat built the first Italian armored cars in 1915. But the Italian title *autoblindomitragliatrice* showed the limited tactical concept that was initially employed: it was literally an armored, self-propelled machine gun, as the name implies. The armored cars took over little of the reconnaissance and skirmish line roles of the cavalry or cyclists, but were assigned to machine-gun units for fire-support missions.[1] By the time of the armistice the Italians had employed about one hundred armored cars in so-called *squadriglia di automitragliatrice.*[2] They were used in the campaign after Vittorio Veneto in 1918, but again with the infantry rather than in the independent role of armored cars on other fronts.

Fiat trucks were also used in a variety of roles, notably as self-propelled guns.[3] The army utilized trucks in almost every conceivable role. Searchlight trucks, ladder trucks for artillery observers, and workshops on trucks were all part of the Italian motorization program. On 1 November 1918 there were 3,000 officers and 115,000 men with 32,000 trucks and 6,000 motorcycles in the Italian army Motor Transport Service.

From 1918 on the history of the tank units became interwoven with that of the motorized units. Italy chose a unique way of directing the development of motor vehicles in its army: a single motor transport corps trained all drivers and mechanics and was responsible for all technical development. The other branches of the army simply used personnel from the Motor Transport Corps if drivers were needed.

The first tank unit per se was the *reparto speciale di marcia carri d'assalto,* special detachment of assault cars, formed in the summer of

1918 with French vehicles.[4] In November 1918 this became the 1st
Independent Battery of Assault Cars with a Fiat 2000, one of two forty-
ton Fiat designed tanks, and three Renault light tanks, presumably the
vehicles brought to Italy in May of that year. This detachment deployed
to Libya in February 1919, where it was used in the renewed fighting
that occurred when Italy tried to regain territory lost during the First
World War.

Although Italy had a policy of using tanks at this point, it did not have
any doctrine for their use. The unit commanders were making pragmatic
decisions. But with the end of the major postwar fighting in Libya, the
army began a general review of its performance. Armored doctrine was
not an immediate concern in this attempt to improve the organization
and operation of the army. However, as soon as the immediate problems,
including the internal political difficulties that led to fascism, were re-
solved, the army embarked on a broader program of experimentation to
formulate a new doctrine.

Assist the Infantry: Doctrine of the 1920s

Italian policy on the use of tanks remained unchanged in the 1920s.
Originally formulated in 1918, when the first decision to produce tanks
was made, tanks were simply support weapons for the infantry. The
armor and firepower of the tank would deal with those obstacles, such
as machine-gun positions, that held up the infantry. The General Staff
now had to establish a specific doctrine for the organization, training,
and operational use of the tank in the Italian army.

This was complicated by the fact that the General Staff itself was
evolving in this period. As a result of the First World War the entire command structure of the army had come under close scrutiny and in the
early 1920s several changes took place. The major change was the establishment of a joint staff to supervise all three services. Nonetheless, the
army did establish a doctrine to implement the established policy. It was
not an innovative set of manuals, nor was there any of the debate and
controversy that was beginning in Britain. A limited number of books
were published in Italy on tanks in the early years. None went beyond
the limits of official policy and most were similar to the manuals in which
doctrine was laid down. In all these works, the tank was an auxiliary to
the infantry, used to destroy obstacles. In general the tactics were universal,

with no reference to specific Italian problems, although some of the commercial books began to discuss the problem of using tanks in the mountains that were now Italy's borders. The doctrine was, however, applicable to any tank operation without regard for terrain. This conventional doctrine was the basis of all tank operations in the 1920s and for the establishment of the first Italian tank units.

The establishment of policy and doctrine was the preserve of the Ministry of War and the *Stato Maggiore* (General Staff). The name of the incumbent minister often identified individual pieces of policy established during the person's tenure. From 1922 to 1925 the Minister of War was, first, Generale Diaz, the Duke of Victory as he had been styled, and then a much less well known politician-general, Antonio Di Giorgio.[5]

In 1925, as Mussolini consolidated his power, he himself became the Minister of War. Early in 1925, Il Duce had become the Minister of the Air Force and on 4 April he became Minister of War *ad interim.* Shortly thereafter he became Minister of the Navy.[6] In each case Mussolini appointed, as the effective head of the Ministry, an undersecretary who was a serving member of the armed force involved. In the case of the army, the *Sottosegretario al Ministero della Guerra* from 1925 to 1928 was Generale Ugo Cavallero, a Piedmontese infantry officer.[7]

In 1923 a council to coordinate defense policy was set up. This was called the *Commissione suprema mista di difesa,* or mixed supreme defense commission,[8] the highest guiding body for Italian defense policy in the interwar period. However, most of the immediate army concerns would be dealt with by the Ministry of War.

There was another change that had a more direct effect on the organization of the Ministry of War. This was the creation of the *Capo di Stato Maggiore Generale* in 1925.[9] When the position was established, Pietro Badoglio assumed it in addition to that of chief of the army General Staff and held both offices until 1929. The senior officer of the army was the *Capo di Stato Maggiore dell'Esercito,* or the chief of the army General Staff, a post created in 1882. Cadorna and Diaz were chiefs of the army General Staff during the First World War; when Diaz stepped down in 1919, he was replaced by his assistant Badoglio. The new responsibilities of the *Capo di Stato Maggiore Generale* sounded formidable. The chief of the Defense Staff, as his new title translates, was the military advisor to Mussolini, the *capo governo,* chief of government. He coordinated the defense plans of the three armed services. In consultation with the chiefs of staff of the armed forces, the chief of the Defense Staff ensured that each service was contributing its best to defense planning and that each was aware of the plans and problems of the others.

The *Capo di Stato Maggiore Generale* had to be an army officer, responsible to the Minister of War for the preparation of the army and its equipment for war.[10] As a result, the chief of the Defense Staff was a superinspector of the various branches of the army. He also had responsibility for the preparation of defense planning studies on all topics, and for the coordination of the annual maneuvers that were a major part of military training. One of his duties was to ensure the cooperation of the army, navy, and air force in these maneuvers, which were the major tests of doctrine and planning for the Italian armed forces.

The *Capo di Stato Maggiore Generale* had no personnel, money, or actual authority. Badoglio, who held the position from its creation to 1940, could not make the studies that were part of the job because he had no staff. Similarly, inspections and coordination of planning for military preparedness was impossible. Actually, the *Capo di Stato Maggiore Generale* was only a figurehead with little to do.[11] Badoglio continued to carry out, in addition, the function of chief of the army General Staff from 1925 to 1929 and then was Governor General of Libya from 1929 to 1933.[12] It was only during the periods of the Italo-Ethiopian war and the campaign in Albania that Badoglio returned to a position of some importance, still as the *Capo di Stato Maggiore Generale.* Despite the multitude of names and the confused paper structure of defense decision making, the army did produce a variety of documents establishing doctrine.

The organization of the army as a whole was controlled by *ordinamenti,* ordinances that defined the number, organization, and purpose of all units in the army. The ordinances were named after the Minister of War currently in office. The basic doctrine was set forth in a series of manuals called either *norme,* norms or rules, or *direttive,* directives. Minor modifications of doctrine, or provisional ones, were published as *circolari,* circulars. These circulars, which would normally be incorporated in the next manual, were distributed as individual publications to the army, and those with sufficient interest were published either in the *Gazzetta Ufficiale,* the official gazette of the government, or in the *Giornale Militare Ufficiale,* the official military journal.

Tactical doctrine in the early 1920s was still that of the First World War. The *Direttive per l'impiego delle grandi unità nell'attaco* and

Direttive per l'impiego delle grandi unità nella difesa, the directives for
the use of major units in the attack and the defense, published in 1918,
gave a straightforward set of infantry tactics.[13] The force was to be divided into a first assault wave, a reserve for that wave, and an exploitation force that would include the cavalry. Artillery, machine guns, and
support troops, including tanks, would help in attacks by dealing with
resistance. The defense was equally conventional but tankless.

Several books showed increased official interest in the new weapon.
When Manlio Gabrielli's book *I Carri Armati* appeared in 1923, the
Giornale Militare Ufficiale informed the army.[14] The journal described
it as a work "that offered a rapid overview of the weapon and showed
the theories in favor of and against the adoption of the new weapon."
It was a brief work of forty-five pages, mostly a straightforward narrative
of the use of tanks in the First World War, with heavy emphasis on the
French experience.

In his conclusion, Gabrielli, an infantry captain, discussed the various
viewpoints on tanks. He mentioned those men who said the next war would
be fought with totally mechanized means. He included Colonnello Augusto
Grassi, commander of the *Reparto Carri Armati* (Tank Detachment), who
was "a determined advocate of tanks."[15] Gabrielli then went on to mention that it was "inadvisable to provide a mass of tanks today—when
tomorrow the military and technical industry will declare them obsolete."[16]
He also advanced the possibility that aerial or chemical warfare would
develop to the point that it would end a war so quickly that no other
means would be necessary.

Gabrielli presented all this information without value judgments.
None of the positions was supported. He presented the official doctrine
as the way to do things, but with no advocacy of progressive ideas. He
argued that Italy should not overdevelop any means of warfare to the
point where the army could not adjust to another type of fighting if the
next war involved a different kind of action than was expected. Gabrielli
added that in any case Italy's next war would "almost certainly begin
in the zone of high mountains where the use of tanks is unanimously
judged to be impossible or of little use."[17]

Colonnello Grassi of the *Reparto Carri Armati* had retired but his successor, Colonnello Enrico Maltese, wrote in 1924 an introduction to tanks
for the Central Military School at Civitavecchia.[18] This combined arms
training center was established under the *ordinamento Diaz* in 1924 for

Figure 1. Colonnello Enrico Maltese. Commander of Reparto Carri Armati, 1924-26. In 1924 he wrote an introduction to tanks for the Central Military School at Civitavecchia that first discussed the concept of self-propelled guns and outlined the Italian method of tank warfare. *Courtesy of the Historical Office of the Italian Army General Staff.*

the "perfection and unity of view of the professional culture of officers."[19] In this treatise Maltese repeated most of Gabrielli's arguments, including that tanks were useless in the mountains. He again emphasized that tanks were not yet proven. The colonel also presented one new point, the concept of the *semovente,* a self-propelled field piece designed to be fired from the carriage without emplacement.[20] This introduction contained the first mention of the standard Italian system of organizing or classifying tanks by weight and purpose.[21] The classes were *carri pesanti* or *di rottura,* heavy tanks or breakthrough tanks, which were in excess of thirty tons and equipped with a medium cannon. *Carri medi* were between ten and thirty tons and had a light to medium cannon; *carri leggeri,* light tanks (also known as *carri d'assalto* or *carri d'accompagnamento,* assault tanks or accompanying tanks), were generally below ten tons. Speed was a minor consideration, since on the field of battle and in close cooperation with the infantry, only very slow speeds would be required.

The next year another commercial book appeared with strong official connections. The author, Edoardo Verse, was a colonel on the staff of the *Scuola d'Applicazione di Fanteria,* the Italian infantry school for officers. His book, again titled *I Carri Armati,* was the longest and most detailed work on tanks thus far.[22] Verse catalogued the advantages of the tank as the ability to approach the enemy without problems, the ability to destroy the enemy with the weapons on the vehicle when the approach was complete, and the economy of personnel involved.[23] The disadvantages listed were that tanks could not be used on all terrain or at night, that their weapons were not accurate or capable of firing in all directions, and that observation and communication were not good in tanks in combat. Verse then discussed the tactical employment of the tank in the various phases of battle. He emphasized the limitations of the vehicle and spoke only in terms of its use on a World War I battlefield. On that ground the tanks would break the enemy line for the infantry attack, deal with emplaced weapons, and similarly assist the main assault force.

In his last chapter, Verse examined the tank forces of other nations. This was one of the continuing phenomena in Italy. Military journals, books, and studies of all types discussed at great length what other countries were doing. The countries most often mentioned were Britain, France, Germany, and the United States. This concern with what others were doing seems peculiar to Italy, since most other countries were concerned with working out their own solutions rather than observing others.

However, this intense interest in developments in foreign lands did give the average Italian officer access to virtually all published developments by the principal powers. This summary offered no judgments beyond that of the inclusion of a given item. A simple précis was presented for interpretation or evaluation by the reader.

The last major work of the 1920s on tanks was perhaps the most important, the manual on the use of the tank, written in 1925 by the Tank Detachment itself,[24] and compiled while Colonnello Maltese was its commander. The basic ideas were similar to previous works, emphasizing the breakthrough and infantry support roles of the tanks. Light tanks would be used as scout vehicles and in support of cavalry units. (Italy at this time had no light tanks for this role, having only the Fiat 3000 medium tank, essentially a modified World War I Renault.)

These four books were the only major works on tanks written in Italy before 1930. More general books on military affairs touched only briefly on tanks. The most famous general work was Colonnello Ettore Bastico, *L'Evoluzione dell'Arte della Guerra* (The Evolution of the Art of War).[25] Bastico was an instructor in military history at the Italian naval academy at Livorno. He dealt with tanks in very much the same terms as earlier writers, seeing them as infantry escorts. He later became an important armor commander.

A more influential aspect of Italian writing in this period was on airpower and its impact in modern war. The most famous writer was Giulio Douhet, an air force officer, who was a powerful advocate of the use of the airplane as a decisive weapon in warfare.[26] His major work, *Il Dominio dell'Aria* (Command of the Air), written in 1921, dealt only in the most general terms with land warfare and, although armored warfare could be fitted into the framework of future war that he described, the air force was the crucial service. Ground troops would hold the borders of Italy while the air force attacked the enemy country.[27]

The Italian air force academy textbook on the art of war published in 1927, however, presented the tank as an important but not exceptional weapon used in attacks and counterattacks only.[28] In these operations it supported infantry and attacked and destroyed obstacles with which the infantry could not deal. The air force text seems to have been based directly on army manuals without any independent consideration of the concepts involved. The author was an army officer attached to the academy.

There were a variety of other official and quasi-official statements on the use of the tank in the Italian army. The *Almanacco delle Forze Armate*, an official almanac of facts and figures concerning the military,[29] had a section on tanks that discussed their history and employment. The tank was an auxiliary of the infantry or the other combat arms— cavalry, light troops, and so forth—when used in attacks of the type infantry carry out. The tanks were to be used in close cooperation with the infantry throughout the attack and with the maximum element of surprise. They were to be used in mass and depth.

For the first time there was an extensive, at least in relation to the length of the article, discussion of antitank defenses.[30] Cannon, mines, and high-powered rifles were discussed, but the tank itself was ignored as a way of combating an attack by tanks. The tank was still conceived to be only a means of attacking and overwhelming fixed positions. Mobile warfare was not yet part of Italian policy nor would it be for several years. However, one of the major considerations of Italian policy was dealt with in a rather oblique way. One of the pictures accompanying the article in the *Almanacco* shows two Fiat 3000s in a mountain meadow and is captioned "A section of tanks crossing an area of peat in the high mountains."[31] Colonnello Maltese, the author, did not mention anything about mountains. He only made a vague statement about using the tanks in suitable terrain. Nevertheless, the question of the Alps and tanks was becoming a major problem in Italian defense planning.

In 1928 a further statement of policy on tanks and infantry appeared in the *Norme per L'Impiego tattico della Divisione*.[32] This basic manual on infantry divisions in combat defined the tactics of tanks in support. The concept of tank use was strictly limited to the attack. Tanks would not march to the assembly area with the infantry. During the attack, they would concentrate on the neutralization of centers of resistance and the destruction of obstacles.

Protection of the tanks from the enemy was a major consideration. Artillery and ground attack aircraft should both be used in neutralizing antitank fire.[33] The tanks would also be deployed on the widest possible front so that the fire of the enemy artillery could not be concentrated on them. This set of standards for the employment of a division remained in effect through the period of the Italo-Ethiopian war and was an important stage in the development of the doctrine in the Italian army from the straight infantry tactics of the immediate post-World War I period to the well-balanced armored divisions of 1939-40.

Thus far all of the manuals and documents examined have emphasized tactics applicable anywhere rather than in any specifically Italian operational theater. But the locations where Italy planned to fight influenced the choice of tactics. The only plan for war that exists today from this period is from 1928.[34] The Operations Office of the General Staff based it on the assumption of a war with Austria and Germany, with the Swiss neutral and the French and Yugoslavs "benevolently neutral." The Italians would conduct defensive operations in this case. The deployment of the tank battalions in 1927-28 conforms to this plan. The avenues of attack from the east and north were blocked by the location of the units.

The examination for officers' promotion also showed the potential battlegrounds. Advancement in the junior ranks of the Italian army, for officers in *servizio permanente effettivo* (regular officers) was by annual examination. The test had sections on tactics, weapons, administration, and geography, among others. In the 1928 test for officers of infantry, cavalry, artillery, and engineers, the geography section quite specifically identified four *teatri d'operazione* with which the officer should be familiar. They were the Italo-French, Italo-Swiss, Italo-Austro-German, and the Italo-Yugoslav fronts. In the test section on the characteristics of foreign armies were the French, Swiss, German, Austrian, and Yugoslavian armies. These five remained, until 1939, the armies on which an officer was tested.[35] Borders with these nations were mountainous but had some areas of open terrain. In the 1920s only France had a tank force and it was behind one of the stronger mountain barriers. At this stage, before Ethiopia, Africa was ignored.

In the same examination only the infantry and the artillery had specific questions on the tanks. The infantry officer was expected to know about the use of tanks in cooperation with cavalry and with motorized and bicycle-transported infantry.[36] The artillery officer was required to know the characteristics of the construction and armament of tanks and armored cars. The design and construction of armored vehicles in the Italian army, along with that of all motor vehicles and weapons, was the responsibility of the Technical Service of the artillery, which was the research and development organization of the Italian army. The artillery was also the main antitank arm. The infantry had a limited antitank role (if they had antitank weapons), while the tanks themselves had no such role, being solely concerned with the destruction of enemy fortifications and obstacles. *Alpini* and *bersaglieri,* the two elite arms mentioned earlier, were, for the purpose of this promotion examination as well as for most of the other administrative functions of the army, considered infantry.

Italian literature in the 1920s lacked the sense of advocacy that was the main theme of British writing at the time. Liddell Hart wrote *Paris or the Future of War* in 1925, and he and J. F. C. Fuller had been writing articles and essays from 1920 on.[37] Italy totally lacked any author advocating a position more progressive than the official one. Britain had authors who, like Verse, wrote histories of tank operations in the First World War. But in Britain a second group of advocates were trying to change policy. Why Italy and the rest of Europe lacked these advocates of change is difficult to say. The great-man theory may be the only explanation: Fuller and Liddell Hart might be original thinkers who just happened to be English, as Douhet was Italian.

The example of Douhet, who became an air force general, imprisoned while a colonel in 1917, for overly aggressive advocacy of his views on military matters, suggests another reason for the lack of Italians critical of official ideas. Douhet had spent much of the war in prison for his views and even his rehabilitation, especially under the Fascists, failed to completely eliminate this fear. Was advocacy of an untried view of armored warfare worth a career? Certainly men like Maltese had ideas in advance of official policy, but they limited their advocacy. The Italian army had no tradition of internal criticism. Italy itself was unstable and there was little general interest in such debate. The battles on policy and doctrine were fought in staff meetings rather than in print.

Lacking innovative ideas, policy and doctrine in Italy were remarkably consistent from the end of the war to 1928, and indeed on to 1935-36. The tank was an infantry support vehicle. It was useful in the attack, but not elsewhere and it could not operate in the mountains. The point was never raised that no one would fight in the mountains if they could help it. The policy on tanks was precise and constant. Organization and equipment were the next step.

The Organization of Tank Units, 1918-28

The development of doctrine was closely involved with the creation of tank units. After the employment of the first tank detachment in Libya, during 1919, a brief pause occurred. In 1923, as part of a general reorganization, an experimental center was established. In 1927 the Ministry of War created four battalions and deployed them across the traditional battlefield in northern Italy. At the same time, the motor service, that branch of the army that provided drivers' and mechanics' training and was responsible for the technical support and development of all motor vehicles, grew at a similar rate.

Together with the development of these units, a broad program of training was developed. Training included an advanced course for officers and a series of armywide competitions in vehicle driving and maintenance for enlisted and officer teams. The increasing emphasis on motor vehicles was the logical development of the policy of motorization the army followed in the 1920s.

The first step after the end of the war was firmly to establish the basic organization of the motor service. Many of the arrangements during the war had been makeshift. In 1919 the motor service was reorganized with a central directorate and ten centers, one for each corps in the army.[38] There was a central depot and a technical directorate at Bologna, which became the center of military mechanization. An interesting comment on the economic situation of the Italian army was that this reorganization made provision to rent military vehicles to other governmental and civilian organizations.[39] At the same time the army formalized training for officers in military vehicle use and maintenance.[40] The first course for captains and majors in 1920 was abandoned due to organizational problems, but by 1921 an advanced course for regular officers was permanently established. This was for officers of artillery, infantry, *bersaglieri,* and engineers.[41]

The next year a course of technical instruction for the officers of all units with assigned vehicles was introduced as well as an expansion of the advanced course.[42] There was further expansion of the tank corps in 1923. In that year a new *ordinamento Diaz* was passed that provided for the establishment of permanent detachments in the new specialties to experiment with and develop new tactics. It authorized, in particular, a detachment of tanks to be formed to allow the development of this new weapon. On 23 January 1923 the Independent Battery of Assault Cars was reconstituted as the *Reparto Carri Armati,* or Tank Detachment, with a strength of 21 regular officers, 4 warrant officers, and 261 enlisted men.[43] This was a somewhat unusual organization, as normal units could be expected to have roughly forty percent of its officer strength be *ufficiale di complemento* (reserve officers). In 1925 the title was changed to *Centro Formazione Carri Armati* (Tank Formation Center).[44]

Attention was called to the new unit by a contest for driving and maintenance, begun in 1925, called the "Cup of the Alps."[45] It was the first in a long series of training and publicity devices that the army was to use in the interwar years. Every unit in the army could submit an entry, which competed over a fixed Alpine course carrying out tasks that the army vehicles would have to perform in wartime. The winning unit received a trophy and enjoyed considerable prestige in the army.

The process of introducing, training, and emphasizing the military role of the motor vehicle continued to grow. The importance of the Tank Detachment in relation to Motor Transport units may be judged by the selection process for the Advanced Course in Motorization. In a class of thirty-two, all captains, majors, or lieutenant colonels, there were to be four general-staff officers, sixteen artillery officers, one officer from the bridging engineers, one tank officer, and ten transportation-unit officers.[46]

In 1927 a major development occurred in the Tank Center. On the first of October the *Centro Formazione Carri Armati* was reorganized as the *Reggimento Carri Armati,* or Tank Regiment.[47] Under this new organization a battalion would be at Rome and a battalion and regimental headquarters at Bologna, which was also the headquarters of the Motorization Board. There were also battalions at Brescia, Udine, and Palmanova and an armored-car group at Udine. Although this seems a major jump in size, it was more a question of semantics than expansion. The Tank Detachment had been growing at the rate of about one hundred men a year from its initial strength in 1923, and although it consisted of five battalions there were still only the one hundred tanks manufactured in 1920-21, which meant the battalions were company sized, approximately twenty tanks and one hundred men per battalion.

It is important to note the location of the battalions. Other than the battalion at Rome, which could serve both an internal security function and as a demonstration unit, the regiment was arrayed across the World War I battlefield of the north. The battalion at Brescia blocked the valley of the Adige, the route of any invader from the Brenner Pass, while the two battalions at Udine and Palmanova were at the crucial neck through which any invader from the east would have to come. The headquarters and the remaining battalion were at Bologna, in the center of the arc and at the center of communications in the Po Valley, where it could reinforce any of the battalions.

Italian development in this period was similar to that in other countries. Britain, France, and the United States were the only countries with tank

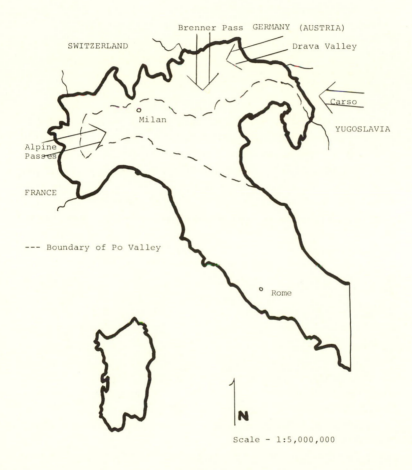

Brenner Pass GERMANY (AUSTRIA)

SWITZERLAND

Drava Valley

Carso

Milan

YUGOSLAVIA

Alpine
Passes

FRANCE

--- Boundary of Po Valley

Rome

N

Scale - 1:5,000,000

Map 1. Avenues of Approach to the Po Valley

units, and they all had battalions that were used in support of infantry. These battalions were all continuations of wartime formations and so had been created ten years before the Italian ones. But they only progressed beyond the Italian units briefly, in 1927 in Britain and 1928 in the United States. Britain formed an Experimental Armored Force in 1927,[48] a combined-arms force of brigade size that was the first true armored formation. Armored is used here to mean a combined-arms organization, with tanks as the main offensive weapon, designed to be used in mobile warfare. The United States formed a similar unit the next year but both were disbanded in 1928.[49]

As the 1920s came to a close the tank was firmly established in the Italian army. The battalions, trained and equipped, deployed to their blocking positions. The motor service furnished extensive support. Together they formed a firm base for further development. The deployment of the battalions showed a firm commitment to tanks. They were located so that they would be a major part of the first reserve if an enemy should penetrate the Alpine fortifications that were the first line of defense. The tanks, however, remained those that had been designed twelve years before. The lack of new and better tanks would be one of the weakest parts of Italian policy in this period.

The First Italian Tanks

The first Italian interest in tanks was at the beginning of 1917. An officer serving with the Italian forces in France observed the operations of French tanks as early as September 1916 and convinced the High Command to try the new vehicles.[50] The officer, artillery Captain (later Major) Alfredo Bennicelli, was also a count and a senator, which probably helped him sell his ideas. In any case, he got the Italian army to import a French Schneider tank for tests. Used on the Carso front, the tank sufficiently impressed the Italians so that further studies of other tanks were undertaken.[51]

The Fiat Company, the major Italian automobile producer, began work on a project of its own. The Fiat 2000 was a large, forty-ton vehicle, well armed and slow moving. Starting from scratch on a vehicle of that size was a long process, and the size left some questions about its usefulness for Italian terrain. In late 1917 the High Command asked the *commissariato per le armi e munizioni* (commissariat for arms and munitions)

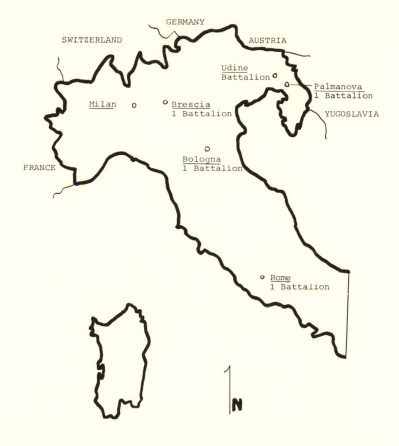

Map 2. Location of Italian Armored Units, 1928

to acquire one hundred Renault tanks and a further twenty Schneiders or the tooling for their production in Italy.[52] This move to acquire tanks immediately preceded the battle of Caporetto. Further action was postponed when the High Command became involved with the problems of that defeat.

Another group of French tanks, three Renaults and a Schneider, did not arrive until May 1918.[53] By this time it had become apparent that the Allies, and in particular the French who produced the Renaults, could not provide for Italian requirements out of their production. After further demonstrations of the Renault, arranged and directed by Maggiore Bennicelli, the Ministry decided to produce a version of the Renault in Italy.

The vehicle chosen was a Renault FT 17, modified in Italy with an improved engine and transmission. Called the Fiat 3000, it was to be produced by the Fiat Company with the assistance of the Ansaldo and Breda companies.[54] Fiat, dominated by Giovanni Agnelli, did the automotive construction.[55] Ansaldo San Giorgio and Company, a Genoa-based steel company primarily involved in shipbuilding, gun founding, railway construction, and the manufacturing of heavy equipment, did most of the work on armor and hull construction in Italian tank building.[56] Ernesto Breda, a Milanese firm primarily known for heavy engines, locomotives, and armaments, produced weapons and other equipment for the vehicles. These firms were among the greatest powers in Italian industry and were normally competitors. Ansaldo and Fiat had been in fierce competition for resources during the early part of the war and only as recently as 1918 had settled a major dispute on the subject.[57]

This consortium was initially given a contract for 1,400 tanks to be produced by 1921. Because of the end of the war, this order was reduced to 100 tanks, which were completed by 1921. The Fiat Company had used its military contracts to gain a predominant position in the Italian motor industry. Of 43,390 motor vehicles accepted by the Italian army in the First World War, 37,019 were Fiats.[58] When the war ended, Fiat got substantial indemnities as a result of canceled contracts. Fiat was well on its way to its preeminent position in Italian military production.

The tank around which all the early developments centered was the Fiat 3000, also known as the Fiat model 1921 or model 21, and later, after modifications in 1929-30, as the Fiat model 21/30. This was a minor modification of the French Renault model 1917, which was the most

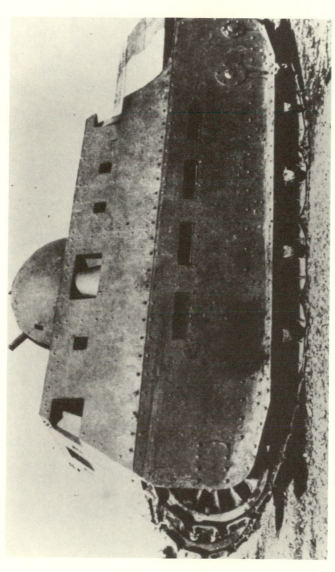

Figure 2. Fiat 2000 (1917) 40 Tons. Two examples built with slight variations. Riveted steel armor 3/4 inch (20 mm) thick. Cast turret. 6 cyl. water-cooled gasoline motor. Speed: road 4.5 mph, cross-country 1.8 mph. Armament: one 65mm cannon, 7 6.5mm machine guns. Crew: 1 officer, 9 soldiers. Ammunition supply: 45 projectiles, 7000 rounds machine guns. *Courtesy of the Historical Office of the Italian Army General Staff.*

Figure 3. Fiat 3000 (1921) 5.5 Tons. Derived from French Renault tank. Riveted steel armor 1/4 and 1/2 inch thick. 4 cyl. water-cooled gasoline motor. Speed: road 13 mph, cross-country 7.4 mph. Armament: 1 or 2 machine guns, 8mm. Crew: 2. Ammunition supply: from 2000 to 5760 rounds. This tank, on maneuvers, is laying a screen from its special smoke device. *Courtesy of the Historical Office of the Italian Army General Staff.*

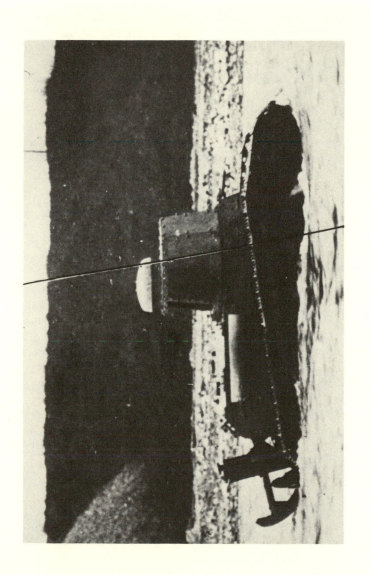

Figure 4. **First Fiat 21-3000 (1921) 5.5 Tons.** Showing the "tail" that prevented back somersaults. This tank is testing its river-fording abilities. *Courtesy of the Historical Office of the Italian Army General Staff.*

widely used tank of the interwar period. France not only used substantial
numbers of the vehicles but exported many. The United States also manufactured the Renault design in quantity. Thus the standard light tank of
the world in the 1920s also equipped the first Italian tank units. The
Fiat model 21 was a two-man vehicle, armed with twin turret mounted
machine guns. Weighing six tons, it was capable of 13 mph (24 kph).[59]
Its machine-gun armament and relatively low speed, coupled with its restricted climbing ability and poor maneuverability, limited the usefulness
of the model 21.

The improvements made in 1930 were few. The use of a cannon was
the significant change in the capability of the vehicle. It also received a
new engine, although due to gearing changes its maximum speed dropped
to 21 kph. Even though no detailed results of the experiments of the
Centro Carri Armati have survived, it is apparent that the Fiat 3000 was
found to be underpowered for cross-country movement. A comparison
with the other Renault FT-type tanks in use demonstrates the continuing
Italian design interests that were to handicap Italian armored warfare.
Both the French and American versions had a top speed of around 5 mph,
compared to the Fiat's 15 mph. From the beginning both countries had
produced cannon-armed as well as machine-gun-equipped versions, similar
to the Fiat model 21.[60] The Fiat was also equipped with slightly thinner
armor than the other models. This fixation with high speed rather than
performance, at least in the sense of cross-country performance, was to
be a design characteristic of the Italian armored fighting vehicles throughout the Second World War.

Although the lack of innovation and development in Italian tank design
has been mentioned, the 1920s were a relatively stagnant period in tank
design worldwide. The fact that World War I tank production had only
achieved full output at the very end of the war created an oversupply of
new vehicles far in excess of the requirements of the much-reduced peacetime armies.

The automotive parts of the armored fighting vehicle were the crucial
consideration in this period. Cross-country mobility is the raison d'être
of the tank and improvement of the mobility of most vehicles was the
major thrust of design and development in the 1920s. The suspension of
the vehicle in particular was the important factor. Most of the new vehicles
that made an impression with their innovations in the period had substantial improvements in suspension. The American Christie tanks are

perhaps the most famous, but Italy also had its Pavesi armored car, the so-called wheeled tank. The Pavesi was a large-wheeled, articulated-chassis vehicle with a much greater degree of cross-country mobility than normal wheeled vehicles. The Italian army, however, only used the design for artillery tractors and did not develop it any further, apparently because of the limitations of the technology available.

* * * * *

Italian tank design and production in this period showed key features that would endure. The major companies could handle tank production but they were the only available producers. Production took time. Independent design projects were infrequent, and government did little to encourage those that were begun. This pattern would continue to the beginning of the Second World War.

Despite these problems in tank design and production, Italy closely approximated her contemporaries. Most countries did little new construction in this period, relying on wartime designs. France had Renault tanks plus a few experimental types manufactured in small numbers. The United States equipped her battalions with Renault-style Ford Six Ton tanks and a few British World War I heavy tanks. Even Russia, when she began tank production in 1927-28, built modified Renaults. Britain had built a new postwar design, the Vickers Mark I and II series. But they were not appreciably superior to the Fiat. They mounted a cannon in a turret and three machine guns, which gave them superior firepower. But their speed was only 15 mph. Britain had 160 Vickers in four battalions; the Italians had 100 Fiats in five battalions.[61]

At the end of this first phase of armor development, Italy had established itself as an armor power. Motorization, Italy's policy, required the use of tanks and other motor vehicles in support of the traditional branches. The army had created a doctrine in keeping with that policy. Tanks were to be used in close support of infantry, to breach defensive lines and neutralize machine guns. Tank units trained in this doctrine were deployed to defend Italy at her most vulnerable point. Despite its relatively late start, Italy had an active and viable armor program the equal of her contemporaries.

There were also flaws in the program. Policy and doctrine were determined with little imagination. The debate on armor policy that raged in Britain was nonexistent in Italy. No advocates of mechanization arose to

propose alternatives to the current policy. Industry showed little interest
in the tank. Fiat and Ansaldo built the Renault but besides the abortive
Fiat 2000 showed no interest in independent design. And the few attempts
at independent design failed without government support. Italy had made
a commitment to armor, but the seeds of its failure were also sown.

Notes

1. *Enciclopedia Militare,* s.v. "Autoblindomitragliatrice"; Pugnani,
Motorizzazione Militare, p. 165.

2. *Enciclopedia Militare,* s.v. "Autoblindomitragliatrice."

3. Giulio Benussi, *Autocannoni, Autoblinde e Veicoli Speciali Del
Regio Esercito Italiano nella Prima Guerra Mondiale* (Milan: Intergest,
1973) is a concise coverage of these vehicles.

4. Pugnani, *Motorizzazione Militare,* p. 184.

5. *L'Esercito e I Suoi Corpi,* 1:272. For personal details, see *Enciclopedia Militare,* s.v. "Diaz, Armando" and "Di Giorgio, Antonio."

6. *L'Esercito tra La Guerra,* p. 62.

7. *Enciclopedia Militare,* s.v. "Cavallero, Ugo."

8. Circolare no. 17, 11 January 1923, *Giornale Militare Ufficiale,
Anno 1923* (Rome: Stabilimento Poligrafico per L'Amministrazione
della Guerra, 1920), p. 87. Circulars normally appear in the *Giornale*
(hereafter cited as *GMU* and year) four to six months after publication
for the army.

9. *L'Esercito tra la Guerra,* p. 56; *L'Esercito e I Suoi Corpi,* 1:273.

10. Howard McGaw Smyth, "The Command of the Italian Armed
Forces in World War II," *Military Affairs,* vol. 15, no. 1, Spring 1951,
p. 40. This article, based on military attaché reports, has many flaws but
is the only work in English on this point.

11. *L'Esercito tra la Guerra,* pp. 56-57.

12. Piero Pieri and Giorgio Rochat, *Pietro Badoglio* (Turin: Unione
Tipografico-Editrice Torinese, 1974), p. 590.

13. *L'Esercito tra la Guerra,* pp. 20-22.

14. Avvisi *GMU 1924,* p. 1110; Manlio Gabrielli, *I Carri Armati*
(Rome: Tipografica Delle Cartiere Centrali, 1923).

15. Gabrielli, *I Carri Armati,* p. 42; *Enciclopedia Militare,* s.v. "Grassi,
Augusto."

16. "Inavveduto il provedersi oggi di una massa—, quando domani la
tecnica industriale e bellica ne dichiaresse inefficace l'impiego ovvero ne
presentassi altri—." Gabrielli, *I Carri Armati,* p. 44.

17. "Quasi certamente inizio in zona di alta montagna e qui l'impiego dei carri e unamimemente giudicato pressoche impossibile o poco redditizio." Gabrielli, *I Carri Armati*, p. 45.

18. Scuole Centrali Militari, *I Carri Armati; Traccia di Conferenza per i Corsi Informativi* (Civitavecchia: Premiato Stab. Tip. "Moderno" di Remo Coltellacci, 1924). It is signed at the end by Maltese. See *Enciclopedia Militare*, s.v. "Maltese, Enrico."

19. *L'Esercito tra la Guerra*, p. 51.

20. Scuole Centrali Militare, *I Carri Armati*, p. 4.

21. Scuole Centrali Militare, *I Carri Armati*, p. 6.

22. Edoardo Verse, *I Carri Armati* (Parma: La Bodoniana, 1925).

23. Verse, *I Carri Armati*, pp. 88-90.

24. Reparto Carri Armati, *Addestramento Delle Unità Carriste, Parte Terza, Addestramento e Impiego Tattico (Stralcio di Regolmento Provvisorio)* (Rome: Libreria dello Stato Maggiore, 1925).

25. Ettore Bastico, *L'Evoluzione dell'Arte della Guerra* (Florence: Carpigiani e Zipoli Editori, 1924-27).

26. *Enciclopedia Militare*, s.v. "Douhet, Giulio."

27. Higham, *Air Power*, p. 68.

28. Regia Accademia Aeronautica, *Sommari di Arte Militare*, 2 vols., prepared by Tenente Colonnello Gian Giacomo Castagna (Leghorn: Belforte, 1927).

29. *Almanacco delle Forze Armate 1927* (Rome: Tipografia del Sanato, 1927).

30. *Almanacco*, p. 353.

31. *Almanacco*, p. 353.

32. Ministero della Guerra, *Norme per l'impiego tattico della divisione*, edizione 1928 (Rome: Provveditorato Generale Dello Stato, Libreria, 1928).

33. *Norme*, 1928, p. 70.

34. Ufficio Operazioni, Memoria Preliminare per Il Piano Di Operazioni alla Fronteria Italo-Tedesca. July 1928. Racc. 232, U.S.

35. Circolare no. 338, 28 March 1938, *GMU 1938*, p. 1053.

36. Circolare no. 181, p. 548.

37. Liddell Hart, *Paris or the Future of War*. See Liddell Hart, *The Tanks*, vol. 1, pt. 2, chap. 2 or Liddell Hart, *Memoirs* (London: Cassell, 1965), vol. 1, chaps. 4 and 5 for a more detailed account of various prize essays and the like.

38. Pugnani, *Motorizzazione Militare*, p. 242; Decreto 2149, 21 November 1919 and Circolare no. 248, 20 April 1920, *GMU* 1920 established these organizations.

39. Circolare no. 175, 23 November 1920, *GMU 1920,* p. 175.

40. Circolare no. 481, 12 August 1920, *GMU 1920,* p. 744.

41. Circolare no. 370, 30 June 1921, *GMU 1921,* p. 348; Circolare no. 478, 8 September 1921, *GMU 1921,* p. 764.

42. Circolare no. 304, 23 June 1922, *GMU 1922,* p. 616.

43. *Memorie Storiche No. 113,* Reggimento Carri Armati, 1, 2, 3, 4, Reggimenti Fanteria Carrista, 1923-1942. "Reparto Carri Armati, Deposito. Memorie Storiche per l'Anno 1923," Rome, 19 January 1924. The *Memorie Storiche* was an annual report of unit activities that each unit had to submit at the close of each calendar year. Those that survived the Second World War are now in bound volumes at the Ufficio Storico. The instruction for preparing *Memorie Storiche* can be found in Ministero della Guerra, Ispettorato Generale Leva Sottufficale e Truppa, *Istruzione per la Compilazione delle Memorie Storiche dei Corpi, No. 3756. Ed. 1939* (Rome: Istituto Poligrafico dello Stato, 1939).

44. *Memorie Storiche,* Centro Formazione Carri Armati, 1926.

45. Circolare no. 110, 5 March 1925, *GMU 1925,* p. 504.

46. Circolare no. 449, 5 August 1926, *GMU 1926,* p. 1591.

47. *Memorie Storiche,* Centro Formazione Carri Armati, 1927. Changes were under Circolare no. 15200, 17 August 1927 and Circolare no. 17900, 1 October 1927. Normally circulars with five digit numbers are major changes in policy and are published as pamphlets rather than in the *GMU.*

48. Liddell Hart, *The Tanks,* vol. 1, pt. 2, chap. 3. Kenneth Macksey, *Armoured Crusader* (London: Hutchinson, 1967), pt. 2, is a biography of Sir Percy Hobart, commander of the force.

49. Mildred Hanson Gillie, *Forging the Thunderbolt* (Harrisburg, Penn.: Military Service Publishing, 1947), chap. 2.

50. Pugnani, *Motorizzazione Militare,* p. 177. Other widely distributed books covering Italian armor are Benedetto Pafi, Cesare Falessi, and Goffredo Fiore, *Corazzati Italiani 1939-1945* (Rome: D'Anna Editore, 1968); *Carri Armati in Servizio fra le Due Guerre,* in the series *Fronte Terra: L'Armamento italiano nella 2^a guerra mondiale* (Rome: Edizioni Bizzarri, 1972). Richard M. Ogorkiewicz, *Armoured Forces* (New York: Arco Publishing Company, 1960). The latter's Italian translation, *I Corazzati* (Rome: Istituto Per La Divulgazione della Storia Militare, 1964), and a second English edition, 1970, which includes some information which appears in the Italian edition but not the earlier English one. All three books are heavily derivative of Pugnani. Henceforth, I will only cite Pugnani for information that appears in all these sources, and they will only appear when their information goes beyond Pugnani.

51. Pugnani, *Motorizzazione Militare,* p. 180.

52. *Carri Armati in Servizio fra le Due Guerre,* pp. 6-7.

53. *Carri Armati in Servizio,* p. 7.

54. *Carri Armati in Servizio,* p. 11 for technical information.

55. *"Fiat,"* A *Fifty Years' Record* (Verona: Arnoldo Mondadori Editore, 1951) is the company version. Valerio Castronovo, *Giovanni Agnelli* (Turin: Unione Tipografico-Editrice Torinese, 1971) serves as both a biography and a history of the company.

56. Emanuele Gazzo, *I Cento Anni dell'Ansaldo, 1853-1953* (Genoa: Ansaldo, 1953) is the only history of the company.

57. Castronovo, *Agnelli,* pp. 146-47.

58. Pugnani, *Motorizzazione Militare,* p. 244.

59. The proliferation of technical books on tanks in all languages over the last few years is amazing. Most contain essentially the same information. In so far as possible I have used Ministero Della Guerra, Centro Studio Motorizzazione, *Caratteristiche Mezzi da Combattimento in Uso nel'Esercito Italiano* (Rome, 1943) for information in the various manuals. For commercial publications, Giulio Benussi, *Carri Armati e Autoblindate del Regio Esercito Italiano 1918-1943* (Milan: Intergest, 1974) is one of the best.

60. For comparative data, I have used Peter Chamberlain and Chris Ellis, *Pictorial History of Tanks of the World 1915-1945* (Harrisburg, Penn.: Stackpole Books, 1972).

61. Ogorkiewicz, *Armoured Forces,* pt. 2.

5
From the Alps to Ethiopia

Military development in Italy during the interwar period often coincided with political development. From 1925 to 1930 Mussolini was establishing and consolidating his control over Italy. When he felt his power was complete, Il Duce began a period of innovation and change, leading to the Ethiopian war in 1935. In military affairs, Mussolini followed much the same pattern. The late 1920s were a period of little change. First World War innovations were tested and integrated into the army.

In the second phase, from 1930 to 1935, Mussolini introduced new ideas and equipment. The army adopted new weapons, uniforms, and helmets. The central theme of these changes was modernization: the Italian army was to be the equal of any army in the world in training and equipment. Several important innovations occurred in armored warfare. A completely new concept of troop organization and employment was introduced that produced a major competitor for the tank units. This idea, the *celeri,* was a combination of cavalry and *bersaglieri* to produce a uniquely Italian unit of mobile troops. This change in policy was quickly translated into doctrine. The idea of two kinds of tank units appeared in the first set of manuals on the employment of tanks. One was for the normal infantry support role and a similarly organized but differently trained unit would support *celeri* troops. This divided the available tank resources between two streams of tactical development. At the same time that the fruits of motorization were being divided, a new major alternative appeared.

Mechanization, a concept developed in Britain, was the reformation of armies to use the motor vehicle as a main weapon of war. The replacement of traditional weapons and tactics with the tank, and tactics designed for its capabilities, would allow a war of maneuver. To implement this policy, armies would have to be radically restructured. All weapons would require mechanized transportation. All personnel would require vehicles. And the entire supply system would need to be organized to support a rapidly moving, demanding army. The Italians noted the new idea but rejected it because of Italy's unusual situation.

At the very end of this phase in armor development, a further change in policy and doctrine occurred. This was a gradual move in the direction of a war of maneuver and away from the defensive mentality the Italians had maintained since the First World War. Signaled first in *I Celeri,* an influential book, official implementation occurred after the beginning of the Ethiopian war, although the concepts had been tested in the 1934 annual maneuvers. The introduction of the idea of a war of maneuver was the first step toward the development of a modern policy of mechanization and "decisive war," a war of strategic rather than tactical maneuver.

To fight the new wars that were being envisaged, Italy constructed new tanks and organized new units in this period. The new tank was the CV 33 series, an armored machine-gun carrier that was initially introduced for mountain operations but quickly became the support vehicle for the *celeri.* New units were organized to use this vehicle both for the infantry and the cavalry elements of *celeri* units. The army also had to organize a number of units in preparation for the war in Ethiopia, which required a large number of armored units and many of the new tanks. The personnel involved had trained in the annual maneuvers held between 1930 and 1935, which emphasized the use of the new vehicle in the Alps. Both new units and new organizations were heavily tested in this manner. The new doctrine was carefully examined before and after its publication.

I Celeri: Doctrine 1928-35

Italian doctrine in the early 1930s was most affected by the new concept of cavalry and *bersaglieri* fighting in integrated units. These *celeri* were a counterpoint to the increased emphasis on tanks and infantry that the First World War had produced. The concept caused a split in the development of armored policy, since the tanks now had to be furnished to two different types of unit. New doctrine had to be developed for the

support of *celeri.* Beyond the *celeri,* the new idea of the decisive war,
a war of maneuver using flanking attacks rather than frontal assault, had
a limited effect initially, but pointed toward major changes in the future.

The concept of the *celeri* was the culmination of several trends in the
use of the cavalry and the *bersaglieri.* The changes wrought in the battlefield by the machine gun and the tank reduced the possible roles for both.
The bicycle gave the *bersaglieri* movement comparable to the cavalry.
And the long pursuits of the defeated Austrians had required cooperation
between the two. But the concept was first enunciated by a well-placed
senior officer.

Generale Ottavio Zoppi was the man who popularized the new idea of
major units of cavalry and *bersaglieri* trained as a maneuver force. Zoppi
wrote *I Celeri* in 1933, a year after their first operational test in the 1932
maneuvers and a year before their use became official doctrine.[1] *I Celeri*
is an example of the way in which most of the new ideas in the Italian
army were presented and popularized. Zoppi was not a military critic
or advocate of the type that was flourishing in the United States, Britain,
or France. He was a Piedmontese, commissioned in the infantry from the
Military Academy at Modena. He had fought in Libya in 1912 and during
the First World War had commanded a brigade, a regiment, and finally
an *arditi* assault division. After the war, Zoppi fought again in Libya during the reconquest, and then held a number of administrative posts in
Italy. He was Inspector of Alpine troops from 1928 to 1930 and from
1933, the year his book came out, to 1935 he was Inspector of the
Infantry branch.[2] The position of inspector in the army was a supremely
powerful one, for the inspectorate controlled virtually everything except
command in the field. It ran the school, made policy recommendations
on organization and equipment, and was responsible for the training and
efficiency of all units of the branch. At this time the *bersaglieri* were
under the Inspector of Infantry and the cavalry under the Inspector of
Cavalry.

Zoppi's book was published in the series "Military Arguments of
Today," with the introduction by Generale Emilio De Bono, one of the
heroes of the First World War and, more importantly, one of the four
Fascist Quadrumvirs who led the March on Rome in 1922.[3] De Bono
commends the book to the people and suggests that the *celeri* had a spirit
similar to the Fascists. De Bono, as did Liddell Hart, lamented the war of
position that Italy had just fought against Austria and pointed to the

Figure 5. Generale Ottavio Zoppi. Inspector of Alpine troops, 1928-30. Inspector of Infantry, 1933-36, author, leading advocate of *celeri* concept. *Courtesy of the Historical Office of the Italian Army General Staff.*

celeri as a way to avoid the repetition of such a stalemate in the future.

Zoppi himself attempted to create a spiritual as well as organizational base for the *celeri*. Again his starting place was the First World War; like many other military writers in the interwar period, Zoppi wanted to break the impasse that was created by the machine gun. However, his solution was to infuse the troops with aggressive spirit. The *celeri* best embodied this spirit. These units, especially in areas like the borders of Italy, could operate in a decisive manner. Their spirit allowed them to overcome the stagnation of trench warfare. Zoppi also felt that tanks were important and that they, along with the close support of aircraft, would be used in the future.

On more technical grounds he wrote that the motor vehicle was not as versatile in the theaters of operations in which the Italians would be active. Only the *celeri* could operate on the fringes of the battlefield. Zoppi makes the *alpini* the *celeri* of the mountains.[4] Thus, theoretically, he covered all of the Italian territory with some *celeri* troops and included the three traditionally morally superior branches of the army in his new elite.

Zoppi's ideas are important not only because of the tactical innovations he proposed, but also because he represented a major effort to re-inspire and convert the army under the Fascist leadership. The Fascists had been attempting to infuse spirit into the Italian people in a number of ways. Often this drive to make Italy into a warrior nation had centered around endless evocations of their Roman ancestry. But within the army itself, people who were in daily contact with the modern methods of war required something more sophisticated. Zoppi tried to supply this by creating a new group based on the historical elites but capable of winning modern wars. The *celeri* were an attempt to adapt the legendary élan of the cavalry and light infantry to modern war by creating a synthesis that would allow it to operate in the situation Italy could expect in the next war. Zoppi's vision was not concerned with armor but with cavalry on horses and sharpshooters in light infantry formations acting together.

The tank units to support the *celeri* were formed as part of the *Guide* Light Horse Regiment at Parma in 1933. The unit commander, Colonnello Gervasio Bitossi, directed the development of these units and established the policy for them. Originally a cavalry man, he became an armor commander in North Africa.[5] Bitossi set the tone of early training with his introductory speech to the regiment.[6] In it he emphasized the *carri*

Figure 6. Generale Gervasio Bitossi. Commander of Reggimento Cavaleggeri Guide,
1° Reggimento Misto Motorizzato and Divisione Corazzato *Littorio.*
One of the most experienced armor commanders, he constantly reminded
his officers of the possibilities of armor and emphasized training, discipline, and cooperation. He kept important records that he included in his
writings (Bitossi Papers). *Courtesy of the Historical Office of the Italian
Army General Staff.*

veloci as a means of introducing motorized warfare to the cavalry without interfering with the traditional tactics and spirit. He declared that unnamed "extremists" had said that the motor would destroy the cavalry, but the creation of tank units within the *celeri* would prove them wrong. The tactical role of the *carri veloci* would be to support the horsed cavalry when it dismounted.

Much of the speech was an attempt to motivate the personnel of the regiment to accept the new vehicles. He likened the tanks to horses in their need for care and feeding. The officers of the regiment especially were urged to learn about the new vehicle and to accept them as alternatives to the horse. This seems to imply the possibility of some problem with members of the regiments accepting the change of role. Bitossi ended with "when the motor and the horse move with a single spirit, the grand voice of our tradition will be heard above the thunder of the living and metal engines for a single glorious future."[7]

With the general outlines of policy for the new units established, actual training began. The *Reggimento Cavalleggeri Guide, Centro Addestramento Carri Veloci* (Guide Light Horse Regiment, Fast Tank Training Center) wrote the guidance document for training the *Addestramento Dei Carri Veloci* (Training of the Fast Tanks), in 1933.[8] Although the training was oriented toward cooperation with *celeri* units, it differed very little from that for the *Reggimento Carri Armati.* The tanks were to be used only in attack or counterattack. They were only one of the means of dealing with hostile positions and were to support the normal units whether they were cavalry or *bersaglieri.* And for the first time there was a very explicit prohibition against the use of tanks in fixed defensive positions. Although the guides do not give a specific reason, the fixed armament on the CV 33 light tank meant it was vulnerable in situations where it could not move. This would be amply demonstrated in Ethiopia, where the very mobile enemy would outflank and immobilize the CV 33s, which were only able to fire to the front. This led to the design of the first turreted tanks since the Fiat model 1921. But for the time being this problem did not enter the new manuals being produced.

The new manuals on tanks appeared in 1931 and were very similar in concept. *Addestramento Delle Unità Carri Armati Mod. 1921-1930* (Training of Model 1921-1930 Tank Units) covered the units equipped with the Fiat 3000,[9] and *Istruzione Provvisoria sui Carri Armati Veloci* (Provisional Instruction on the Fast Tank) those with the Carden-Loyd

Figure 7. **CV-29 (Vickers: Fiat Ansaldo) Carden-Loyd (1929) 1.7 Tons.** CV (Carro Veloce). Riveted steel armor 1/4 and 3/8 inch thick 4 cyl. Ford Model T water-cooled gasoline motor. Speed: road 24 mph, cross-country 9 mph. Armament: 6.5mm machine gun. Crew: 2. Ammunition supply: 1500 rounds. The numbers and symbols indicate the tank's position in the platoon and company. *Courtesy of the Historical Office of the Italian Army General Staff.*

CV 29, which was just being introduced.[10] There were no startling changes in policy. The tank was an offensive weapon only used in counterattacks during the defensive phases of the battle.[11] The concept of tanks fighting other tanks is completely absent. Artillery was the answer to tanks and the Italians assumed that since tanks would not be employed in the defense there was no chance of tank-versus-tank combat.[12] A paragraph on the use of tanks in the mountains was very circumspect.[13] Tanks could be used but the terrain had to be suitable for them to maneuver. And the tank could deal with objectives that were relatively close. The paragraph placed no prohibitions on the use of tanks in the mountains other than the natural ones of terrain.

Istruzione Provvisoria sui Carri Armati Veloci devoted a majority of its pages to technical information on the new Carden-Loyd tank and its operation. The only significant change from the manual on Fiat 3000s was that the *carri veloci,* the term for the Carden-Loyd CV 33 light tank family, were especially suited for cooperation with the *celeri,* that is, the cavalry and *bersaglieri,* who were becoming identified as a separate special type of troops because of their mobility.[14] The *carro veloce* was ideally suited for use with these troops because of its speed. For the first time reconnaissance was introduced as a tank mission.[15] This merely indicated the use of the tank in close cooperation with the troops to which it was assigned. Since the *celeri* were the reconnaissance troops of the Italian army, the tank was still used only as an adjunct of the conventional military unit.

In 1935, the *Stato Maggiore* published a new manual, *Direttive per L'Impiego delle Grandi Unità* (Directive for Use of Major Units).[16] Beginning with an inspirational message from Mussolini, the *Direttive* discussed the war of movement and the need for boldness, initiative, and a decisive victory. The innovative commitment for a war of maneuver is important; it marks the first time the *Stato Maggiore* moved beyond World War I tactics and strategy. The *Direttive* nevertheless remained conservative in the use of weapons. The new means of war did not change the fundamentals of war. The tank and its contemporaries were only an aid to the traditional branches of the army.

In unofficial works the major debate at this time was the emergence of the twin concepts of mechanization and motorization. Generale Angelo Pugnani, Inspector of Motorization from 1929 to 1936, in his pioneering work on military vehicles in the Italian army, *Storia della*

Motorizzazione Militare Italiana, identifies the two ideas in Italy as early as 1921-22.[17] But contemporary documents indicate that the terms came into use about 1930. The most definitive statement appears in the *Enciclopedia Militare,* published in 1933,[18] where two articles covered the different approaches in detail. Motorization was the more prudent approach, for the individual would always be important on the battlefield. This is often confused with the Fascist emphasis on individual heroics and is used as a reason for the failure of Italy to mechanize. It is true that the Fascists glorified the Italian as a superior fighting man, the descendant of the Roman legionary which many authors have seen as the reason for the Fascists deemphasizing the machine in warfare.[19] However, Mussolini was determined to prove Italy was a modern nation, as advanced as any in Europe. Many of the popular heroes of the First World War, often deified by the Fascists, had used technology. Italo Balbo, the hero of transatlantic flights, is the best example.

In 1933 the *Enciclopedia* said that Britain was the only country in Europe that followed the path of mechanization.[20] While Italy was paying close attention to all developments in the field of motor vehicles, the situation in Italy must determine Italian developments.[21] The probable theaters of operations in which the Italian army would be involved were mountainous and did not present many opportunities for the use of tanks. *Enciclopedia* writers concluded that "today we can consider Italy inclined more toward motorization than mechanization."[22]

Fascism affected more than just the concept of the individual in combat. A Fascist reorganization and domination of the military journals began about 1930. Before then there were a straightforward set of professional journals in Italy. *Rivista di Fanteria* (Infantry Review) and *Rivista di Artiglieria e Genio* (Artillery and Engineer Review) were the only branch publications of note, while *Rivista Militare Italiana* (Italian Military Review) covered the entire field of military affairs.[23] *Esercito e Nazione* (Army and Nation) was the journal of the National Association of Officers Not on Active Duty.[24] There were a substantial number of officers in this situation because of the mobilization needs of the army and the enormous numbers of officers remaining from the First World War.

In the period 1929-33, when Italy was developing a new policy and a new tank, these journals closely followed official doctrine. There were a limited number of articles on tanks and they were on such subjects as "A Tank Company in the Attack by an Infantry Battalion" or "A Defensive

System against Tanks," developing only slightly the material in official manuals.[25]

The most interesting part of these journals is, however, their review and "current publications in other journals" section. By this means the Italian army could examine virtually everything that was being written or done in the field of armored warfare. George Patton, J. F. C. Fuller, and B. H. Liddell Hart were all reviewed and discussed.[26] But the general attitude toward these men, and indeed toward all developments that were different from those in Italy, was that Italy's situation was unique as far as tank development was concerned.

The year 1934 saw significant new publications. As the army was implementing the *Direttive per L'Impiego delle Grandi Unità,* Colonnello Sebastiano Visconti Prasca published *La Guerra Decisiva* (The Decisive War).[27] Visconti Prasca, an infantry officer, was an instructor at the military academy and was a favorite of the royal family. *La Guerra Decisiva* advocated a war of movement with maximum use of the supporting arms to allow the main combat units to maneuver. Prasca felt that the tank was one of the means to be used to open the way for the cavalry and the infantry, but again it was not a primary means of attack. Artillery and air power were given major roles in the attack, and the idea of balanced combat teams was presented, but they were still built around and heavily dependent on infantry. Along with the war of movement, moral superiority is emphasized. The troops have to believe that they are superior to the enemy and have the spirit of victory and of the "decisive war" in order to win.

The introduction of the ideas of the *celeri* and of the decisive war were both to have far-reaching effects. The *celeri* units were to develop into a force equal in size to that of the armored units at the beginning of the Second World War. This was an important diversion of resources that the Italians could ill afford. The concept of decisive war was a step forward, however. A war of mobility gradually became official doctrine, finally and officially proclaimed in 1938 as the *guerra di rapido corso.* But in immediate terms, doctrine made no improvements in this period. There was no major change in the use of tanks, as had occurred in Britain.

Battalions for War

The changes that occurred in tank unit organization between 1928 and 1935 were directly related to the changes in doctrine and the political situation. Some changes were also the result of the introduction of the first new tank since the production of Fiat 3000s stopped in 1921. All these developments were caused by Mussolini's push to modernize the army and establish Italy as a power. In the early stages the expansion of units was experimental, but from late 1934 on it was preparation for war that led to the increase in the number of tank formations.

This period began with the creation of an experimental unit for the new Carden-Loyd tankettes that were being tested for adoption. Italy had followed the developments in Britain in some detail. After testing a Carden-Loyd Mark VI, four were purchased from Vickers in 1929. In July of 1930 a *Sezione Carden-Loyd* was created and attached to the battalion at Udine.[28] Conventional armored-car squadrons (*autoblindi*) had been organized for the tank battalions in the north in 1929. The new fast-tank unit was attached to the 4th Armored Car Squadron, which was part of the 4th Tank Battalion. The Carden-Loyd section was involved with the entire *Reggimento Carri Armati* on maneuvers during the summer of 1930. The tanks worked with infantry units; the armored cars and the Carden-Loyds operated with the cavalry and cyclist units.[29]

At the end of summer maneuvers, the General Staff transferred the Carden-Loyds to the armored car squadron at Rome. Rome being the seat of government and the Ministry of Defense, it was the site of many displays and tests of new equipment and the Carden-Loyds were no exception. During this period the government made the decision to produce a number of Carden-Loyds in Italy.

Within the army itself further testing of the new vehicles continued. The *Sezione Sperimentale Carri Veloci* (Fast Tank Experimental Section), as it was called, remained at Rome during the winter of 1930-31.[30] In the spring, the 4th Tank Battalion, to which the Carden-Loyds had originally been attached, was transferred to regimental headquarters at Bologna. A battalion of armored cars, made up of the squadrons that had been in the tank battalions, was formed at Udine in its place. It was in this unit that the new tanks were formed into companies for the summer maneuvers.

In 1932 the organization of the *Reggimento* remained stable except that the Armored Car Battalion now had moved to Codroipo, a northern town midway between Pordenone and Udine. The 4th Tank Battalion, which had been moved from Udine to Bologna in 1931, was now moved to Bassano del Grappa. This town was near the famous World War I battleground of Monte Grappa, at the mouth of the Val Brenta, which was one of the two main exits onto the plain of the Po for invasions through the

Brenner Pass. A battalion located there would be able to block the Val Brenta and was also in a reserve position for the battalions on the Carso front.

In April and May of 1933 the Minister of War, Generale Pietro Gazzera, visited the *Reggimento Carri Armati* to watch tests with the first new Fiat Ansaldo CV 33.[31] The *Reggimento* by this time contained 84 regular officers, 9 reserve officers, 143 noncommissioned officers, and 1,168 enlisted men, who were from the classes of 1910 and 1911. At this time there were 60 regiments of infantry, 9 regiments of *alpini,* 12 of *bersaglieri,* and 12 of cavalry.[32] So out of roughly 94 combat regiments in the Italian army, one was a tank unit. The personnel of even that small unit were subject to rapid turnover. In 1933 the policy was that the class of 1910 would be released and the class of 1912 called up. Half of the enlisted personnel would be returning to civilian life and half the regiment would have to be trained from scratch. This was the constant two-year cycle of military life in Italy. While it shows the *Reggimento* had become a well-established unit, the constant turnover meant that few well-trained tank crewmen were available at any time.

The concrete changes that occurred in armored organization in 1934 were those surrounding the creation of the first cavalry tank unit. The formation of these special *carro veloce* units had been recommended as a result of the 1932 summer maneuvers. The idea was implemented by a series of directives from the Ministry of War in late 1933. The 1st *Gruppo* (battalion) of the *Cavalleggeri Guide* (Guide Light Horse Regiment) was to be converted into a *Gruppo Carro Veloce.*[33] *Guide* was one of the most famous of Italian cavalry regiments. Although listed as nineteenth in order of precedence in the cavalry, the Guides were not originally a regiment of the line. It had been formed as a unit of couriers and scouts and only after some years became a regular regiment. In 1933 it was the most junior cavalry regiment in existence.

Initially only one *gruppo* was created, the *1⁰ Gruppo Carri Veloci,* but a second and third were formed in April and June 1933 respectively. The three groups were named *San Marco, San Giusto,* and *San Martino,* and were all under the headquarters of the *Guide.*

The acceleration of tank units in late 1934 and then the rapid changes in 1935 were inextricably involved with Italian intervention in Ethiopia. Planning had, of course, started as early as 1932 for Italian operations in Ethiopia.[34] However, the first development in tank policy that could be

attributed to Ethiopia only came in November 1934.[35] The army had
also undergone a mobilization scare over German interference in Austria
in the summer of 1934, but this had passed by the time the new tank
units came into being. Their formation in November and December coincided directly with the beginning of preparations both in Italy and in the
colonies for what would become the Ethiopian war.

   This first development was the establishment of a number of new units,
utilizing the newly produced CV 33-35s, for the army corps and for the
cavalry regiments. The battalions (forty-six tanks) of the army corps would
be of *carri d'assalto* and technically part of the infantry *Reggimento Carri
Armati*.[36] The squadrons (thirteen tanks) in each cavalry regiment would
be of *carri veloci* and part of that cavalry regiment. All the units would,
of course, be equipped with the same vehicle and have the same table of
organization, whether squadrons of *carri veloci* or companies of *carri
d'assalto*. A new *gruppo carri d'assalto* would be formed at Palmanova,
replacing the armored car squadron that had been there, to train the
personnel for the battalions. Once the decision to organize these units
had been made by Generale Federico Baistrocchi, the *Sottosegretario*
of the Ministry, and Generale Alberto Pariani, the *Capo di Stato Maggiore*
(Chief of Staff), new vehicles had to be allotted.[37] The priorities for the
distribution of vehicles were established by Generale Baistrocchi. On 28
January 1935, the first three cavalry regiments were to have their full
complement in time for the summer maneuvers. The thirteen army corps
were only to have one company each.[38] For the autumn maneuvers three
more cavalry regiments were to be equipped, and by July and August
1936 the vehicles for the colonies were to be ready. This was the first
mention of overseas deployment. The next directive on the subject, a
month later on 27 February, had the priorities rearranged.[39] The units
for the colonies, now identified as two groups of three squadrons each
for the East African exigency, were to be equipped before 15 May 1935.
The remainder of the units were kept on the same schedule. All the supporting material was to be issued before March 1935.

   Tanks for these units were to come from new production and initially
there would only be enough for one vehicle for each of the corps units
and half the authorized strength for the squadrons destined for Ethiopia.
Most of the officers were to come from the *Reggimento Carri Armati*.[40]
The vehicles came direct from Ansaldo to the units. As fast as the units
could be equipped and trained they were to be shipped out. The 5th

Group received its vehicles in the middle of May and they were to be ready to deploy by 20 June 1935. All this was happening nearly five months before Italy attacked Ethiopia.

The next units to be organized were three battalions of *carri d'assalto.*[41] These battalions were to consist of eleven companies, one for each of the divisions in Eritrea. With the tanks coming direct from Ansaldo, the General Staff hoped that six of the companies could be completed by 20 August so that they could go on maneuvers. The creation of these units gave Italy a major tank force at the beginning of the Ethiopian war. Based on tactics that had changed little since the introduction of tanks, they were nonetheless a powerful and effective force. Like all developments in Italy, a slow, cautious process of experimentation had led to the creation of these units. Each unit was carefully organized to provide an adequate number of vehicles and support personnel to carry out the mission it would be expected to perform, whether it was with an infantry unit or assigned to the *celeri.* The difficulties that were to occur came not as a result of faults in the units themselves, but because of flaws in the doctrine.

The Tank for Italian Terrain

Introduction of a new tank made possible the expansion of Italian tank units for the war in Ethiopia. The older Fiat 3000 was underpowered and unwieldy in mountainous terrain. The new, smaller tank was supposed to eliminate these problems.

The production of the new tank demonstrated the weaknesses of Italian industry that plagued armored policy throughout the Second World War. A consortium of two manufacturing firms was the only organization capable of producing the tanks. These companies were also involved in many other defense contracts and in substantial civilian work. In addition, raw material acquisition and the supply of workers were both limited by national policy. Mussolini's drive for self-sufficiency under the names of the battle for grain and *autarchia* limited both the import of raw materials and the movement of workers from job to job.[42] The decision to produce new tanks under these difficult circumstances went back to the 1929 maneuvers.

The annual maneuvers were the traditional testing ground for new tactics and equipment. For tanks, the 1929 maneuvers were to be a crucial

Figure 8. Fiat Ansaldo L3/33 (1933) 3.1 Tons. L-Leggero (Light). Riveted steel armor 1/4 inch floor, deck, roof; 5/16 inch sides; 1/2 inch front and rear. 4 cyc. water-cooled gasoline motor. Speed: road 26 mph, cross-country 9 mph. Armament: 6.5mm machine gun. Crew: 2. Ammunition supply: 2400 rounds. This tank is on maneuvers. The drop is about 4 feet. *Courtesy of the Historical Office of the Italian Army General Staff.*

Figure 9. Fiat Ansaldo L3/33 on Maneuvers. Tanks were equipped with a pump to drain the interior when fording water courses. *Courtesy of the Historical Office of the Italian Army General Staff.*

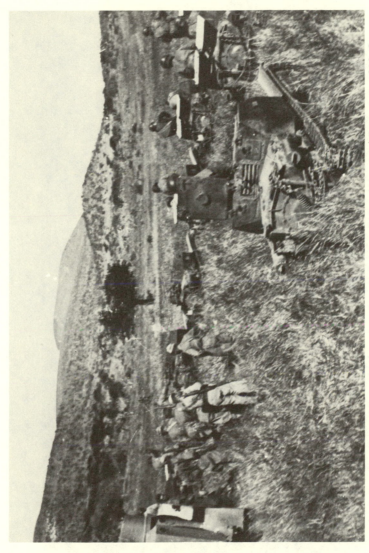

Figure 10. Fiat Ansaldo L3/33. Awaiting battle before the heights of Mega (Abyssinia) Ethiopia in 1936. *Courtesy of the Historical Office of the Italian Army General Staff.*

Figure 11. Fiat Ansaldo L3/33 at Vigologano, Spain. L33 and L35 models were also used in Greece, Albania, Yugoslavia, and Crete, among other places. *Courtesy of the Historical Office of the Italian Army General Staff.*

turning point. In that year they were held in the Val Varaita, a valley in the Maritime Alps that runs from the upper end of the valley of the Po due west toward the French border. The terrain is typical of the border area. Elements of the *Reggimento Carri Armati* worked with *alpini* in the mountains. The ultimate conclusion was that the Fiat 3000 was inadequate in the mountains.[43] The important point to note is not that tanks could not be used in the mountains, but that the tanks used, twelve years old, fast, and with low power-to-weight ratio, were inadequate.

As a result of the performance of these tanks in the 1929 maneuvers, changes were made in the Fiat 3000 series that produced a more powerful version. The important development, however, was the decision to buy a new type of tank better suited for Italian terrain. This would be a derivative of the Carden-Loyd tankette.[44] The Carden-Loyd, the most important development of an armored fighting vehicle in the 1920s, was not completely new. The adaption of existing designs and automotive technology produced a vehicle that was to be eminently successful. This tank was cheap, easily maintained, and suited most countries' concept of tank operations. It was an ideal infantry support vehicle.

The term tankette is normally used to mean a vehicle smaller than a light tank, generally without a turret. That was exactly what the Carden-Loyd was, a very light (1,400 pounds) two-man vehicle armed with a single machine gun. The crew sat side by side and the machine gun was on a limited traverse mount directly in front of the gunner's position. The vehicle also had detachable armored covers, and, because of the rudimentary machine-gun mount and lack of permanent overhead cover, the tankette could mount any machine gun that a country desired to use. The Carden-Loyd tankette Mark VI was the major production model, sold to many countries. The two-man, single, forward-firing machine-gun design had remained the same, although the weight had increased substantially, as the performance and reliability were improved to produce a salable vehicle.

The Fiat Ansaldo *Carro Veloce* 33 was a direct descendant of the Carden-Loyd Mark VI imported for tests in 1929.[45] After an intensive development program by Ansaldo, the new design (CV 33) was a three-ton vehicle with one Italian machine gun and a more powerful engine, both by Fiat. It retained the general design of the Carden-Loyd, having in the first model a boxlike superstructure that contained the crew and the single machine gun. It had a top speed of 26 mph. After prototype field testing, the CV 33 was further modified and full-scale production of the new model (called the CV 35) was undertaken. The total output was 2,500 vehicles, including those for export sales. The CV 35 was slightly faster than the CV 33, but the main improvement was that it now had two machine guns, still mounted in a barbette in front of the gunner's seat. Fiat Ansaldo, whose first involvement in tank production had been the Fiat 3000 series in 1921, constructed the CV 35.[46]

One of the continuing problems of Italian tank development was the predominance of these two concerns in Italian industry. They were the only firms capable of producing tanks. However, they were busy with other more profitable products, which tied up a majority of their capacity. The Ansaldo Company was also having a variety of other problems. It was a diverse company, originally developed by a family of Genovese capitalists named Perrone.[47] Like Fiat's Agnelli family in Turin, they owned a newspaper and a variety of other interests in the city as well as the Ansaldo complex (which involved shipbuilding, foundries, locomotive works, and related industries).[48] In 1928 Ansaldo appointed Generale Ugo Cavallero as general manager.[49] Cavallero came directly from his position as *Sottosegretario* at the Ministry of War. This move was followed by a heavy increase in Ansaldo's defense work, both military and naval. Whether or not Cavallero was using his position and connections, the production capacity for vehicles of this type was so limited in Italy that Ansaldo and Fiat were probably the only companies with the equipment and expertise.

However it may have been arranged, Ansaldo manufactured twenty-four Carden-Loyd tankettes under license.[50] The entire group of Carden-Loyds was given the designation *Carro Veloce 29* (after the year of their introduction). Along with the production of the CV 29, Ansaldo also undertook a program to develop an Italian version of the tankette with which to equip the Italian army.

The production of the CV 33-35 series vehicles was an important step forward for the Italians. These tanks enabled the army to create a large number of units, which gave them much practical experience. From this experience, both in maneuvers and in actual combat, the General Staff developed the modern and effective doctrine under which Italian armored divisions and an armored corps were formed in 1938.

Alpine Maneuvers

The maneuvers held between 1929 and 1935 had important ramifications. We have already seen the effects of the 1929 maneuvers on the
decision to replace or supplement the Fiat 3000 tanks and the testing of
the Carden-Loyd in the 1930 maneuvers before its adoption as the basis
for the new tanks of the CV 33 series. The testing of both the CV 33 and
the new organizations for the use of that tank were the main theme of
the remaining maneuvers in this period.

All tank units were used in the 1931 summer maneuvers. From the
18th to the 25th of August the 3rd and 5th Battalions, equipped with
Fiat 3000s, were a part of the "enemy" forces in maneuvers in the area
of the Valtellina and Val Camonica.[51] These valleys were major avenues
of movement from the Po Valley north toward Austria and Germany.
The three battalions made up of Fiat 3000s held maneuvers with the
infantry divisions located at Turin, Novara, and Padova.[52] The two companies of CV 29s that had been formed by this time conducted maneuvers with the cavalry divisions that were in a defensive role on the Yugoslav border. These maneuvers were unremarkable except for the emphasis
on mountainous terrain and the first connection of tanks with cavalry
units.

The 1932 maneuvers are important for a number of reasons. Two
platoons, one of Fiat 3000s from Bologna and one of CV 29s from
Codroipo, took part in landing and embarkation operations with the
Italian navy in the area of Barletta and Brindisi at the southern end of
the Adriatic. The other elements of the regiment took part in maneuvers
with various units throughout Italy. The after-action reports show that a
number of problems occurred.[53] The *carri veloci* were generally well
liked. They were seen as a rapid, efficient way to deal with the machine
guns and artillery that were a particular hazard to the cavalry and cyclists.
Without suggesting the elimination of the horse cavalry, the tank was to
be part of the cavalry. The report mentioned that the tanks had difficulty
in the mountains and that the problem was often not only that there was
not room to deploy the tanks and use them in the attack, but that the
trails were so narrow that the tanks could not even be moved from place
to place in the mountains.

The most important recommendation in the report was that a few weeks of summer maneuvers were not enough for the troops to become trained in cooperation with the tanks. Tank units, therefore, should be permanently assigned to the divisions so they could train continually with the troops they would support in any future war. This would make the troops familiar with mechanical means of war and accustom them to work with tanks. Prior to this time, the units of the *Reggimento Carri Armati* had been independent, carrying out their own training and only working with other units during the summer maneuvers.

In February 1933, two squadrons of armored cars, displaced by the Carden-Loyds, were sent to Fiume to train cavalry officers in the use of armored vehicles. This was the beginning of the gradual process by which the *celeri* acquired armored vehicles. In July the battalions of the regiment assembled for maneuvers at San Pietro del Carso (now called Pivka by the Yugoslavs), due east of Trieste. The possibility of a Yugoslav invasion was always a danger, and these maneuvers were intended to determine the use of armored vehicles in that event. The corps at Trieste wanted light tanks and armored cars in their organization for use as part of the screening forces although they were not ready to make final disposition of the units. However, they would definitely have a role.[54]

The maneuvers of 1934, which were in the Apennines, south of Bologna, signaled a major change in policy. The new *Direttive per L'Impiego delle Grandi Unità,* not published until the next year, was the basis for the exercise.[55] The directive adopted a war of maneuver as the basic tactical doctrine of the Italian army. The idea was to test, in particular, methods of initially breaking through the enemy front line in order to begin the war of movement. Then in the second phase would occur the actual battle and the exploitation of success.

In the maneuvers, the *carri veloci* and *carri d'assalto* were used in the attacks. Despite severe problems of coordination the General Staff analysis was generally favorable. Recommendations for change were made but none of the offending commanders were relieved. There is no sense of urgency in the report. The Italian army had had these problems for many years and improvement would be slow. But there seemed to be no awareness of the importance of the tank in breaking through the enemy line. The tanks were just another tool in the commander's selection of support weapons, not a decisive means of leading the attack. The tank unit would not operate independently nor was it intended to be used against targets the tank officers thought were important. The tank was in every sense

subordinate to the infantry. In such a limited role the full potential of
the tank would never be realized.

The *celeri* in the same exercise were praised for their speed and élan,
but apparently were not as successful as the high command would have
liked due to failures in reconnaissance.[56] Throughout the report on the
1934 maneuvers, no matter what failure or flaw was reported, the élan
of the troops received favorable comment. The moral force of the troops
had become more important than their effectiveness in battle. The Fascist
regime attempted to instill pride and a sense of purpose in the Italian
people as a whole. In the military, these feelings were manifested in the
spirit and élan of the troops, so such observations became important. But
the equipment and training remained inadequate, preventing any real
feelings of confidence.

The 1935 maneuvers were largely devoted to the training of the units
that would soon be going to Ethiopia. The training areas ranged from the
Brenner Pass to the Po Valley. All available elements of the *Reggimento
Carri Armati* and the *carri veloci* units were involved, as was a new motorized division.[57] The tank units and the *celeri* divisions received favorable
reports, but the motorized division, the first large formation in the Italian
army to be completely motorized, received mixed reviews while exciting
much interest.

The maneuvers in the early 1930s continued to affect tank policy until
the beginning of the Second World War. The lessons that these maneuvers
had taught the army about the *celeri* and about the war of maneuver were
incorporated in the *ordinamento* of 1934 that established the three *celeri*
divisions.[58] And the performance of the tank units in Ethiopia had a
profound effect not only on Italian policy but on the policy of Britain
and other European countries.

*   *   *   *   *

The early 1930s also saw changes in both policy and equipment by the
other European powers. In Britain in 1929 the manual *Mechanized and
Armoured Formations* gave tanks a role in a war of maneuver. *Modern
Formations,* the 1931 revision, developed the idea further and in 1934
a tank brigade was created to employ these tactics.[59] France was also
creating its first fully mechanized unit in 1934, the *Division Legere Mech-
anique.* Both these developments moved beyond the limited position the
Italians took. Britain and France had created tank units that were capable

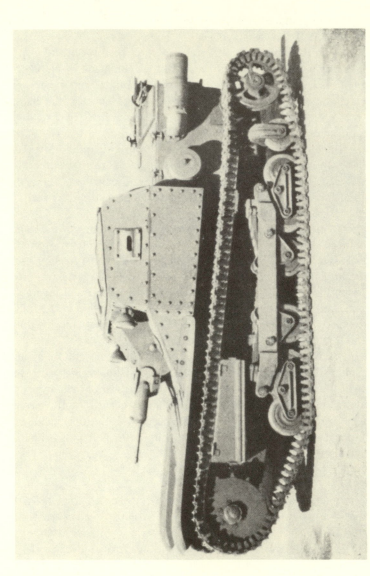

Figure 12. Fiat Ansaldo L3/35. Slightly faster, in top gear, than 1933 model. Carried 2 8mm machine guns. Otherwise similar. Crew: 2. Speed: road 28mph, cross-country 9mph. *Courtesy of the Historical Office of the Italian Army General Staff.*

Figure 13. **Fiat Ansaldo L3/35 on maneuvers in Italy 1939.** About 2500 model 33 and 35 three-ton tanks were produced, including exports. Some were armed instead with flame-throwers or 20mm antitank guns. Others, unarmed, were radio-equipped command tanks. *Courtesy of the Historical Office of the Italian Army General Staff.*

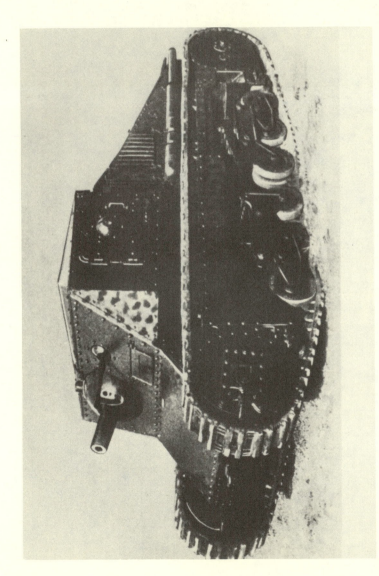

Figure 14. Ansaldo-Experimental (1935) 12 Tons. (Breakthrough or "di rottura"). Riveted steel armor, probably about 1 1/4 inches. Fiat 6 cyl. water-cooled naptha motor. Speed 14mph. Armament: 1 45mm howitzer, provision for 4 8mm machine guns. All in ball mounts. Crew: 3. Ancester of medium tank 11/39. *Courtesy of the Historical Office of the Italian Army General Staff.*

of independent action, which Italy would only do in 1937 and then in a tentative way.[60]

But it was in vehicles that Italy really began to fall behind at this time. The CV 33-35 series gave Italy a larger force of new tanks than any other country. Britain, for example, was experimenting with new designs continually, but in lots of twenty or fifty vehicles for a total of perhaps 200 tanks in the early 1930s compared to 2,500 in Italy in a much shorter time.[61] But the Italian CV 35s were all of one type.

Italy lagged in the crucial areas of progress and experimentation. In Britain, starting in 1930 and continuing through the end of this period, Vickers and the government's Royal Ordinance Factory built a series of light tanks based on the Carden-Loyd.[62] In 1935 the government began development of a medium tank. In France, 1935 also saw the government establish a specification for two series of tanks, one light and one medium. Germany was the most dramatic innovator in tank design. Starting virtually from scratch in 1935 she set requirements for two types of light tank and two types of medium tank, vehicles that were to be used during the Second World War with great success. These were the changes that left Italy behind.

Italy's achievements in armor policy in this period were substantial. New doctrine specified the role of the tank on the battlefield. The *celeri* used tanks in a long-range cavalry role, giving more breadth to their employment. The production of the CV 33 gave Italy an ample supply of fast tanks that fitted her doctrine. The formation and dispatch of the tank units for the Ethiopian war demonstrated the emphasis on tanks and the ability of the Italian system to quickly produce armored forces. A general interest in military affairs presaged more debate on policy. Visconti Prasca's *La Guerra Decisiva* pointed to the increasing interest in a war of maneuver that led to the complete change of doctrine in the late 1930s.

On the other hand, the problems demonstrated in the 1920s had not been dealt with and new problems arose. The introduction of the *celeri* caused an immediate dispersion of effort in armor development. The existence of two kinds of tank troops would necessitate two types of tanks in later periods, a further demand on production. Even the production of the CV 33 caused problems. Italy now had a large inventory of one tank, which impeded the production of new designs because all units were fully equipped.

Nonetheless the 1930s were a step ahead for Italian armor. New tanks in numbers meant that tactics could be fully tested. Substantial numbers of crews could also be trained. The Ethiopian war meant combat experience and further testing of doctrine. At this point, there was no reason to believe there were any drastic problems in the development of Italy's armored forces.

Notes

1. Generale Ottavio Zoppi, *I Celeri* (Bologna: Nicola Zanichelli Editore, 1933).

2. *Enciclopedia Militare*, s.v. "Zoppi, dei conti nob. Ottavio."

3. *Enciclopedia Militare*, s.v. "De Bono, Emilio."

4. Zoppi, *I Celeri*, p. 77.

5. Bitossi wrote, after he escaped from the collapse in North Africa, a history of his involvement in Italian armored development. Called *Frammenti di Una Espirienza Decennale di Guerra Motorizzata 1933-1943*, it was prepared in ten copies. Part of it is a personal narrative and the remainder simply documents he kept and included. Henceforth Bitossi Papers will be used to identify records from this collection. I consulted a photographic copy at St. Antony's College, Oxford.

6. Speech, "Innesto degli Squadroni Carri Veloci Nei Reggimenti di Cavalleria," 8 June 1934, Bitossi Papers.

7. "Quando motori e cavalli, si muovono con anima unica, la gran voce delle nostre tradizione si amplifichi al di sopra del rombo possente dei motori umani e metallici per le glorie di una unica avvenire." *Ibid.*

8. Reggimento Cavalleggeri Guide, Centro Addestramento Carri Veloci, *Addestramento dei Carri Veloci* (Parma, 1934), Bitossi Papers.

9. Ministero della Guerra, Comando del Corpo di Stato Maggiore, *Addestramento delle Unità Carri Armati, Mod. 1921-1930* (Rome: Istituto Poligrafico dello Stato, Libreria, 1931).

10. Ministero della Guerra, Comando del Corpo di Stato Maggiore, *Istruzione Provvisoria sui Carri Armati Veloci* (Rome: Istituto Poligrafico dello Stato, Libreria, 1931).

11. *Addestramento*, pp. 12-13.

12. *Addrestramento*, pp. 16-17.

13. *Addestramento*, pp. 61-62.

14. *Istruzione*, p. 16.

15. *L'Esercito tra la Guerra*, p. 94.

16. Ministero della Guerra, *Direttive per L'Impiego delle Grandi Unità*, (Rome: Istituto Poligrafico dello Stato, Libreria, 1935).

17. Pugnani, *Motorizzazione Militare*, pp. 295-97.

18. *Enciclopedia Militare,* s.v. "Meccanizzazione" and "Motorizzazione."

19. Mazzetti, *Politica Militare,* p. 138.

20. *Enciclopedia Militare,* s.v. "Meccanizzazione," p. 33.

21. *Ibid.,* p. 29.

22. "In somma, oggi l'Italia possiamo considerla incamminata, piut-
tosto che verso la meccanizzazione verso la motorizzazione." *Ibid.,* p. 33.

23. *Rivista di Fanteria* (Rome: Ministero della Guerra) monthly, 1887-
present. Different format 1933-40; *Rivista di Artiglieria e Genio* (Rome:
Ministero della Guerra) monthly, 1866-present. Different format 1933-
40; *Rivista Militare Italiana* (Rome: Rivista Militare Italiana) monthly,
1856-1932, 1946-present.

24. *Esercito e Nazione, Rivista per l'Ufficiale Italiano in Servizio Attivo
ed in Congedo* (Rome: Esercito e Nazione) monthly, 1925-1936, then
Nazione Militare, monthly, 1936-sometime during war.

25. Domenico Barbato, "Una Compagnia di Carri Armati nell'Attacco
di un Battaglione di Fanteria," *Esercito e Nazione,* June 1930, pp. 533-
40; G. Battista Pelosio, "Sistemazione difensiva contro carri armati,"
Esercito e Nazione, January 1931, pp. 36-40.

26. For example, Maggiore di Cavalleria Patton, "La Motorizzazione in
cavalleria" (from the *Cavalry Journal,* July 1930), *Rivista Militare Italiana,*
October 1930, p. 1680.

27. Colonnello Sebastiano Visconti Prasca, *La Guerra Decisiva* (Milan:
Arti Grafiche Ubezzi e Dones, 1934).

28. *Memorie Storiche,* Reggimento Carri Armati, 1930.

29. *Memorie Storiche,* Reggimento Carri Armati, 1929.

30. *Memorie Storiche,* Reggimento Carri Armati, 1930.

31. *Memorie Storiche,* Reggimento Carri Armati, 1933.

32. *L'Esercito tra la Guerra,* allegato 34.

33. *Memorie Storiche,* Reggimento Cavalleggeri Guide, 1933.

34. Giorgio Rochat, *Militari e Politici nella Preparazione della Campagna d'Etiopia* (Milan: Franco Angeli Editore, 1971), pp. 23-30.

35. Memorandum from Ministero della Guerra, Gabinetto to Comando
del Corpo di Stato Maggiore, 29 November 1934. Subject: Carri Veloci-
Carri d'assalto. Racc. 750, U.S.

36. *Memorie Storiche,* Reggimento Carri Armati, 1935.

37. Promemoria per La Superiore Autorità, Ministero della Guerra,
Stato Maggiore, Ufficio Ordinamento e Mobilitazione, December 1934.
Subject: Carri Veloci-Carri d'assalto. Racc. 750, U.S.

38. Ministero della Guerra, Gabinetto to Ispettorato del Materiale
Automobilistico, 28 January 1935. Subject: Comesse Carri veloci Mod.
33. Racc. 751, U.S.

39. Ispettorato del Materiale Automobilistico to all corps commanders, 27 February 1935. Subject: Formazione di nuove unità di carri da combattimento. Racc. 235, U.S.

40. Annex one to the letter in n. 39, filed as a separate document. Racc. 235, U.S.

41. Ispettorato delle Truppe Celeri to Ufficio Ordinamento e Mobilitazione, 28 May 1935. Subject: Reparti di carri veloci per esigenza A. O. Racc. 752, U.S.

42. Castronovo, *Agnelli*, p. 533.

43. *Carri Armati in Servizio*, p. 54.

44. Chamberlain and Ellis, *Tanks*, pp. 770-78.

45. All production information and technical data from Benussi, *Carri Armati e Autoblindate del Regio Esercito Italiano*.

46. *Carri Armati in Servizio*, pp. 54-55; Benussi, *Carri Armati*, pp. 30-35.

47. Gazzo, *I Cento Anni dell'Ansaldo*, chap. 1.

48. Gazzo, *I Cento Anni*, p. 498.

49. Benussi, *Carri Armati*, p. 34.

50. *Memorie Storiche*, Reggimento Carri Armati, 1931.

51. *Memorie Storiche*, Reggimento Carri Armati, 1932.

52. Comando della 2ª Divisione Celere, "Relazione sull'Azione della 2ª Divisione Celere Durante le Esercitazioni a Grande Unità contraposte nell'Appennino Umbro-Marchigiano-Agosto 1932, Osservazione e proposte," p. 37. In special file, prepared for Avvocato Lucio Ceva, U.S.

53. Corpo di Stato Maggiore, Ufficio Operazioni to Corpo d'Armata, Bologna, 31 December 1933. Subject: Provvedimenti in relazione ad un'ipotetica agressione improvviso jugoslava." Racc. 207, U.S.

54. *L'Esercito tra la Guerra*, p. 85.

55. Ministero della Guerra, Comando del Corpo di Stato Maggiore, Ufficio Addestramento, *Ammaestramento Tratti dalle Grande Esercitazioni sull'Appennino Tosco-Emiliano del 1934*.

56. Circolare no. 7500, p. 22.

57. Ministero della Guerra, Gabinetto to Comando del Corpo di Stato Maggiore, 5 July 1935. Subject: Promemoria inteso a definire questioni in atto-armi e materiali recentmente adottati. Racc. 752, U.S.

58. *L'Esercito tra la Guerra*, pp. 82-83.

59. Liddell Hart, *The Tanks*, vol. 1, pt. 2, chaps. 5 and 6.

60. Ogorkiewicz, *Armoured Forces*, p. 65.

61. Chamberlain and Ellis, *Tanks*, pp. 85-89.

62. *Ibid.*

6
Combat Experience

Italy began its gradual change from a policy of motorization to mechanization in the mid-1930s. There was a period of transition from 1935 to 1937. Combat experience and maneuvers combined to point the new direction. Until the beginning of the Ethiopian war in 1935, the army had firmly adhered to the idea of motorization. The motor vehicle replaced animals and men in the movement of certain weapons and supplies. Beyond the creation of new motor units and the reduction of horse units, the new concept of motorization had no impact on the structure or tactics of the army.

Mechanization made its first appearance as a new idea imported from Britain and in competition with motorization. The Ethiopian war and the Italian involvement in the Spanish Civil War overshadowed the initial appearance of mechanization in Italy. But the events of these wars, coupled with experimentation, gradually forced official policy toward mechanization. Beginning with the creation of a motorized regiment, the Italians experimented with increasing numbers of men and vehicles. This culminated in the 1937 maneuvers, when an armored brigade demonstrated its potential. Both the wars and the maneuvers contributed to the eventual decision to adopt mechanization as the official policy.

Italian efforts in the first war, in Ethiopia, were divided into four phases, of which only one involved armored vehicles.[1] The first phase, from October to December of 1935, was a march to contact. Both armies involved, despite Italian claims, were ill equipped; they had very limited motor transport and long distances to cover. The Ethiopians counter-attacked in the second phase while the Italians held their positions. The initial phases had been launched prematurely for political reasons. The Italians had to stop and rectify deficiencies in supply and transport, which gave the Ethiopians an opportunity to attack.

The third phase, a general offensive, began in February 1936 and included the majority of the actual battles as the Italians slowly destroyed the opposing armies. The final phase was the exploitation of the victories of the third phase. In accordance with existing tactical doctrine, the Italians used tanks primarily in the offensive phase of the operations. This limited their effectiveness, since much of the defended terrain was not suitable for armored operations. In keeping with Mussolini's emphasis on presenting a modern image, press photography often showed tanks. Unfortunately, instead of convincing the world of the modernity of the Italian army, the use of tanks showed a barbarity that appalled world opinion.

The tank units committed to the war in Ethiopia did more than pose for photographers, however. One incident in the war made an important comment on Italian policy and equipment. The only loss of more than one tank at a time was in December 1935.[2] In the area near Adowa an Italian column with a platoon of tanks attached found that they were cut off from friendly forces by infiltrating irregulars who occupied Dembeguina Pass. The tank commander decided to withdraw without infantry support and fight his way back through the pass. The terrain was rocky with little space to maneuver and the enemy held no fixed positions for the tanks to charge. In this fluid situation the CV 35s were unable to use their speed. The unit officers dismounted to act as ground guides. The enemy was soon able to approach the vehicles from the rear and disable first the tracks and then the guns. The twin machine guns were susceptible to being bent and could not be changed from within the vehicle. The entire six tanks were destroyed in this manner. The disadvantages of this type of glorified machine-gun carrier were all too evident in this case.

The major impact of the Ethiopian war on Italian policy was the increase in the use of motor vehicles in general rather than just tanks. The rigors of transporting supplies and personnel in that area proved the need for total motorization of the army. This idea of increasing the mobility of the army led to the commitment of a motorized force to the Spanish

Civil War when Italy entered the war in support of Franco a few months after the end in Ethiopia.

Two months after it began (in October 1936), the first Italian troops fought in the Spanish Civil War.[3] The first group of volunteers consisted of tank crewmen and artillerymen, two areas in which the Spanish Nationalists were weak. These army volunteers, released from active duty, served in Spain first as instructors, then with small units. They began arriving at Vigo in the last days of September and the first of October.[4]

The volunteers brought artillery and *carri veloci* with them. They were moved into the line at Madrid and fought there from the 21st to the 29th of October. The tanks and artillery apparently fought as a support unit for Nationalist troops in the battles on the southern flank of the Madrid salient. A sergeant in the tank unit was the first wounded Italian and received the *Medaglia d'argento al valore militare,* the second highest decoration for valor in the Italian army.[5] One of the first soldiers killed was also a tank crewman.

The visible Italian armored troops in Spain were only the most demonstrable instance of the highly motorized *Corpo di Truppa Volontaria.* The experience of this relatively small force, motorized to a much greater degree than the army as a whole, coupled with the experimental force in Libya and the use of the armored brigades in maneuvers, gave the General Staff the information needed to reconsider policy. This transitional period did not see real changes, but only the beginning of debate and the accumulation of information.

Motorization's Last Stand

Motorization had been Italy's official policy since the end of the First World War. In this transitional period, while mechanized tactics and units were first being tested, a senior general, Angelo Pugnani, conducted a final defense of motorization. Official manuals also continued to adhere to motorization. The only changes were minor ones based on the Ethiopian war. While policy and doctrine did change in this period, mechanization made sufficient impression to be attacked by a highly placed decision maker. But even as this attack was launched a changing of the guard occurred within the General Staff and Ministry of Defense that brought to power the men who would mechanize the Italian army.

The structure of the Ministry of Defense and the army high command

Figure 15. Generale Federico Baistrocchi. Army Chief of Staff and Under-Secretary, Ministry of War, 1934-36. *Courtesy of the Historical Office of the Italian Army General Staff.*

Figure 16. Generale Alberto Pariani. Army Chief of Staff, 1936-39, and Under-Secretary, Ministry of War. He introduced mechanization as military policy. *Courtesy of the Historical Office of the Italian Army General Staff.*

had not undergone any major changes since the 1920s.[6] Theoretically,
the Chief of the Defense Staff, the *Capo di Stato Maggiore Generale,*
Maresciallo Pietro Badoglio, was superior to the Ministry of War. Although
he had been away from effective control of the army since 1929, Badoglio
had made a dramatic return in Ethiopia. The first commander of the
Italian forces had been Emilio De Bono, as much a political as a military
general. Mussolini relieved De Bono as a result of the fiasco of supply
and organization that struck the first months of the Ethiopian campaign.
Badoglio returned to take command in Ethiopia and lead the army to
victory. Despite this, Badoglio's position remained the same. The *Capo
di Stato Maggiore Generale* had little real power. For example, he was
opposed to the creation of the smaller binary division, a major structural
change, but was unable to stop its implementation.

Mussolini himself had become the Minister of War again.[7] Under him
were Federico Baistrocchi, the *Sottosegretario,* who was also the *Capo
di Stato Maggiore dell'Esercito,* and Ubaldo Soddu, the head of the
Ministry Staff. The *Sottocapo di Stato Maggiore dell'Esercito,* Generale
Alberto Pariani, actually ran the army General Staff. All these men remained in positions of power until the beginning of the Second World
War. Pariani succeeded Baistrocchi as *Capo di Stato Maggiore dell'Esercito*
in 1937. Soddu became the *Sottocapo di Stato Maggiore Generale* (army,
navy, and air force) and, at least in the eyes of Mussolini, the effective
head of the *Stato Maggiore Generale.* Indeed, all of this group was on ex-
ceedingly good terms with Mussolini and his followers, which Badoglio
was not.

Under Pariani, the army *Stato Maggiore* had three staff sections doing
the various operational and administrative tasks. Two groups of special
staff dealt with specific areas of army operations. One group consisted
of the technical and administrative directorates. These included the
Ispettorato di Motorizzazione, where Generale Angelo Pugnani was still
chief, and *Direzione Generale di Artigleria,* which controlled the acquisition of tanks.

In the second group of inspectorates were those who controlled the
training and organization of branches of the army. In addition to infantry,
artillery, and engineers, a new inspectorate had been formed in 1934, the
Ispettorato di truppe celeri, under Generale Vittorio Ambrosio, who
would rise to be *Capo di Stato Maggiore* of the army.[8] The establishment
of an inspectorate was the ultimate sign that a specialty in the army had

been accepted. Pariani and his associates, trusted by Mussolini, made the decisions on Italian armored policy in the next four years. These men, and especially Pariani, introduced mechanization as military policy and largely determined doctrine under the new policy. The first shot for the new policy—or rather the last defense of the old—came from Pugnani, the leading expert.

La Motorizzazione dell'Esercito e La Conquista dell'Ethiopia by Generale Pugnani was more an argument for motorization than an account of the events in Ethiopia.[9] Pugnani had been most intimately involved with the history of motor vehicles in the Italian army, as Director of Motor Material in the 1920s and for much of the 1930s as Inspector of Motorization. In that position Pugnani was the officer in charge of all preparation of tanks and trucks for the Ethiopian war. In 1936, at the end of the Ethiopian war, he retired at the age of sixty-six, after forty-six years of service.[10]

La Motorizzazione contains a good deal of Fascist rhetoric about the importance of Italy and its military power. It developed some very well substantiated arguments on the course of military mechanization in Italy. Pugnani presented a detailed discussion of the alternatives, either mechanization or motorization, one of the first times this had appeared in print in Italy.[11] Pugnani argued persuasively for motorization (represented by the artillery tractor) as opposed to mechanization (symbolized by the tank).

Pugnani said that the school of motorization believed that tanks were only infantry support vehicles. Mechanization enthusiasts, on the other hand, believed that the tank should be used in mass and as the most important element of the army, with the infantry conforming to the tanks' requirements rather than vice versa.[12] According to Pugnani the tank was an essential weapon to support both the infantry and the *celeri.* It could break the enemy line and defeat enemy machine guns.[13]

Despite this relatively primitive view of the tank, Pugnani's book was a strong blow in favor of the motor vehicle in Italy. It brought the army use of tanks and other vehicles to general attention and argued for the increase of motor vehicles in general. The Ethiopian war and the publicity around it brought motorization and the tank to the forefront of public consciousness.

Official publications of this period also took notice of the war in Ethiopia. The Ministry of War quickly reacted to the defeat at Dembeguina Pass. Seventeen days later the *Norme per L'Impiego delle Unità Carriste* (Norms for the Use of Tank Units) appeared.[14] This was a brief set of instructions on the use of the tank. Much of what is said was standard. The tank was for use in attack and counterattack, as a weapon of movement and not part of a static defense. It was not a replacement for existing weapons but should be used in conjunction with them. But the major points in the *Norme* were drawn from the battle at Dembeguina Pass. Tanks should never be employed without reconnaissance, with security elements in front and in the rear, and in coordination with attacking infantry if possible. Reconnaissance elements must be used to prevent surprise. The crew of a tank must never leave that tank—it is just as cowardly as the soldier who abandons his weapon on the battlefield. All future manuals on tank training and operations included these basic ideas. The Italians, like everybody else, had a very limited knowledge of tank combat, but they had learned a lesson the hard way and did not intend to have it happen again.

In contrast with the tank battles of the Second World War, six tanks lost in a battle seems inconsequential, but Italy, using tanks for the first time, had no frame of reference for casualties. The defeat increased emphasis on the close cooperation of tanks and infantry, and on turreted vehicles in research and development projects.

Except for the *Norme,* armor doctrine underwent no changes as an immediate result of Ethiopia. The army used tanks in accordance with regulations, and no experience had occurred that modified regulations. This lack of impact or haste to reform affected the entire army, not just tanks. The changes that did occur as a result of the Ethiopian war took a year after its conclusion to be implemented. Infantry divisions underwent major organizational change from the tertiary division to the binary. The Italian infantry division had consisted of three regiments, but on the basis of experience in Ethiopia it was found to be too cumbersome.[15] After long debate the transition began so that the majority of Italian divisions in the Second World War had only two regiments. Although only one example, the delay in reorganizing the divisions indicated the slowness of any reform in the Italian army. Armored units suffered no more than the army as a whole. The army could not absorb reforms fast enough to make the lessons of Ethiopia valuable.

These lessons had little impact on the new manuals published in 1936. *Impiego ed Addestramento Carri d'Assalto*[16] and *Addestramento ed*

Impiego dei Carri Veloci,[17] one for infantry and one for *celeri,* vary only in a few administrative details. Tanks should still be used as close-support vehicles for the conventional troops. The use of *carri veloci* in reconnaissance, a traditional cavalry role, was the only change. Both manuals incorporated the advice included in the *Norme* issued on 1 January about losing tanks in close terrain and when not escorted by ground troops.

There was also a *Norme per il Combattimento della Divisione* published in 1936.[18] This replaced the *Norme* in force since 1928. The manual covered both ordinary infantry divisions and *celeri* divisions. The instructions for these infantry divisions contained nothing new. It discussed the *divisione celere* in some detail.[19] In normal employment, the division would be divided into two distinct groups. The cavalry, motorcyclists, and tanks would be used as a maneuver element in operations requiring agility, while the truck-borne and bicycle-borne *bersaglieri,* with the artillery, provided a unit for use in conventional attacks. The tactics of the armored division had been created and now it only required an armored division instead of a *celere* division to carry them out.

Nonofficial publications late in 1936 and the first part of 1937 were singularly barren. The only article of any note on the tanks in the professional journals was a brief introduction to the *fanteria carrista* that appeared in *Nazione Militare* (Military Nation), which was the new Fascist-controlled version of *Esercito e Nazione.*[20] This piece closely followed official policy: tanks supported infantry units in dealing with those obstacles the infantry could not handle on its own. The new formations only allowed more infantry units to be supported.

Although policy and doctrine remained the same in this period, the first evidence of mechanization had appeared. Despite Pugnani's defense, motorization as national policy had a serious competitor. Doctrine, however, remained untouched by the new idea. The tactics of the *celere* divisions approached the use of armored forces in the mechanized war, but no one had a clear perception of the use of armored fighting vehicles as a main combat weapon. The tank would still support the infantry.

Thus the Ethiopian war contributed little of immediate importance to doctrine. Although motor vehicles in general would become more important as a result of the transportation and supply difficulties of the war, this innovation would have to go through the Spanish Civil War before emerging as a radical change in Italian policy.

The First Mechanized Units

The Italian tank and armored-car units in Ethiopia were formed under the policy of motorization. They were support units for the conventional combat troops. But even while replacements were being formed for Ethiopia, the General Staff created the first completely motorized units, capable of operating in a mechanized war. These units, first a regiment and then a weak brigade followed by a strong brigade, demonstrated the value of completely motorized formations. Although organized under a doctrine based on the policy of motorization, these units could operate independently and provided the basis for the eventual mechanization of the Italian army.

The first half of 1936 saw little change in units in Italy. The *Reggimento Carri Armati,* depleted of much of its trained manpower by the Ethiopian war, served as a training and replacement center.[21] The army normally formed a *battaglione di complemento,* or replacement battalion, from which draftees would be found for units in the field. Both the *Reggimento* and the *Cavalleggeri Guide,* the *carri veloci* training center, had replacement battalions.[22] The *Reggimento Carri Armati* also trained reserve officers during the summer of 1936.[23] These *ufficiale di complemento* were officers who had done their initial service with the *Reggimento* and were now assigned to be mobilized with it. Normally they would, along with enlisted men in the same category, form complete companies within the battalions on mobilization. The enlisted men were not normally called up for summer training, although in some circumstances specialists were called either for training or, in an emergency, to fill active units.

During the summer of 1936 the army also attempted to recruit a number of volunteers for the regiment (the infantry tank service) and for the *carri veloci* (the *Guide,* or cavalry-oriented) groups.[24] The requirements included a number of skilled workers, automobile mechanics, radiator repairmen, and other automotive experts. Most notably the army wanted 170 drivers for the tanks, and another 350 for the infantry of the motorized divisions and the *bersaglieri.* This was the first in a long series of requests of this type. Few Italian draftees could drive before they entered the army, so they had to be found outside of the *chiamati* (those called up). The army had little skilled manpower because it had to rely on unskilled draftees for the majority of the enlisted personnel. They could not teach any of these skills in the short eighteen-month period of the draft. Consequently getting specialists quickly required volunteers.

The Reggimento Cavalleggeri Guide also trained new personnel during this period.[25] The *Guide* directed its efforts toward the training of the new squadrons of *carri veloci* for each of the cavalry regiments. The officers and noncommissioned officers, trained by the *Guide,* then returned to their regiment and trained draftees that made up the bulk of the squadrons.[26] The *Guide* did this for six regiments at a time in the winter of 1935 and the spring of 1936.

However, the important events that were occurring in tank doctrine were taking place in Libya. As part of the reinforcement of the colonies, a new regiment was formed containing infantry and tanks, with as much motor transport as possible.

Colonnello Bitossi of the *Guide* commanded the *1° Reggimento Misto Motorizzato* (First Mixed Motorized Regiment). This integrated unit contained motorcyclists and motor machine-gun units in addition to infantry and tanks. Bitossi trained them together and emphasized operations in rough terrain. He attempted to train his unit as something more than just a normal regiment supported by tanks. He recognized that the CV 33 was only the first step in the development of tanks for the Italian army and that the tactics used should be universal tank tactics.

Although only a temporary formation, *1° Reggimento Misto Motorizzato* led to the beginning of true mechanized formations in Italy. The *Brigata Motomeccanizata* (Motor-mechanized Brigade), formed on 1 June 1936, consisted of the *5° Reggimento Bersaglieri, XXXI Battalione Carri Veloci,* and a *Gruppo Leggero Motorizzato.*[27] The army still suffered under the impact of Ethiopia and the *Brigata* did not conduct maneuvers in 1936 due to lack of means. The *Brigata,* the first integrated armor combat unit in Italy, became the *1ᵃ Brigata Corazzata* in July 1936, with two additional tank battalions. This important unit was the first integrated, balanced, armor infantry unit in the Italian army, the basic unit of mechanized war.[28]

Before that occurred a number of other changes in the organization of tank units came about. The availability of the CV 33s delivered in the spring of 1936 allowed the formation of new units. The strength of the *Reggimento Carri Armati* underwent a tremendous expansion. In May 1936 a ministerial dispatch reorganized existing units and created new ones. This increased the table of organization to twenty-four battalions of tanks, five equipped with the Fiat 3000 tank and nineteen with *carri veloci.*[29] Ten independent units included a battalion of armored cars and various independent companies.

Of the units, three battalions and most of the smaller units served overseas, including those in East Africa and the elements of the *1° Reggimento Misto.* The remainder, located in northern Italy with the exception of a company in Sardinia, remained under the *Reggimento.* The *5th Bersaglieri* controlled one battalion, the *XXXI,* which would be in the *Brigata Motomeccanizata.*[30] By the summer the two motorized divisions, just created, would control two other battalions. The availability of units thus allowed the experimental use of a variety of possible organizations. The experience gained with these units provided the information for eventual mechanization.

In August the Ministry disbanded the *Reggimento Carri Armati* and assigned the battalions to four newly established regiments on the basis of geographical location, while local commands controlled those units overseas. In Italy four *reggimenti fanteria carrista*[31] (infantry tank regiments) became the headquarters. These regiments served, as their name implies, as infantry support units, still under the supervision of the Inspectorate of Infantry. Those battalions assigned to work with major units came permanently under the control of the unit's own headquarters while the General Staff controlled the *Reggimenti Fanteria Carrista.* Each of the *Reggimenti Fanteria Carrista* had four battalions, normally one of Fiats and three of CV 33s. In keeping with the changing political alliances of Italy, the army distributed the new units somewhat differently than had been the case since the organizing of the first battalions in the 1920s. The First Regiment was in the western Po Valley, forming an arrowhead pointing at France.[32] The arrowhead battalions stationed at Turin, Vercelli, and Alessandria had a reserve at Monza, near Milan.

The Second Regiment had battalions at Bolzano, Verona, Trieste, and Udine, thus controlling the eastern Po Valley.[33] This disposition of units against Germany made an interesting comment on German-Italian relations. Two battalions blocked the Brenner Pass route from Germany into Italy; the same number defended against the Yugoslavs. The Third Regiment, the direct successor of the *Reggimento Carri Armati,* controlled four battalions at Bologna, one at Florence, and one at Treviso.[34] These six battalions could reinforce either the First or Second Regiment. The Fourth Regiment, at Rome and in the south,[35] indicated a new orientation

GERMANY

SWITZERLAND

<u>Treviso</u>
1 Battalion
3rd Regiment

<u>Bolzano</u>
1 Battalion
2nd Regi-
ment

<u>Udine</u>
1 Battalion
2nd Regiment

<u>Milan</u>

<u>Monza</u>
1 Battalion
1st Regiment

<u>Trieste</u>
1 Battalion
2nd Regiment

<u>Verona</u>
1 Battalion
2nd Regiment

<u>Alessandria</u>
1 Battalion
1st Regiment

YUGOSLAVIA

FRANCE

<u>Bologna</u>
4 Battalions
2nd Regiment

<u>Florence</u>
1 Battalion
3rd Regiment

<u>Turin</u>
1 Battalion
1st Regiment

<u>Bari</u>
1 Battalion
4th Regiment

<u>Rome</u>
3 Battalions
4th Regiment

<u>Vercelli</u>
1 Battalion
1st Regiment

<u>Anagni</u>
1 Battalion
4th Regiment

N

<u>Palermo</u>
1 Battalion
4th Regiment

SICILY

Map. 3. Location of Italian Armored Units, 1936

in Italian foreign policy, the concentration on Africa. Of the Fourth Regiment, Rome had three battalions while Bari, Agnani, and Palermo had one each. Where the previous deployments had been directed against the possibility of invasion from the north, Italy was now concerned about the possibility of fighting on any of her borders or in her territories with these tank units.

However, the next employment of tanks occurred many miles from the frontiers of Italy, in Spain. On 26 January 1937 the Ministry requested for Spain the first tank unit, a battalion of *carri d'assalto,* CV 33s. The *Ispettorato* of infantry had to "urgently prepare" a battalion trained in infantry cooperation for Spain. This initial Italian contribution to the Nationalist cause was made up of 141 men and 31 tanks.[36] The *4° Reggimento Fanteria Carrista* prepared the tank troops sent to Spain in southern Italy, from where the troops departed.

A request for a heavy mobile workshop followed on 27 January. The workshop of the *Trento* Motorized Division, the division first organized in 1935, with its equipment and as many of its personnel as would volunteer, formed the basis of this unit.[37] The Italian commitment was going to be heavily motorized, rather more so than the Italian army at home. On the 29th, the first of a long series of requests for civilian drivers went out.[38] The Spanish expedition required two hundred at first, but on the 30th it was raised to four hundred.[39] The army's lack of trained drivers again manifested itself. While the tank battalion was being prepared for Spain the total number of tanks and tank troops in Italy remained the same, as units were being repatriated from Ethiopia.

In April 1937 Italian tanks first fought in a major battle at Guadalajara. An Italian column, moving toward Madrid, attacked at Guadalajara, on the road between Madrid and France. (As a result the Italians generally list this battle as the *Strada di Francia.*[40]) The Republicans repulsed the Italians and hailed it as a great victory. The *Corpo di Truppa Volontaria* (Corps of Volunteer Troops) consisted of the *Littorio* (Lictor) infantry division and the tank battalion, along with some Italian-officered Spanish troops, among others. The tanks were used in their infantry-support role and a platoon leader, Luigi Fuccia, who led his tanks in two assaults on the enemy line, was awarded, posthumously, the first *Medaglia d'oro al valore militare* in Spain.[41] (The *Medaglia d'oro* is Italy's highest decoration for valor and was awarded twenty times in the Spanish Civil War to volunteer army personnel, of which five were to tank crewmen.[42]) The

Raggruppamento Carristi of the *Corpo,* a combination of the first tank units sent to Spain and the *battaglione carri d'assalto* formed in January 1937, had a strength of about sixty tanks at the time of Guadalajara.[43]

The battle at Guadalajara was the only major event of 1937 in tank operations in Spain. During their first six months there, Italian tank troops had received a good deal of publicity. The tank unit had both the first casualty and the first hero. This vanguard role of the *carristi* demonstrated the effectiveness of the tank. Even if it didn't win Italy any new friends in the Western world, the Italian army commitment to the tank was demonstrated to the Italian people and the world. The organizational changes occurring in this period clearly demonstrated both the interest in armor vehicles and the problems of the Italian army. The formation of new units, the highly motorized force of Spain, and the deployment of tanks to defend Italy all pointed to the importance of armor warfare. The army moved pragmatically toward mechanization, while doctrine and policy remained static. The lack of trained personnel, both as crews and for support, showed the weakness in suitable skills that would plague development. Only in equipment could Italy handle her requirements and this temporary situation resulted from the mass production of the CV 33 series light tanks.

Nothing to Offer: Italian Tanks in the Mid-1930s

Italian armor development stagnated in this period. The army had enough tanks for its immediate requirements and other deficiencies required attention, so tank technology fell by the wayside. After the Dembeguina Pass battle, leisurely development of a new tank began, but without priority by the high command. The army did adopt an antitank gun, the first in Italian service. This major step forward indicated a final realization that the enemy would also have tanks.

Only during the Ethiopian war did Italy ever have a sufficient number of tanks. CV 33s, called CV 35s in the two-machine-gun version, filled the new units, while the larger, fifteen-year-old Fiat Model 21/30s formed the breakthrough battalions. As a result, limited research and development took place in Italy. Production for the war absorbed all industrial capacity, the army had its units complete, and the General Staff had its hands full. No one pursued the design of new tanks. Unfortunately, these designs fell well behind those of Italy's contemporaries. When the Ministry of War requested an exchange of information on tank development with the United States, the American military attaché at Rome recommended rejection on the grounds that Italy had nothing to offer.[44]

Fiat and Ansaldo began work on a new tank in 1936. They remained the giants of industry and were involved in virtually all aspects of Italian rearmament. Consequently, tank development was only one of many urgent projects. Ansaldo shifted the tank work to a subsidiary, Giorgio Fossati, located with Ansaldo in the industrial suburbs of Genoa.[45] Although it took nearly three years to develop a new tank, the design concept would be a turreted, cannon-armed vehicle, a necessary, albeit slow, step in the right direction.[46]

The battle of Dembeguina Pass, where tanks had been destroyed because they could not protect themselves, caused this design change. Thenceforth, the Italians designed tanks to the same standards as the other European powers. The special-purpose vehicle, with fixed forward fire for mountain warfare, had shown it could not do the job.

The lack of force in Italian planning for the material of armored warfare extended beyond a lack of impetus in tank design. In armored combat the tank and defense against tanks are essential elements. An effective armored force must have a thoroughly developed defensive plan as well as an offensive plan. The Italians had none until 1939. There had been no development of an antitank weapon up to 1935. In that year the Ministry decided to manufacture under license an Austrian design, the Bohler 47-mm antitank gun, used in Italy under the title *cannone contro carro da 47/35*.[47] Even in 1935 a weapon of moderate performance, the Bohler design was also used in a number of other countries.

Italian introduction of the weapon proceeded slowly. To provide the divisions with their authorized antitank company for the 1936 maneuvers, the Ministry assembled instructors and students from the schools teaching the use of the gun into companies.[48] The introduction of this antitank gun exemplifies much of the process by which Italy developed its armored force. Although a correct concept, general inefficiency and a lack of command emphasis led to the task being poorly done and then having to rush to scrape together an improvised force at the last minute. The new antitank gun did not herald a policy or even a doctrinal change. No new emphasis on antitank defenses appeared. Antitank measures remained a secondary role for units actually under attack. The mechanized warfare concept of independent armored maneuvers, requiring special defenses, had not appeared.

The wars, particularly that in Ethiopia, had taken too much out of Italy. Technological improvements in armor warfare did not occur because neither the army nor industry had time, money, or industrial capacity for them. Only when preparation for another war began in earnest in 1937-38 did Italy have time for tanks. Fortunately the equipment on hand enabled the army to experiment in the annual maneuvers.

Testing the Armored Brigade

After a year's absence due to the war in Ethiopia, annual maneuvers made their return in 1937. That year's exercises pointed in the direction of the future. The armored brigade, understrength and ill prepared, operated under the old doctrine. The *celere* division and the new motorized divisions also took part. The information and recommendations from these maneuvers formed the basis of practical experience for the policy change from motorization to mechanization that occurred in 1938.

The *Prima Brigata Corazzata* (First Armored Brigade), created on 15 July 1937, consisted of the *31st Reggimento Fanteria Carrista* and the *5th Reggimento Bersaglieri,* plus a company of motorcycles, one of 47-mm antitank guns, and one of engineers, and a battery of 20-mm antiaircraft guns.[49] The *5th Bersaglieri* had been in the *Brigata Motomeccanizzata,* while the Ministry organized the *31st Fanteria Carrista* especially for the brigade on 7 July 1937.[50] It consisted of three battalions, the *I* and *II Battaglione carri di rottura* and the *II Battaglioni carri d'assalto,* which had been in the *Brigata Motomeccanizzata* as part of the *5th Bersaglieri.* The brigade was organized under the guidance of circular number 10600 (of 20 July 1937), which established major changes in Italian armored policy.[51] The brigade was created as "an instrument of high penetrating capacity, designed to open a breach in a solid enemy line." The armored brigade would eventually be reinforced with supporting units and other types of weapons so that it could be used as a maneuver element against the flanks of the enemy, and in cooperation with "other special divisions," that is, *celeri* and motorized divisions. The new formation was to be tested in the 1937 grand maneuvers.

The brigade was in the course of organization and although Pariani asked that it be kept at its home station for as long as possible, there was only one month in which it could prepare before the maneuvers. It participated as part of the Red Force, against the Blue, in a series of conventional infantry war-games operations.

The report on the operation of the First Armored Brigade in the 1937 maneuvers was very important since it was the basis for the further development of armored units in the Italian army. The Ministry of War letter covering the copies of that report circulated to the General Staff described it as *"alcune considerazioni e proposte sulla costituzione e sull'impiego della divisione corazzata"* (some considerations and proposals on the constitution and on the use of the armored division).[52] This report discussed the use of the armored brigade in the maneuvers and then made recommendations for change.

The report states that the armored brigade was handicapped in the maneuvers by only having twenty of ninety *carri di rottura,* less than half the men for the antitank unit, and other deficiencies. In addition the commander did not use it in an independent role, but in support of the motorized division; nonetheless the brigade opened a hole of sufficient width in the enemy lines. The report made the important recommendation to make the 47-mm antitank guns mobile, preferably on tracks, and to improve the tanks. The tanks were severely limited in their cross-country ability and this, of course, handicapped the whole purpose of the brigade. In particular the terrain along the French and German borders with Italy was mentioned as a place where better cross-country ability would be required. The report further recommended that artillery not be assigned to the armored brigade in the breakthrough role, since it could use the support of the other major units in the area. The brigade itself was already large, and its own artillery would burden it further. However, if the brigade (or any armored unit) was going to be used as a maneuver element, breaking through the enemy's line or maneuvering around the flank of the opposing force, then it would require motorized infantry, at least two groups of medium artillery, and air support. Thus, the report ended on an ambiguous note. The armored brigade was all right as constituted, but if it was going to be made into an armored division, then it would require additional troops. The report could thus be used to defend expansion or nonexpansion. The commander of the troops in Sicily, Generale Vittorio Ambrosio, who was to be one of the leading staff generals during the Second World War, and briefly *Capo di Stato Maggiore,* signed the report.[53]

A second series of maneuvers that summer involved the troops in the *IV Corpo d'armata* in northeast Italy, the operational and administrative command with responsibility for the Italo-Austrian border. The maneuvers in this area involved a testing and comparison of the motorized division and the *celere* division.[54] The after-action report consisted of observations on the units actually employed and recommendations for changes in the organization of *celere* and motorized units. In the maneuvers the tanks were often used independently or retained as a reserve. If kept as a reserve, the commander frequently used them as a covering force in case of withdrawal. The commanders of the tank units failed to carry out proper reconnaissance and to arrange for cooperation with infantry. The commander of the supported unit, that is, the infantry commander, should determine the use of the tanks. He should be in close contact with the tank commander and insure that the tanks were carefully used. The employment of tanks in unsuitable terrain was a waste of men and equipment, according to the reporting referees.

The *carri veloci*, supporting the *celeri* troops, should be trained more like the infantry tanks. The tanks in *celeri* units tended to be kept as a reserve and used in situations where covering forces were required. Motorized detachments provided the best units for penetration of the enemy line and for rapid movement. The army had trouble providing security during marches, a responsibility of the *carri veloci*. Although the remarks on the motorized units and the tanks were in close proximity, in the report there was no combination of the two. The tank was not included in the operation of the motorized detachment but remained a vehicle for use in the infantry assault.

Despite the uninspired thinking on the use of tanks, the recommendation section of the report, a synthesis of the ideas of the commanders involved, did make some interesting suggestions. It advanced the idea that motorized units are ineffective in the presence of mechanized means of combat, and that if this is the case, tactics and organization would have to be changed. In particular, they mentioned a number of relatively limited changes, such as attaching tanks to each infantry unit for use as support against enemy defenses, just as the attached infantry guns are used. It said that the idea of using motorized units in combat with mechanized units ought to be reconsidered. The report made one major recommendation, that a new tank with a cannon was essential and that it ought to be included in the *celeri* tank units as well as the infantry tank units. This was an important recognition of the need for cannon-armed tanks in support of all units.

Although the report on the 1937 *celeri* and motorized maneuvers contains several incisive judgments, it concluded on a reactionary note. The ultimate recommendation was that "in the present state of technology there are insurmountable difficulties, so that for now it is not possible to adopt a mechanized vehicle the equal of the horse, either as a fast means of transportation or as a weapon." Once again the horse had emerged as a viable weapon of modern war, at a time when an armored brigade was in existence in the same army.

The 1937 maneuvers, despite occasional lapses, propelled Italian policy in the direction of mechanization. The recommendations emphasized the use of tanks in greater numbers and in more independent roles. The armored brigade distinguished itself and showed the potential of mechanized warfare. From these events, Italian planners began work on the policy and doctrine that would appear the next year as the *guerra di rapido corso*, mechanized warfare as envisioned by Mussolini. The reactionary generals included their ideas on the usefulness of the horse, but economic necessity rather than generals would keep the horse in the Italian army.

*   *   *   *   *

The period from 1935 to 1937 in Italy saw little progress on the road to mechanization. The Ethiopian war and then the Italian participation in the Spanish Civil War occupied the attention of the army and the nation as a whole. These wars required major efforts by the army and industry, which left little time for experimentation. Only after the end of hostilities in Ethiopia could the army experiment with new tactics. The lower level of Italian effort in Spain enabled the General Staff to conduct large-scale maneuvers. These maneuvers (rather than the corps in Spain) saw the testing of armored brigades and motorized divisions. The results directed planners' attention to new methods of warfare.

Despite these signposts toward the future, the Ministry of War still had motorization as official policy. Tactics and organization provided tanks in support of conventional infantry attacks. And although Generale Pugnani used his book on Ethiopia to further support this idea, even he had to admit that mechanization was a viable alternative to motorization.

Equipment remained stagnant in this period. The large number of CV 33 light tanks filled all units, leaving no urgent need for equipment. Industry had sufficient orders to keep it busy on other projects. The General Staff only purchased new antitank guns and they had a low priority. Solely in the new units formed, based on the abundant light tanks, did Italian armor progress in this period. New units meant more experience. And more experience, in maneuvers and in war, led to change.

Notes

1. *L'Esercito e I Suoi Corpi,* vol. 1, pp. 148-50.

2. Report of Military Observer with Italian Armies in East Africa, Report number 7 by Norman E. Fiske, Major, Cavalry, 24 July 1936. File 2022-611/141, Records Group 165, Records of the War Department General and Special Staff, NA.

3. Ministero della Guerra, *Volontari dell'Esercito nella Guerra di Spagna* (Milan: Tipo-Litografia Turati Lombardi e C, 1939), p. 8.

4. *Volontari dell'Esercito,* p. 10. Hugh Thomas, *The Spanish Civil War* (New York: Harper and Row, 1961) says the first were on 23 October (p. 308) but the Italians had already awarded a medal for valor by then.

5. *Volontari dell'Esercito,* p. 12.

6. *L'Esercito tra la Guerra,* chap. 4.

7. *L'Esercito e I Suoi Corpi,* vol. 1, p. 274.

8. Ministero della Guerra, *Relazione Sull'Attivita Svolto per l'Esigenza A.O.* (Rome: Istituto Poligrafico dello Stato, 1936), p. 219.

9. Angelo Pugnani, *La Motorizzazione dell'Esercito e La Conquista dell'Etiopia* (Rome: Edizione della "Rivista Transporti e Lavori Pubblici," 1936).

10. *Enciclopedia Militare,* s.v. "Pugnani, Angelo," vol. 6, p. 336.

11. Pugnani, *Etiopia,* pp. 29-51.

12. Pugnani, *Etiopia,* p. 37.

13. Pugnani, *Etiopia,* p. 100.

14. Ministero della Guerra, Gabinetto, *Norme per L'Impiego delle Unità Carriste* (Rome: Tipografia del Comando del Corpo di Stato Maggiore, 1936).

15. *L'Esercito tra la Guerra,* p. 124.

16. Comando del Corpo di Stato Maggiore, Ufficio Addestramento, *Impiego ed Addestramento Carri d'Assalto,* Circolare no. 10500, 15 August 1936 (Rome: Tipografia del Comando del Corpo di Stato Maggiore, 1936).

17. Ispettorato Truppe Celeri, *Addestramento ed Impiego dei Carri Veloci,* Manual no. 3025, 16 September 1936 (Rome: Istituto Poligrafico dello Stato, 1936).

18. Ministero della Guerra, *Norme per il Combattimento della Divisione* (Rome: Istituto Poligrafico dello Stato, 1936).

19. *Norme per Divisione,* pp. 113-28.

20. Luigi del Mauro, "Fanteria Carrista," *Nazione Militare,* August-September 1936, pp. 581-84.

21. *Memorie Storiche,* Reggimento Carri Armati, 1936.

22. *Memorie Storiche,* Cavalleggeri Guide, 1936.

23. Circolare no. 76, 8 January 1936, *GMU 1936,* p. 44.

24. Military Attaché Report, No. 15481, from Military Attaché, Rome, 1 September 1936. File 2022-564/75, RG 165, NA.

25. *Memorie Storiche,* Cavalleggeri Guide, 1936.

26. Circolare no. 647, 27 June 1935, *GMU 1935,* p. 1673.

27. *Memorie Storiche,* Brigata Motomeccanizzata, 1936.

28. *Memorie Storiche,* Brigata Motomeccanizzata/Corazzata, 1937.

29. *Memorie Storiche,* 3ª Reggimento Fanteria Carrista, 1936.

30. *Memorie Storiche,* Reggimento Carri Armati, 1936.

31. *L'Esercito e I Suoi Corpi,* vol. 2, pt. 1, pp. 420-23.

32. *Memorie Storiche,* 1º Reggimento Fanteria Carrista, 1936.

33. *Memorie Storiche,* 2ª Reggimento Fanteria Carrista, 1936.

34. *Memorie Storiche,* 3ª Reggimento Fanteria Carrista, 1936.

35. *Memorie Storiche,* 4º Reggimento Fanteria Carrista, 1936.

36. Letter, Ufficio Operazioni, 26 January 1937. Subject: Costituzione di una battaglione carri d'assalto per O.M.S. Racc. 756, U.S.

37. Letter, Ufficio Operazioni, 27 January 1937. Subject: Costituzione officina pesante mobile per esigenza O.M.S. Racc. 756, U.S.

38. Letter, Ufficio Operazioni, 29 January 1937. Subject: Ingaggio autisti civili per esigenza O.M.S. Racc. 756, U.S.

39. Letter, Ufficio Operazioni, 30 January 1937. Subject: Ingaggio autisti civili per esigenza O.M.S. Racc. 756, U.S.

40. Thomas, *The Spanish Civil War,* pp. 381-83. Olao Conforti, *Guadalajara* (Milan: Mursia, 1967) is the best Italian account.

41. Conforti, *Guadalajara,* pp. 146-47.

42. *Volontari dell'Esercito,* pp. 49-59.

43. *Volontari dell'Esercito,* p. 18. The best account of the Raggruppamento in action is in Conforti, *Guadalajara.* Dino Campini, *Nei Giardini del Diavolo* (Milan: Longanesi, 1969) is supposed to be a history of Italian armour but has only a superficial, two-page account of the Spanish Civil War.

44. Letter, Colonel J. G. Pillow, Military Attaché, Rome to Chief, Military Intelligence Division, War Department, 9 July 1936. Subject: Exchange of Information Between the United States and Foreign Countries Concerning Light Tank Developments. File 2450-E-20, RG 165, NA.

45. Gazzo, *I Cento Anni dell'Ansaldo,* p. 492.

46. Pugnani, *Storia della Motorizzazione,* p. 356.

47. Peter Chamberlain and Terry Gander, *Anti-Tank Weapons* (London: MacDonalds and Jane's, 1974), p. 3.

48. Letter, Baistrocchi to Ufficio Addestramento, 1 August 1936. Subject: Compagnie Pezzi da 47. Racc. 755, U.S.

49. *Memorie Storiche,* 1ª Brigata Corazzata, 1937 and Comando De-

signato d'Armata, Napoli, Direzione manovre in Sicilia Anno XV, Rossi, Parte III, Composizione del Partito. Racc. 228, Anno 1937, Manovre in Sicilia, U.S.

50. *Memorie Storiche,* 31° Reggimento Fanteria Carrista, 1937.

51. Although Circolare no. 10600 is mentioned in all works on this era (for example, Pafi, Falessi, and Fiore, *Corazzati Italiani, 1934-45,* p. 10), I could find no surviving copy. This is an extract contained in Stato Maggiore, Stralcio e Promenoria sulla Divisione Corazzata, 10 May 1938. In special file for Avvocato Ceva, U.S.

52. Letter, Ministero della Guerra, Gabinetto, to Stato Maggiore, 8 November 1937. Subject: Costituzione ed impiego divisione corazzata. In special file for Avvocato Ceva, U.S.

53. *L'Esercito e I Suoi Corpi,* vol. 1, p. 274.

54. Comando IV Corpo d'Armata, Bolzano, Relazione sulla Esercitazione di Divisione Celere e Divisione Motorizzata Anno XV, Testo-Parte I e Parte II. Racc. 758, U.S.

7
Divisions and Corps

Italy changed from a policy of motorization to mechanization in 1938.
Italian perceptions about the next war had changed radically as a result
of the Ethiopian war, the Spanish civil war, and the changing alliances
that resulted. Italy could no longer depend on Britain. The embargo over
Ethiopia had shown that. France, an ally since 1859, also opposed Italian
aggression. Together these countries had protected the Mediterranean
and colonial areas so that Italy could concentrate on Europe. Now Italy
had to think of war against a European power in Africa as well as worry
about the Mediterranean shores that England had protected.

The supply and transportation problems of the Ethiopian war and the
exposure to new tactics in Spain further changed Italian concepts of future
wars. Together the strategic realignments and tactical innovations required
mechanization. The new policy first emerged in debate over the organization of armored divisions in the service journals in the spring of 1938.
After a long battle the Ministry of War made mechanization official policy
by announcing a war game of maneuver in the fall of 1938. Simultaneously,
new manuals and the organization of new units implemented the doctrinal
changes.

Under the new doctrine, an armored corps of two armored and two
motorized divisions formed a striking force in the Po Valley, Italy's major
strategic target for an enemy. These units grew out of the brigades that
had been tested in 1937 and formed maneuver elements the equal of any
in Europe, at least on paper. Unfortunately Italian industry, under no
pressure from the army, had not produced any new vehicles. The grand

new divisions had to prepare for a war of maneuver with twenty-year-old light tanks in place of what should have been medium tanks and machine-gun carriers.

The preparation took the form of the annual maneuvers and the study and terrain reconnaissance of operational plans. Italy had had plans for its operations in the next war since at least 1928. But these new plans hypothesized new strategic situations. Previous plans considered a defense of the Alpine frontier with Austria and Yugoslavia as most likely. Now the General Staff formulated plans for war against virtually every European power both on the continent and in Africa. New priorities required new plans.

Although much of the decision making on army policy was carried out within the Ministry of War, the *Commissione Suprema di Difesa* established priorities in defense matters. Traditionally the choice of priority had been the defense of northern Italy. This area had been the target of invasions from Roman times. More particularly the area had been the scene of the majority of the fighting in the Napoleonic wars. Furthermore, all the World War I fighting on the Italian peninsula took place in this area.

The end of this fighting left Italy with two major potential foes, Austria and Yugoslavia. Both countries had legitimate complaints about the demarcation of their borders with Italy and both had historical traditions of fighting against the Italians. The Po Valley, the immediate objective of any invasion by land, contained a major segment of the Italian people and, more importantly, virtually all of her industry. The industrial triangle of Milan, Turin, and Bologna held the majority, not only of industrial plants, but also of workers. With Genoa, these cities were centers of trade and of raw materials. These vital resources, largely imported, came by sea with few exceptions.

The importance of the industrial area and the likelihood of the next war being against one of these traditional enemies dominated Italian military thinking. The contingency plans involved invasions from the north. An alliance had been made with Hungary to outflank the Austrian and Yugoslav foes. The new tank battalions of 1927-28 and three of the four new tank regiments of 1936 had been deployed to that area.

But the period after the Ethiopian war showed an increase in the importance of the Mediterranean in Italian thinking. The navy and air force became the first priority in defense appropriations. Mussolini directed

this action, and Pariani could only try to lessen the effect on the army.
Libya also became a major consideration in defense planning. This policy
began to gain influence in 1937, but emerged as the first priority in 1938.[1]
The *Commissione Suprema di Difesa* normally made the decision in this
case, but it was a very complex problem. Since the final subjugation of
the Libyan resistance in 1929, Italy invested tremendous amounts of
money in Libya. A large number of Italian emigrants settled there in an
attempt to relieve the overpopulation of Italy itself and build a strong
presence on the southern shore of the Mediterranean, the so-called
fourth shore of Italy.

Libya not only became important because of the economic and strategic importance that Italy attached to it; the reorientation of Italian
alliance also increased the emphasis on Libya. With Germany as an ally,
and especially after the Anschluss, her two major European foes of the
First World War became Italy's friends. This left as potential land enemies
the Swiss, who even the Italians would have to admit were no great threat,
and the French, assessed as a relatively minor threat with the Alps as a
barrier. The other possibilities were the Yugoslavs and, in North Africa,
the French and British.

The German alliance made the Italians feel secure in Europe. The
British and French would not attack Italy with Germany as its ally. The
Yugoslavs presented more of a threat, since they could operate against
the Italians with less risk of major-power intervention. But the main
Italian fixation was the joint British-French threat to Libya. The Italian
investment in Libya and the projected role of Libya in Italian strategic
and economic planning made any threat to Libya important. On the other
hand, in the context of European politics in 1938, serious French or
British aggressive plans toward Libya seem farfetched. The German threat,
the Spanish Civil War, and the effects of the depression would seem to
have been enough for the two countries to worry about without waging
a war to take an unprofitable wasteland from the Italians.

Nonetheless, the Supreme Defense Commission designated Britain and
France in Libya as a major threat, along with the Yugoslavs on the Dalmatian front. Germany remained a potential enemy. With these priorities,
the Ministry of War and the General Staff made their plans.

Brigade or Division: Mechanization Arrives

The acceptance of mechanization as policy sparked a public debate
over motor-vehicle policy and doctrine. The official acceptance of mech-

anization followed, and doctrine appeared simultaneously in a number of manuals. Although presented as a unique Italian concept, the *guerra di rapido corso* differed only in detail from mechanized warfare in other countries. In Italy, economic and geographic considerations limited the extent of mechanization initially but the army firmly grasped the concept. Debate on mechanization stemmed from the experience of the previous year's maneuvers.

The *Brigata Corazzata* had been tested in the maneuvers of 1937. A second brigade existed in cadre form. The use of these brigades had been tested and the idea of creating armored divisions out of these brigades was advanced. Apparently there was disagreement within the high command over the exact organization that should be used. This debate spilled over into the pages of the *Rivista di Fanteria.* Beginning in the January 1938 issue there was a series of articles proposing various formations for the new divisions.

The first of these articles was "In tema di Grandi Unità Corazzate" (On the theme of major armored units) by Generale di Brigata Edoardo Quarra.[2] Quarra had been the commander of the *Reggimento Carri Armati* from the early 1930s until the regiment was divided in 1936.[3] At the time of the article he was the assistant division commander of an infantry division. Quarra advocated the use of tanks in mass, to break enemy lines. He wrote that experience in Spain had shown that the use of tanks in small groups or independently was ineffective.[4] This was the first discussion of tanks in Spain that appeared in any Italian military journal. Quarra also cites examples from the First World War in building his case for the use of tanks in accomplishing and exploiting the breakthrough.

The main point of his article was that, given the important role of the tank on the battlefield and its use in the exploitation phases, the large armored unit must have a substantial motorized infantry element and its own artillery, preferably self-propelled. At this time, of course, the two armored brigades, the First at full strength and the Second in cadre form, had no artillery and only two battalions of truck-mounted infantry. As a result, they were really infantry-support units, since they could not operate effectively beyond the range of the artillery of the infantry units they were supporting.[5] Similarly, the infantry in the armored units had to be able to keep up with the tanks and be in sufficient numbers to allow the tanks to penetrate the enemy line. Without its own infantry the armored unit could only penetrate as far as the supporting infantry units, which in the Italian army, of course, would not be motorized. Quarra

Figure 17. Generale Edoardo Quarra. Commander of Reggimento Carri Armati, 1933-36. First commented on the experience with tanks in Spain. He was the author of a 1938 article advocating the use of tanks in mass. *Courtesy of the Historical Office of the Italian Army General Staff.*

argued that these changes were essential to the creation of truly effective means of mechanized warfare and that, by implication at least, the armored brigades as constituted were ineffective.

The following month another article appeared in the *Rivista,* "Conviene trasformare la Brigata Corazzata in Divisione Corazzata?" (Is it worthwhile to change the armored brigade into an armored division?). The author, Generale di Brigata Carlo Di Simone, also an infantry officer, commanded the Second Armored Brigade.[6] The Second Brigade had not carried out any full-scale maneuvers, but had studied and restudied the results of the First Brigade's maneuvers and conducted map exercises and staff studies on the employment of an armored brigade.[7] Di Simone, a gradualist, suggested a number of changes in the structure of the brigade to make it efficient, and then, when the equipment and financing became available, the conversion of the brigades into armored divisions. His argument, more technical than Quarra's, mentioned the equipment of the existing units. Because only a few tanks had cannon rather than machine guns, Di Simone emphasized the need for more antitank cannon in the armored unit.[8] He also wanted to increase dramatically the tank strength of the brigade, nearly doubling it from 120 to 210. Other changes would help to increase the strength of the supporting arms, which Di Simone found the greatest weakness. Di Simone looked forward to the introduction of the new tanks under development by Ansaldo because they would remove many of the problems of the existing vehicles.

When possible Di Simone would convert the brigade into an armored division with more firepower. The main addition would be two armored self-propelled groups of artillery.[9] The *bersaglieri* regiment would have one more battalion, and all troops would be motorized if not armored. An attack aircraft squadron might be assigned. But the crucial point of Di Simone's argument was that the existing plan, which was under discussion by the General Staff, would utilize unsuitable artillery. And if a reorganization of the armored brigades into divisions used out-of-date artillery it would damage the image of the armored division and cause people to lose faith in the concept.[10] For this reason he felt that the armored divisions should not be formed at that time. The editor of the *Rivista* followed the article with a note saying he was happy to publish the personal views of Generale Di Simone and that as long as the subject was being studied by the General Staff, the *Rivista* would be happy to publish the view of any competent writer. The next author, Generale

Paolo Berardi, who had not served with the tanks, was the commander
of artillery for the First Army Corps along the French frontier at this
time. He later became *Capo di Stato Maggiore* in the confusion after the
Italian surrender.[11] In his article, titled *"Della Brigata Corazzata o Divisione che dire si voglia"* (Of the armored brigade or division, whichever
one wants to call it), Berardi suggested that the tank was not as crucial
to the initial breakthrough of the enemy lines as had been advocated and
was more effective in the exploitation phase of the battle.[12] Berardi
wanted the armored brigade to have armored vehicles for troop transport for use after the initial breakthrough rather than for the assault itself.

His major point was that the tank was not as essential to breaking the
enemy's line of trenches or fortifications as the doctrine led one to believe. While Di Simone's articles had been followed by a statement that
the *Rivista di Fanteria* would be happy to publish further views on the
subject, the editor followed Berardi's article with a rather sharp remark
that normally he preferred to leave the discussion of such questions to
"great captains" rather than minor commanders, but he would make an
exception in this case.[13] It would appear that the General Staff did not
appreciate Berardi's attack on policy. Most of Berardi's differences may
be attributed to his being an artillery officer rather than an infantry
officer with tank experience like the others.

Generale Quarra immediately wrote a rebuttal to Berardi's article.
In his *"Brigata o Divisione Corazzata"* (Armored brigade or division)
Quarra repeated his earlier arguments in favor of the division.[14] He did
not directly rebut either Di Simone or Berardi, but he presented a view
of the requirements of the army that contradicted Di Simone on the need
to wait and Berardi on the role of the tanks in breaching the enemy line.

Despite the variations in these articles, they showed some important
trends appearing in Italian military thought at this time. All three authors
agreed that the army needed armored divisions with a capability for independent action. They also agreed on the employment of the armored
units in the exploitation phase following a breakthrough. A consensus
had emerged about the nature of armored forces. They had moved beyond the infantry-support role that had been the doctrine since the First
World War. Now the army was intellectually prepared to create true
armored formations. The authors only debated the detailed organization
and the chronology of the changes.

Although most of the working papers on the new armored division

Figure 18. Generale Paolo Berardi. Artillery Office who in 1938 wrote articles discussing the policy of new brigades or divisions of armor, prompting Generale Quarra to reply. *Courtesy of the Historical Office of the Italian Army General Staff.*

produced by the General Staff have not survived, one dated 10 May 1938 has. This *Stralcio e promemoria sulla Divisione Corazzata* (Extract and promemoria on the armored division) began with a discussion of the *circolare* of July 1937, which established the armored brigade and suggested the development of divisions.[15] The study stated that the development of antitank weapons had reduced the usefulness of the tank in breaching defenses and increased its importance in the exploitation phase of the battle. To this end, the types of tanks had been revised so that there were light, medium, and heavy tanks, all still under development by Fiat Ansaldo. The new armored divisions would be equipped with these vehicles under a new organization. Four medium-tank battalions, used as the mass of armored power in the division, would be particularly important in a war of maneuver, although they could also be used in attacking hasty enemy defenses. There would also be one battalion of heavy tanks to be used against strongpoints during the maneuver phase of the battle or to attack defensive lines. Since none of these vehicles were available at the present time, the divisions would be provisionally equipped with one regiment of four battalions of Fiat 3000s, the twenty-year-old Renault design. The armored division also contained a *bersaglieri* regiment of two battalions of two-seat motorcycles, a company of armored cars, an artillery regiment of two groups, one company of antitank guns, and two batteries of 20-mm antiaircraft guns. The armored division combined modern concepts and some of the worst of traditional Italian military organization. The most notable flaw, of course, was equipment. The tanks were a major problem, but virtually every nation struggled with the need for new tanks. The idea of all the infantry in the division being mounted on motorcycles was a legacy of the bicycles and motorcycles used by the *bersaglieri* in the First World War.

All wheel-drive, military trucks were in production for the Italian army, most notably the Fiat *Dovunque* (anywhere), which Quarra and Di Simone had advocated. But the *bersagliere* on his motorcycle with his plume blowing in the wind was a powerful image to Italians, including that old *bersagliere* Benito Mussolini. The other deficiencies more directly related to equipment availability. Only a limited number of antitank weapons and towed artillery pieces existed.[16] In the rush to rearm Italy, there simply were not enough guns to go around, and at this stage the armored divisions were no better equipped to deal with tanks than the ordinary infantry division, nor did they have even the equivalent artillery support of an infantry division, although they had more modern guns than the World War I relics in the infantry divisions.

This May 1938 proposal, for the new armored division, made no accommodation for the arguments of Quarra, Di Simone, and Berardi. The division would have only one antitank company and limited, antiquated artillery support. Although the division was designed as a maneuver element, the staff study made no other attempt to deal with the criticisms already published in a leading military journal.

As the 1938 maneuvers approached, much progress had been made. The armored division was under serious discussion both by the General Staff and in the professional press. Armored brigades had been tested and would be further tested in the upcoming maneuvers. The Spanish Civil War provided useful information on armored operations. On the negative side, however, the vehicle situation was critical. The delivery of new tanks designed for infantry support more than for armored combat was still some distance in the future.

Mussolini and the Ministry of War made their final decision in the fall of 1938. Mechanization became official policy with the publication of *La Dottrina Tattica nella Realizzazioni dell'Anno XVI, Circolare 9000* (The tactical doctrine in realization in the year 16 [of Fascism]) of the *Stato Maggiore* on 28 October 1938.[17] This circular signaled the adoption of the doctrine of high-speed mobile warfare as the official strategic and tactical concept of the Italian army. The circular began by saying that the Italian principles of war had not changed, because the conditions under which Italy could fight a war had not changed. However, the doctrine had evolved and developed. The changes tested in the annual maneuvers, concluding with those of 1938, were now ready for implementation.[18] *La guerra di rapido corso* (the war of rapid course) would be a war of maneuver, using what the British military critic B. H. Liddell Hart had called the strategy of the indirect approach.[19] The army would maneuver against the flank of the enemy. In the Italian concept, mechanized and airborne weapons would be important aspects of war, and the essential principles of their use had to be learned. Exploitation by motorized forces would follow the use of the maximum mass available to break the enemy line. This was, in essence, a standard *blitzkrieg*. The new manual on the use of armored units, *Impiego delle Unità Carriste,* outlined the new doctrine, based on the *guerra di rapido corso,* simultaneously with the reorganization.[20] This 1938 manual, the crucial turning point in the development of armored policy in Italy, established the basic principles.

The manual enumerated clearly defined tasks for the various tank units. It differentiated between tanks that were to be used to support infantry, *celeri,* and motorized units and those that were part of the armored division.[21] Supporting tanks gave fire support to the appropriate unit and dealt with strong points and other centers of resistance. Armored divisions were, however, maneuver elements in which the tank was the main weapon.[22] All units in the armored division supported the tanks in their attack. The division either maneuvered against the flank of the enemy or, if that was not feasible, made an overwhelming attack against his line.[23]

Whether the tanks were in an armored division or supporting the infantry they should be used in mass.[24] Artillery and antitank guns protected the tanks against other tanks and against hostile artillery. The instructions for tank units cooperating with *celeri* units differed only in their use in reconnaissance. And although they would be used like the infantry tanks in the breaching of the enemy line, it was to enable the *celeri* to penetrate the enemy line rather than to destroy that line itself.[25]

The tank had finally come into its own in the Italian army. At last a clear distinction existed between the use of tanks as infantry support weapons and the use of the tanks as a major battlefield weapon, capable of decisive action on its own. This was the sine qua non of creating a modern army in the 1930s. With this new doctrine and the creation of an armored corps, the Italian army should have been on the way to establishing an important and effective modern army.

Unfortunately there were several flaws. The new concept still did not adequately deal with the problem of tank-versus-tank combat.[26] The armored division had no major role in combat with the enemy's tank force. Antitank guns remained the primary means of dealing with tanks, and Italians had only the Austrian Bohler 47-mm model. The tank would attack the enemy artillery where possible.[27] The destruction of hostile artillery was important of course, but the use of the tanks against emplaced artillery was disastrous if maneuver was not properly used. The tank remained a replacement or substitute for the traditional arms, in this case the artillery, rather than a major weapon of a new and radically different type.

The progress made in the fall of 1938 and early 1939 was rather less than the changes in policy required. The army procured no new tanks.

Designs started in 1936 would not be ready for issue until the fall of 1939. Although *Impiego delle Unità Carriste* in November 1938 included the basic characteristics of the new medium tank,[28] the new armored divisions had the twenty-year-old Fiat tanks in their medium-tank battalions, the main striking force of those divisions.

The combination of *La Dottrina Tattica* and the *Impiego delle Unità Carriste* created the theoretical base for Italian mechanization. The next war would be a war of maneuver using highly mobile armored forces to outflank the enemy. The old idea of mass attacks against the enemy line with the tank dealing with obstacles became secondary. It would still be used in some situations, but the grand stroke of a mechanized "strategy of the indirect approach" would be the preferred method of operation. New units would be required and they were the next priority.

The *Ordinamento Pariani*

The new mechanized war needed units organized for rapid movement and independent action. The new *ordinamento* authorized a field army of two corps. The *Armata Po* would defend the Po Valley with seven divisions, three *celeri,* two armored, and two motorized. One corps contained the *celeri* and the other the mechanized units. Even under the new policy, the *celeri* remained a major element in the army.

Generale Alberto Pariani, the *Sottosegretario* of the War Ministry and Chief of the General Staff of the army, gave his name to the new *ordinamento.* The *ordinamento Pariani* reorganized the whole army with substantial increases in the number of divisions and of higher headquarters.[29] Most importantly, it created a number of headquarters units and divisions especially designed for the *guerra di rapido corso.* The *ordinamento* organized an army of two corps, the *Armata Po* (an armored corps) and a *celere* corps. Four divisions, two armored and two motorized, would be under the armored corps. The three *celeri* divisions that had existed since 1934 would be under the *celere* corps. Twenty new divisions, plus a number of headquarters units, further increased the strength of the whole army.[30]

The *Armata Po* controlled the four armored and three *celeri* units.[31] From November 1938, Generale Ettore Bastico, a *bersaglieri* officer born in Bologna, commanded the Army of the Po. He had served throughout the First World War as a staff officer and had published a work on military history as well as serving as commander of the *Scuola Centrale di Educazione Fisica* (Central School of Physical Education) in the 1920s. In addition to his formidable record as an army staff officer and as one of the most intellectual of Italian general officers, he had also been an instructor at the naval academy and editor of *Rivista Militare Italiana*. A favorite of Badoglio, Bastico commanded a division and later a corps in Ethiopia. He then commanded the *Corpo di Truppa Volontaria* in Spain, where he was promoted again for "merit in war."[32]

Thus the *Armata Po,* the army of maneuver that was to be the modern striking force of the Italian army, was given one of the most experienced and brilliant commanders in the army. Under his command were the two corps previously mentioned, the *Corpo d'Armata Corazzato* and the *Corpo d'Armata Celere.*[33] The former contained the two motorized infantry divisions that had been in existence since 1935 and two armored divisions to be organized from the two existing armored brigades.[34]

All three higher headquarters had experienced commanders. Generale Fidenza Dall'Ora would command the Armored Corps at Mantova. A supply officer, Dall'Ora rose from being a colonel at the beginning of the Ethiopian war in 1935 to Corps commander in 1938.[35] He belonged to the anti-Badoglio faction at the War Ministry. So a *bersagliere* with an extensive staff and command background, who gained prominence under Badgolio, commanded the *Armata Po,* while a supply officer, from the anti-Badoglio faction, commanded the armored corps.

The *celere* corps contained the three *celeri* divisions authorized in 1934, but which were not operational as divisions.[36] The individual regiments existed often in cadre form, but these divisions and the corps would only become active on mobilization. Generale Giovanni Messe would command the *celere* corps. Messe, a cavalryman, had previously been the inspector of *celere* troops.[37]

Although nothing was done about the organization or activation of the *celeri* divisions at this time, the fall of 1938 did see a great deal of activity toward organizing the armored divisions. The *1ᵃ Brigata Corazzata* was the only active armored formation. The Second Brigade (*2ᵃ Brigata*) consisted only of a staff, while the assigned *bersaglieri* regiment and the battalions that would make up the armored regiment carried on independent existences. The promulgation of the *ordinamento Pariani* changed not only this situation but the composition of all units of *fanteria carrista.*

The four *regimenti fanteria carrista* established under the 1934 *ordina-*

mento were reduced to three.[38] The second regiment, redesignated the 32nd, became a regiment of the Second Armored Brigade, which was finally formed as an active unit on 15 November 1938.[39] The General Staff organized a third regiment, the *33ᵃ Regimento Fanteria Carrista*, from battalions in the three original regiments.[40] The ultimate results of these changes, six regiments of tanks, had two different missions. The infantry-support regiments acted as headquarters for the battalions that would be attached to corps and divisions in war. These regiments had varying numbers of battalions assigned to them. The other three, 31st, 32nd, became a regiment of the Second Armored Brigade, which two of *Fiat Mod. 21/30 carri di rottura,* and two of CV 35 *carri d'assalto.*[41] Although the new tanks had not arrived, the *battaglione carri di rottura* were renamed *battaglione carri medi* and the *battaglione carri d'assalto* became *battaglione carri leggeri.*[42] These name changes symbolized the evolution in tactical concepts that had occurred in the army.

Even the organization of the new units was a slow process. Pariani directed the first priority to be the constitution of one armored division, one *celere* division, and the two motorized divisions.[43] Initially the two armored brigades would be gradually built up to strength while they retained their identity as brigades.[44] The first division (based on the Second Brigade), the *132ᵃ Divisione Corazzata,* was established on 1 February 1939.[45] The *Prima Brigata* was only brought to full strength in early April, and officially redesignated as the *131ᵃ Divisione Corazzata* on 20 April 1939.[46] Both of the new armored divisions had the same commanding officer they had had as brigades, the 131ᵃ under Giovanni Magli and the 132ᵃ under Di Simone.

The slow development of these units resulted from the many problems that would plague the Italian armored formations throughout their history. The lack of modern vehicles has already been mentioned. Manpower was to be another major problem. The Ministry directed the *Armata Po* to be manned to fifty percent strength.[47] This was the standard level in the Italian army, where the short period of conscripted service made the active units essentially training organizations that would be filled with called-up reserves on mobilization. When in April 1939 the invasion of Albania was about to begin and Europe was coming progressively closer to war, the General Staff brought the *Corpo d'Armata Corazzato* to eighty percent strength.[48] This involved the calling up of the class of 1912, all the reservists for that entire year. The officers also had to be called up from civilian life. In most cases this meant seventy-five percent of the officers in a unit would be recalled officers, many of World War I vintage. The draft provided the enlisted men. But as already mentioned, few recruits had the skills necessary for the tank units.

The lack of money and oil presented even greater problems. In the midst of the creation of the armored divisions, on 1 April 1939, the financial crush required the reduction of the order for new tanks.[49] The General Staff reduced the armored regiments in each division by a third and then the battalions by another third, which reduced the total order for the new medium tank, still not delivered after three years of planning, by fifty percent.[50] The supply of fuel remained a problem. No other unit in the Italian army required as much fuel as the armored divisions, and the Corps, with its two armored and two motorized divisions, would use a tremendous amount of fuel. The Ministry initially assigned the divisions only enough fuel for 250 to 300 kilometers.[51] This enabled them to move to the borders of Italy from their home stations in the Po Valley. Fuel depots for the armored units were also to be constructed in Libya, so that sufficient fuel would be on hand if the armored units were deployed to that colony.[52]

With the implementation of the *ordinamento Pariani,* the Italian army had the basic structure for mechanized war. Although small in relation to the whole army, the *Armata Po* and, in particular, one of its parts, the *Corpo d'Armata Corazzata,* formed a potent striking force. They would be quite capable of defending the Po Valley against any presumed enemy. And the largely unmechanized colonial forces that threatened Libya would pose no problem. But the inclusion of the *celeri* units weakened the army as a whole. The horsed troops did not have enough firepower or support troops to survive on a mechanized battlefield. Furthermore, the weaknesses in equipment and fuel in the armored corps prevented it from becoming fully effective. The General Staff had devised the plans for modern units and a mechanized war. The economy and Italian industry now had to provide the means for those units to conduct that war. For the time being the *Armata Po* could only train with its outdated tanks and wait.

1938 Maneuvers

The army conducted maneuvers in both Italy and Libya in 1938. The training in Italy was limited in scope and interest. The new doctrine had not yet appeared and the armored brigade only conducted limited infantry-support operations. In Libya, under the colorful maresciallo dell'Ariazone (Air Marshal) Italo Balbo, the maneuvers involved airborne operations in addition to extensive testing of tank-infantry cooperation. The use of assigned tank battalions with the infantry divisions had been doctrine for several years. In Libya the divisions had organic tank battalions and the units trained together, making them much more effective than in Italy.

At the same time, the General Staff and the officers of armored units worked on operational plans for war. The Italians had a number of plans for any contingency. In 1938 for the first time the General Staff conducted staff tours of the intended battlefields. At each site the staff made detailed appreciations of the use of armored troops, showing exactly what was planned for the new units, in addition to maneuvers as close to the areas as possible.

For the 1938 maneuvers the two Italian corps in Libya fought a sham battle in the area southwest of Tripoli. The XX Corps, the attacking force, consisted of one air-infantry regiment, *Reggimento Fanti dell'Aerea,* with Italian officers and Libyan enlisted personnel.[53] The rest of the maneuvers were straightforward ground operations: the two corps fought each other. The total tank force involved was six battalions, four battalions assigned to infantry divisions and two to the two corps.[54] At this time the divisions in Libya, and for that matter the corps, were the only units that had organic tank battalions. This was primarily because the troops in Africa were under a separate command system and so the battalions had been assigned to some higher headquarters for administration. In Italy, although tank battalions existed for each of the corps, they had remained grouped under the four *reggimenti fanteria carrista.* These acted as administrative headquarters for the tank battalions in Italy but also had the unfortunate effect of segregating the tank units from the daily training of the infantry units they supported. The only tank units that were integral with other units in Italy were the two battalions that were in the motorized infantry divisions, and the battalions in *1ª Brigata Corazzata.*

Despite the close relationship that existed between the tank battalions and their divisions in Libya, the 1938 maneuvers involved normal infantry tactics.[55] The tank battalions only supported the infantry in the approved manner. The appreciation written after the maneuvers emphasized the airborne aspects of the maneuvers, which of course were the most dramatic. One battalion of one division was motorized, while the air-transported division moved completely by air. This was another example of the problems of innovation in the Italian army. It was experimenting with the most modern means of military transport, yet it could not equip its infantry units with motor vehicles that had been introduced twenty-five years before.

The tank battalions and the motorcycle companies in each division were the only fully motorized units beside this battalion in Libya. The manpower report stated that they were of insufficient strength for the jobs required. And rather dramatically, the appreciation of the tanks (CV 35s) ended with the statement that they were inadequate both in number and quality. The report went on to say that the command use of the motorized units, especially in a reconnaissance role, lacked understanding and emphasis. The detachments were used with insufficient strength and speed.

The deficiencies in the use of armored and motorized elements was to be a major critique of Italian military tactics for some years to come. However, the Italian emphasis on the use of an air-transported division and the weakness of the tank units makes an interesting contrast to the deployment by the British of a mobile division to Egypt in September 1938, some four months later. This British division, which was to become the 7th Armoured Division, spent the two years before the outbreak of war in the Western Desert training, while the Italians continued to work on airborne units, but did not substantially reinforce the tank units in Libya.

The Libyan maneuvers followed one of several contingency plans in effect. These plans showed the exact intention of the General Staff for the use of the armored units. Mobilization plans in the Italian army were called *piani di radunata,* or assembly plans, although they normally involved not only the assembly of the units, which would have been dispersed at their home stations, but also the initial operations, whether they were to be the assumption of defense positions along a border or offensive operations. These plans were commonly known by their initials and a number. For example, P.R. 12 was the plan for the troops in Libya in case of war with Britain.[56]

While the plans were very detailed and essentially military, there were also large scenarios for the next war that established the presumed enemies and conditions of war. These were called *ipotesi,* or hypotheses; they might involve several plans. *Ipotesi B* was the hypothesis of war against Britain and France, with Yugoslavia neutral. *Ipotesi B* would then involve several *piani di radunata,* including P.R. 12 for Libya, another for the Franco-Italian border, and one for the Italo-Yugoslavian border. These hypotheses changed according to the international situation, and the plans changed both with the hypotheses and with army intentions and capabilities.

In the fall of 1938 and the spring of 1939, the last twelve months before the Second World War, the following hypotheses were in effect. A German attack through the former Austro-Italian border was the oldest of the hypotheses. A Franco-British conflict, with operations both along the European border and the Libyan borders of these countries with Italy, was rapidly becoming a favorite. And the Yugoslavs were considered a definite threat, either in alliance with the British or French or with one or both as unfriendly neutrals. Some of these possibilities had been the main focus of Italian military planning since the First World War while others, most notably the Libyan defense question, had only emerged in the late 1930s.

Although there is evidence of the planning of fuel depots for the use of armored units in Libya, no copies of the plans for their use have survived from the winter and spring of 1938-39. However, a substantial amount of information remains on European planning, particularly at this time, on the preliminary planning that would determine the use of the armored units. These plans consisted of staff tours of the Italo-German and Italo-Yugoslavian borders. The armor representatives on these tours were Di Simone, as commander of the Second Brigade, and Generale Carlo Vecherelli, who was attached to the *Corpo d'Armata Corazzato* and who would become the commander of the 132nd Division in rapid succession to Di Simone.[57]

Against Yugoslavia the Italians would occupy a large part of Croatia and, in particular, block the north-south communications from Fiume and from Ljubljana.[58] There was no particular problem about the employment of armor in this *ipotesi C* since the area involved was fairly open. The main objective would be Zagreb.

On the German frontier the problems were much greater.[59] The extreme ruggedness of the terrain presented substantial problems in the employment of armored units. Di Simone decided that the best avenue of movement would be in the valley of the Drava River, east toward Spittal. He also said that this would depend on the arrival of new tanks, as "with the M.21/30, you could not get one more hour of work." The *celeri* divisions would also be used in the region, which would be the area of the main thrust. The defense of the other main pass, the Brenner, would be only a blocking action, apparently because of the heavy Italian defenses and reasonable expectation that it would be the main objective of the enemy.

The 1938 maneuvers and the operational plans show both the development of armored warfare and the weaknesses. On both the European and colonial fronts, the army planned the use of tanks and armored units as a main feature of operations. In Italy the armored corps formed the spearhead of the attack. In Libya the infantry would have close tank support. On the other hand most units had not trained with tanks (those in Libya were unique). But there were still doubts about the use of tanks in mountains. The staff studies did not investigate the use of tanks to the fullest extent. The tank commanders had to convince the corps and army commanders that tanks could be used; the higher commanders had doubts.

* * * * *

With this change in policy, Italy moved ahead of most other nations. Although Britain and France had more experience in tanks and a larger proportion of their army motorized, they did not have an armored striking force that the Italians now possessed. The United States had even less theoretical background than the British and French. Only one brigade of quasi-armored troops existed in the United States. Germany, Italy's putative ally, had a superior armored force but was more concerned about other countries.

In 1938 Italy made its decisive move in armored warfare. The change from motorization to mechanization brought Italy into the first rank of nations in military policy and this forward-looking policy could have given Italy the impetus to create an army second to none. The basis for such an army existed in policy and doctrinal statements issued in the fall.

But economic and industrial inadequacies limited the possibilities. The Fiat Ansaldo combine had not yet produced new vehicles to fill even the reduced requirement. The small armored force initially planned had to be cut back. Italy could not provide the money for the necessary vehicles and their operation. A fifty percent reduction in the armored force severely limited the achievement of the goals of Italian planners. Further troubles resulted from the selection of antipathetic commanders for the new units.

Nonetheless, training and planning indicated the definite Italian commitment to armored warfare. Contingency plans depended heavily on the use of armor. Maneuvers involved close cooperation of tanks and infantry. The army had accepted mechanization. It only needed the equipment and financing.

Notes

1. Ministero della Guerra, *XV Sessione Della Commissione Suprema di Difesa, Sintesi degli argomenti tratti da S.E. il Sottosegretario di Stato nella riunione del 25 Novembre 1938*, U.S.

2. Edoardo Quarra, "In tema di Grandi Unità Corazzate" *Rivista di Fanteria*, Anno V, No. 1, January 1938, pp. 1-10.

3. *Memorie Storiche*, Reggimento Carri Armati, 1933-36.

4. Quarra, "In Tema," p. 5.

5. Quarra, "In Tema," p. 11.

6. Carlo Di Simone, "Conviene trasformare la Brigata Corazzata in Divisione Corazzata," *Rivista di Fanteria*, Anno 5, No. 2, February 1938, pp. 79-88. For his assignment, see *L'Esercito e I Suoi Corpi*, vol. 2, pt. 1, p. 68.

7. *Memorie Storiche*, 2ª Brigata Corazzata, 1938.

8. Di Simone, "Conviene," p. 80.

9. Di Simone, "Conviene," p. 87.

10. Di Simone, "Conviene," p. 88.

11. *L'Esercito e I Suoi Corpi*, vol. 1, p. 374.

12. Paolo Berardi, "Della Brigata Corazzata o Divisione che dir si voglia," *Rivista di Fanteria*, Anno 5, No. 5, May 1938, pp. 213-18.

13. Berardi, "Della Brigata," p. 218.

14. Edoardo Quarra, "Brigata o Divisione Corazzata," *Rivista di Fanteria*, Anno 5, No. 5, May 1938, pp. 219-22.

15. Stato Maggiore, Stralcio e promemoria sulla Divisione Corazzata. In special file for Avvocato Ceva, U.S.

16. *L'Esercito tra la Guerra*, pp. 280-90 shows the deficiencies that still existed a year later.

17. Ministero della Guerra, *La Dottrina Tattica nella Realizzazione dell'Anno XVI* (Rome: Stato Maggiore, 1938).

18. *La Dottrina Tattica*, p. 7.

19. See B. H. Liddell Hart, *Strategy* (New York: Praeger, 1967).

20. Comando del Corpo di Stato Maggiore, *Impiego delle Unità Carriste* (Rome: Istituto Poligrafico dello Stato, 1938).

21. *Impiego delle Unità Carriste*, pp. 3-4.

22. *Impiego delle Unità Carriste*, p. 31.

23. *Impiego delle Unità Carriste*, p. 35.

24. *Impiego delle Unità Carriste*, pp. 4, 6.

25. *Impiego delle Unità Carriste*, pp. 19-20.

26. *Impiego delle Unità Carriste*, p. 28.

27. *Impiego delle Unità Carriste*, p. 38.

28. *Impiego delle Unità Carriste*, p. 2.

29. *L'Esercito e I Suoi Corpi*, vol. 1, p. 217; *L'Esercito tra la Guerra*, pp. 130-33.

30. *L'Esercito tra la Guerra*, p. 131.

31. *Memorie Storiche*, Armata Po, 1939.

32. Araldi, *Generali dell'Impero*, pp. 45-50.

33. *L'Esercito tra la Guerra*, p. 130.

34. Letter, Ministero della Guerra, to Comando Corpo d'Armata Corazzato, 20 November 1938. Subject: Denominazione di unità corazzate. Microfilm T-821, roll 375, frame 211, NA.

35. Carlo De Biase, *L'Aquila d'Oro* (Milan: Edizioni del Borghese, 1970), p. 395.

36. *Memorie Storiche*, Corpo d'Armata Celere, 1939.

37. *L'Esercito e I Suoi Corpi*, vol. 2, pt. 2, p. 455.

38. *Memorie Storiche*, 2ª Reggimento Fanteria Carrista, 1938.

39. *Memorie Storiche*, 2ª Brigata Corazzata, 1938 (the existence for one month in 1938 apparently did not warrant a separate *memorie storiche*).

40. *Memorie Storiche*, 33° Reggimento Fanteria Carrista, 1939.

41. Letter, Ministero della Guerra, Gabinetto, 15 November 1938. Subject: Riordinamento dei reggimenti di fanteria carrista. Microfilm T-821, roll 375, frames 205-7, NA.

42. Comando del Corpo di Stato Maggiore, *Impiego delle Unità Carriste*, Circolare no. 18000, 1 December 1938.

43. Letter, Pariani to Generale Viscontini, Capo di Ufficio Operazioni, 28 November 1938, covering matters of urgency in the new "ordinamento." Racc. 759, U.S.

44. Letter, Gabinetto, 20 November 1938. Subject: Denominazione di unità corazzate. Microfilm T-821, roll 375, frame 211, NA.

45. *Memorie Storiche*, 132ª Divisione Corazzata, 1939.

46. Letter, Stato Maggiore to Comando del Corpo d'Armata di Firenze, 5 April 1939. Subject: Approntamento immediato di unità. In special file for Avvocato Ceva, U.S.

47. Promemoria per Il Sottocapo di Sm.m per le Operazioni, 1 February 1939. Subject: Promemoria di S.E. Bastico circa "Efficienza Armata Po." Racc. 756, U.S.

48. Memorandum of meeting of Stato Maggiore, 3 April 1939, dated 12 April 1939. Subject: Armata Po. Racc. 756, U.S.

49. Promemoria per Il Sottocapo di Sm.m per le Operazioni, 17 March 1939. Racc. 208, U.S. Letter, Sottocapo per le Operazioni a Sottacapo per Intendente, 21 March 1939. Subject: Programma provvista carburanti e costruzione depositi carburanti in Patria e in Libia. Racc. 208, U.S.

50. Promemoria, 17 March 1939.

51. Promemoria, 1 February 1939. Subject: Promemoria di S.E. Bastico circa Efficienza Armata Po.

52. Letter, 21 March 1939. Subject: Programma provvista carburanti e costruzione depositi carburanti in Patria e in Libia. Racc. 256, U.S.

53. All details of the 1938 maneuvers are from Governo Generale della Libia-Comando Superiore Forze Armate Africa Settentrionale, Esercitazioni Anno XVI in Libia. Special File, U.S. See also Nino Arena, *I Paracadutisti* (Modena: Stem Mucchi, 1972), pp. 22, 60-61.

54. Esercitazioni Anno XVI in Libia, pt. 3 Considerazioni.

55. *Ibid.*

56. Piano di Copertura e Radunata 12 (P.R. 12), March 1940. Copy in Imperial War Museum, London (Imp. W. Mus. Reference No. AL 1511).

57. *L'Esercito e I Suoi Corpi,* vol. 2, pt. 1, p. 68.

58. Promemoria per S.E. Il Capo di Stato Maggiore, 6 April 1939. Subject: Radunata Armata Po alla frontiera orientale. Carteggio Storico-Armata "PO", U.S.

59. Promemoria per S.E. Il Capo di Stato Maggiore, 26 January 1939. Subject: Ricognizioni alla frontiera settentrionale. Carteggio Storico-Armata "PO", U.S.

8
Prelude to War

Between Italy's creation of a mechanized policy in late 1938 and her entry into the Second World War on 10 June 1940, the Fascist government and the General Staff tried to modernize Italy and its army so that it could survive in the next war. The major thrust of these attempts was the introduction of a new national automotive policy, designed to motorize Italian society. Mussolini wanted to increase the use of the automobile in Italy to stimulate the automotive industry. The industry would then be more capable of military production in time of war.

This effort followed an equally important change in army policy. Beginning in November 1938 the Italian army attempted to create a modern armored force. The adoption of the new idea of mechanized warfare led to the creation of an armored corps and two armored divisions. The General Staff established the framework of mechanized warfare. However, it furnished only limited guidance on tactical doctrine. The staffs of the new armored units developed detailed tactics for the employment of their formations.

At the same time, the army needed many new vehicles if the bold plan of Mussolini's *guerra di rapido corso* was to be effective. The armored force urgently required new tanks to replace the inadequate ones currently available, and Italy did not have any of the support material required. She lacked natural resources of petroleum and rubber and had only limited deposits of iron and coal. In consequence, the government had difficulty in providing the material for the construction and maintenance of the armored force. Mussolini's Italy failed to provide this technical support and, as a result, the military innovation failed.

Italy also moved dramatically in world affairs in 1939, and these events deeply influenced the development of armored warfare. In April, Italian troops returned from Spain while another expeditionary force supported the Italian annexation of Albania. In September the Second World War began, involving Italy's allies and neighbors. While the war did not at once directly effect Italy, it did show what the future held.

Events in Spain and Albania had direct and immediate effects. The return of the *Corpo di Truppa Volontaria* reduced expenditures and provided a pool of trained, experienced men. The army quickly found uses for this experience. Many senior officers joined or rejoined units, where they took a leading role in teaching the new concepts. The major infantry unit in Spain was reformed as an armored division in the Italian army. But as the army gained these men, it lost more to the expedition to Albania.

Albania had been in the Italian sphere for many years, but Mussolini chose the spring of 1939 to annex the country and depose the man Italy had helped become king. The ensuing military operations strained the army nearly to its limits. The difficulties of supporting a major force across so short a distance as the Adriatic proved nearly insurmountable. Equipment and clothing revealed a number of flaws; the *Centauro* armored division, equipped with ten- and twenty-year-old tanks, hardly distinguished itself, although it did beat the Germans by several months as the first armored division operationally employed.

The German use of armored divisions in opening the Second World War had little immediate effect in Italy. Although Italy had common borders with two of the belligerents in Europe and with a third in Africa, Italian neutrality meant no major involvement. Troops in Libya maintained lookouts along the border. Beyond that little disturbance occurred, and indeed the contingency plan against Germany remained in effect along with those against Britain, France, and Yugoslavia.

Italy could hardly help being deeply interested in what went on in Europe, but by the time the Germans proved conclusively that mechanization was the wave of the future, Italy had been embarked on a desperate attempt to achieve a mechanized nation for almost a year. Despite the mechanization of the army, society remained unmotorized. And because of this, and not the understanding or lack of understanding of the German success, Italy failed as a mechanized power. It was the late introduction of Mussolini's automotive policy and the inherent weaknesses of the Italian industrial base that prevented the development of a mechanized army.

La Politica Automobilistica

Mussolini and his government belatedly recognized that Italian society could not support the kind of army that they wanted. In February 1939 they developed a new national policy called *politica automobilistica in funzione militare* (automotive policy in its military function). Italy had to become a motorized society so that it could support and supply its army. To this end the government abolished many restrictions on the use of cars. It attempted to find new sources of fuel. It mandated an integrated national system of design and construction to make the motor vehicles produced in Italy militarily useful.

Prior to this in the interwar years, Italy had no automotive policy, although a policy of subsidies had existed before the First World War. The central government expended no effort to rationalize the automotive industry or insure the availability of adequate production facilities for military purposes. Only in 1937 was a standardization scheme for heavy trucks introduced. There seems to be no explanation of this lapse, except that the automobile manufacturers generally opposed government interference and the government made no concerted effort to implement such a policy.

The *Commissione Suprema di Difesa* formulated and implemented the new automotive policy. The *Commissione*, already mentioned briefly, was the supreme consultative body on national defense.[1] It consisted of a president (Mussolini, the *capo di governo*) and the ministers of state. All these men had votes in the decisions of the *Commissione*. However, of the sixteen ministerial positions, Mussolini held five and his son-in-law, Galeazzo Ciano, another. On questions relating to their ministries, the *sottosegretario* of each had a vote, along with the *Capo di Stato Maggiore* of each of the three services. Several other senior officers also had consultative roles.[2] As the main discussion and decision-making body, it dealt with many questions relating to mechanization. For many questions the actual agency that implemented the decisions was the *Commissariato Generale per la Fabbrica di Guerra*, which was the position held by Generale Alfredo Dallolio, who had directed Italian war production in World War I.[3] He now would briefly try to do the same in World War II.

Fabbriguerra, as this organization was commonly called, was responsible for the control of industrial capacity and raw materials in support of the war effort. Dallolio had been quite successful in the First World War in

balancing the limited resources available with the needs of the nation,
but much of the difference between supply and demand had been filled
by Britain and the United States. Now Italy had to deal with the demands
of mechanization with virtually no support.

The February 1939 meeting of the *Commissione* attempted to come
to grips with the problems of mechanization. Mussolini directed a discussion with Badoglio, Dallolio, and Paolo Thaon di Revel, the Minister of
Finance.[4] They discussed the difficulty in getting petroleum and rubber
and the foreign exchange problems involved. The members lamented the
difficulty of supplying the necessary raw materials for the manufacture
of motor vehicles. Badoglio discussed the inability of industry to manufacture the necessary number of vehicles. They then discussed the plans
to requisition civilian vehicles for military use. Dallolio and Thaon di
Revel argued that enough cars and trucks could be obtained to supply
the army without damaging civilian businesses. Badoglio replied that the
army could not go to war in two-seat Fiats and that the "taxis of the
Marne" had been a unique event that the Italians could not repeat.

Then Mussolini rose to speak. He announced a new civilian policy to
help mechanize the army. "It was," Mussolini said, "evident that it was
necessary to motorize the nation."[5] Italy had spent millions on her
beautiful roads, now the roads needed cars. He said that Italy could only
have about five or six hundred thousand cars in peacetime, that was all
the economy would support. But Italy had to have that many to create
the industries that could supply the necessary vehicles in time of war.

To implement this, Mussolini initiated the policy of motorization.
The first step was the removal of the gasoline tax, which was designed
to limit consumption. He also pursued other means of reducing the cost
of gas, including synthetic fuels. Mussolini focused on automobile transport since Italy had little motorization in agriculture. The few tractors
were concentrated in limited areas like the Po Valley. This meant that
motorization would have to emphasize the private ownership of cars.
Italian agriculture, based on grapes and olives cultivated on small plots
in most areas, was not a fertile field for increased vehicle use.

Four months after the policy of mechanization for the army had been
announced, Mussolini initiated his attempt to motorize Italian society.
It was not possible to make society catch up with the demands of modern
war in the manner that Il Duce suggested. Italy had only three hundred
thousand of the cars he wanted. The reduction of the gasoline tax simply

was not enough to double the number of cars in a year or two. It would be several years before Italy was motorized.

A year later, in February 1940, the *Commissione* held another discussion on automotive policy.[6] In this meeting, Pariani, as *Sottosegratario di Stato per la Guerra,* covered the changes implemented in the past year and planned for the future. Pariani first reaffirmed that "automotive policy is a fundamental element of preparation for war"[7] and of great importance to the Ministry of War.

Pariani stated that the areas of concern were the introduction of standard designs, the renovation of old material, increased production, and the conservation and development of fuel supplies. These problems were tied together in a comprehensive program. The list of solutions indicated the depth of the crisis the Italians were trying to overcome. The conception of standard designs for vehicles so they could be quickly integrated into an army had been used before the First World War in Italy as well as many other countries. In February 1940 standards for trucks over six tons, which had been introduced in 1937, were the only ones in effect. The *Commissione* would now implement standards for all other classes of vehicles. Thus on the declaration of war only a very limited number of trucks of the civilian economy could be quickly integrated into military service; to change this would require much-increased production.

Increasing production and replacing and updating old vehicles depended on stimulating the use of motor vehicles in the civilian economy. To this end, the government reduced taxes on road use as well as on gasoline. The attempts to save petroleum products centered around the introduction of electric buses; the population was encouraged to use them, rather than their own cars, for urban transportation. This demonstrates that many of the objectives of *politica automobilistica* were mutually antagonistic.

Pariani ended by requesting that the *Commissione* direct that this policy be given maximum support and that the responsible ministries accelerate their parts of the program. Because of the complexity of the Fascist government several ministries had jurisdiction over automotive affairs. For example, the Ministry of Finance, the Ministry of Corporations, and the Ministry of Communication all had to agree on the modernization of old vehicles. The concept of needing a motorized society to support a motorized army was undoubtedly correct. But in February

1940 all of Europe was already at war. Italy could not have caught up
if she had had five years instead of five months before she too became
embroiled.

Spain and Antitank Warfare: Italian Doctrine in 1939

Experience in Spain and the use of armor in other armies formed the
basis of the discussion of armored doctrine in Italy in the first year and
a half of mechanization. Policy remained as laid down in *La Dottrina
Tattica nella Realizzazione dell'Anno XVI.* The army investigated the
details of armored use to determine the tactical doctrine under this policy.
From this the army produced an informal doctrine with which Italian
armor units went into the Second World War.

The major shift in emphasis in these studies was toward a substantially
greater emphasis on antitank warfare. After considering the Spanish Civil
War and the armored forces of other nations, the Italians concentrated
on antitank warfare and in particular on the use of the armored division
and its tanks against similar forces. Previously, the Italians had neglected
antitank defense as a feature of mechanized war. The traditionally superb
artillery had the task of antitank defense and combat between tanks during a war of maneuver was not considered. Now as a result of the Spanish
Civil War and the new alignment of Italy with Germany against two
armored powers, Britain and France, the General Staff placed a high
priority on antitank defense.

Although the Germans used the Spanish Civil War as a testing ground,
the Italians had not regarded Spain as an example of what the next war
would be like. Italian officers felt that the war in Spain was one that followed "a middle way between a colonial war and a war between regular
armies."[8] They expected the next war to include more heavy artillery,
tanks, chemical warfare, and well-prepared fixed defenses. The lack of
these in Spain meant that it was not a true test of the next war. On a
more realistic plane, the army felt that the lack of training, equipment,
and the inability to maneuver of the Republican forces limited the value
of Spain as a testing ground. These preconceptions of the Italian officers
prevented them from learning the lessons of Spain.

The army did learn the need for antitank defense. The Russian tanks,
armed with a 55-mm cannon, proved too heavily armored for the Bohler
47-mm guns, but could be destroyed by the 65-mm infantry gun in the

infantry regiments. Even this depended on a good shot. They praised the 65-mm gun primarily for its light weight and "omnipresence."[9] Despite the obvious inadequacy of the Bohler 47-mm antitank gun adopted in 1934, Italy made no concerted effort to replace it. The Italians were indeed barely able to equip all units with the obsolescent design.

While the criticism of the antitank defenses was muted, everyone admitted the ineffectiveness of the CV 35 light tank. The officers who observed the CV 35 in Spain acknowledged that it was obsolete. Small-arms fire penetrated its armor. Shrapnel at close range knocked it out. Everyone praised its speed and agility, but recognized the need for a new cannon-armed vehicle. Gervasio Bitossi, formerly of the *Guide* and the *Reggimento Misto* in Libya, said that it was a first-generation vehicle, not the final design, but a step on the road.[10] Bitossi had commanded the army infantry division in Spain and would soon command an armored division.

The General Staff drew one other lesson from Spain: that the day of the horse was not over. In January 1939 Pariani, *Capo di Stato Maggiore* of the army, directed that studies be undertaken on converting at least one of the *celeri* divisions from its limited motorization to being entirely horse drawn.[11] He gave as a reason that "the news from Spain shows the difficulty of movement when motorized." After due consideration, Pariani directed that the 3rd *Celere* Division exchange its motorized artillery units with the horse-drawn elements of the artillery in the other two *celeri* divisions.[12] This gave Italy one all-horse division for employment in those areas where motor vehicles could not operate. This division later went to Russia and made *L'Ultima Carica*. The Italians had read the lessons of Spain much differently than the Germans.

In 1939 the Italians also considered expanding their armored force by converting the *celeri* divisions to armored divisions.[13] Several studies appeared, but the lack of tanks prevented the conversion of these divisions. The army did prepare for possible expansion of the armored units by requiring all units in the army to submit a list of officers with tank experience or those who would be suitable for assignment to tank units.[14]

The Italian General Staff studied German military organization as well as those of other powers in this period. While the military journals and the military intelligence service published general studies, the armored division staffs undertook special examinations of the foreign armored units to evaluate the Italian organization.[15] They found that the Italian

divisions, although smaller than those of any other country, were capable
of conducting armored operations successfully. They also recognized
that because of "our imperial destiny," Italy would fight in terrain un-
like the mountains of the north.

Beyond that, the study emphasized that the armored division was designed for flanking attacks in a war of maneuver, the *guerra di rapido
corso,* and not for frontal attacks except in the most exceptional cases.
In these frontal attacks, the enemy antitank guns could easily destroy
the tanks, as they would at El Alamein three years later.

When the Germans used flanking movements in the campaign in Poland,
their success provoked immediate interest. By this time (1939) the
Italian army had established a special relationship with the Germans
through exchange officers and an Italian-German military commission
that met periodically to share information. Even before the Polish campaign, the Italians requested information on German armored units. At
the July-August 1939 meeting of the automotive subcommittee, the
Italian members asked for information on tanks and their equipment,
training schools, and the schools' curriculum.[16] The Italians also conducted meetings of this type with the Hungarians, their principal ally in
central Europe. This subcommission exchanged substantial information
about armor. In this case the Hungarians wanted to know all about Italian
armor while the Italians were less interested. With Germany it was the
Italians who were eager and the Germans who were less excited.[17]

After the *blitzkrieg,* in the fall of 1939 and the spring of 1940, the
Italians requested information immediately from the Germans. The
Germans sent an officer, Major Eugenio Midolla, who had participated
in the campaign and also had previously spent three years with the Italian
army. He gave a detailed lecture,[18] emphasizing training, equipment, and
tactics, three things the Italians already had trouble with. He said German
maneuver tactics were similar to the Italian *guerra di rapido corso,* which
they were, in style if not in execution. And the major finished with a
brief discussion of moral factors, especially the importance of aggressive
spirit on the part of the attacker, and the fact that the Poles lacked a
winning spirit.

The information received was of little help to the Italians. They did
indeed believe in a war of maneuver similar to that the Germans had used,
but in the other aspects, the Italians could not hope to approach the
Germans. While the German officer talked of good equipment, well-trained

men, and efficient supply units, the Italians could do nothing; they could not afford these essentials.

The result of these various influences on Italian doctrine were twofold: a new policy on antitank protection and a new emphasis on morale in the armored troops. The new studies on antitank defense recognized that every nation had adopted mechanization to some degree.[19] This meant that armored formations would meet on the battlefield. Drawing heavily on the German experience in Poland rather than the Italian experience in Spain, the authors of the various studies opted understandably for the German ideas of antitank guns well forward. These guns should ideally be self-propelled, and they rather than the tanks themselves should fight the enemy tanks.

Morale had always been an important point in the Italian army. D'Annunzio and Mussolini glorified the spirit of the *bersaglieri* and the *arditi*. Even the studies of foreign armored units emphasized the importance of the moral force of the Italian soldier, which would help him triumph. The new manuals on the operation of the CV 33 series light tanks, first issued seven years after the vehicle, had a page on the moral importance of the commander. He must do everything with audacity and assurance; his moral force will lead the unit to victory. This is one of the continuing examples of the Italian attempt to substitute moral superiority for technical equality.

The Italians could not utilize much of what they learned from Spain and the German campaign in Poland. They already had a tactical and strategic concept of armor employment that was similar to the Germans. The Italian weaknesses in training, equipment, and spirit could not be remedied by observing the actions of another army. The Italians could only try to improve in detail those flaws that were too large to correct.

Continuing the Traditions of Spain

With no changes in doctrine or policy, no major changes occurred in the organization of armored troops in Italy. The changes recommended by various staff studies, such as self-propelled antitank gun units in the armored divisions, could not be carried out for lack of equipment. The only changes directly attributable to Spain involved the transfer of some artillery battalions and the reorganization of the 3rd *Celere* Division into a horse-drawn division already mentioned.

The Italian expedition to Albania caused the only other change in the organization of armored troops in 1939. The *Centauro* armored division deployed to Albania on 21 April.[20] In June the *Littorio* infantry division became the third armored division in the Italian army. The General Staff converted it to fill the gap in the *Corpo d'Armata Corazzata* created by the departure of the *Centauro*.

The *Littorio* had originally been the army division in Spain. There had also been a Fascist militia division. When the Spanish civil war ended the army brought the *Littorio* into the regular establishment to recognize and continue the traditions of the Italian volunteers in Spain. After two months as an infantry division, the *Littorio* became the third armored division, numbered the 133rd, after the 131st and 132nd.[21] The armored regiment assigned to the new division, also numbered 133, had been organized the year before at the same time as the regiments for the first two divisions. Gervasio Bitossi, one of the most experienced Italian armor leaders, continued to command the division, as he had the *Littorio* in Spain.

Despite the increase in the number of armored divisions, the *Littorio* received no new vehicles. The newest tank in the division had been manufactured when Bitossi still commanded the *Guide* in 1935. The CV 35s, as they were now called, were abundant if nothing else. Some had been lost, either in Ethiopia or Spain, and some had been sold to Hungary and other countries, but the majority of the 2,500 produced remained available. They formed the light-tank battalions, while the older Fiats, all manufactured between 1920 and 1930, formed the main striking force, the medium-tank battalions. Yet all the reforms would not improve the chances of Italy in the least without new vehicles.

New Tanks at Last

In 1939, after three years of experimentation, the Italian army finally received its first new tank design since 1933. By the time this, a medium tank armed with a cannon and two machine guns, appeared it was three years behind the designs of other countries. The economic problems of maintaining a mechanized army loomed so large that they obscured the arrival of this new vehicle. The Italian government, in the form of the *Commissione Suprema di Difesa,* had considered the lack of tanks and motor vehicles for the army and discovered that the society as a whole lacked the prerequisite of mechanization so that the army had no place to turn.

The new tank was the Fiat Ansaldo M 11/39, an eleven-ton tank adopted in 1939.[22] Ansaldo designed it to fit a General Staff requirement for a tank to be used in the Carso region north of Trieste, where much of the World War I fighting had occurred. The General Staff expected the Yugoslavs to come through the Carso when they tried to recover the lands formerly controlled by their component groups.

The M 11/39 had a cannon mounted low in the hull and machine guns in the turret. This design presupposed fighting as an infantry vehicle, where the cannon would deal with fortifications while the machine guns in the turret could traverse against troops. This would prevent another Dembeguina Pass. Unfortunately, exactly the same thing had happened to the M 11/39 that happened to the CV 33. They were both designed to deal with a tactical situation that had changed. The Italians now needed a cannon in the turret to deal with moving vehicles.

The failure to produce an adequate tank was a joint failure of the army and industry. Neither took the lead in designing and producing new vehicles. Industry, without the impetus of army orders and specifications, devoted little time to tanks. The army, with an abundance of CV 35 tanks, did not encourage the development of new designs. Although comparisons are difficult because of problems in determining what variations constitute a new and separate vehicle, roughly stated, Italy designed eight new tanks in the interwar period, of which four became first-line equipment.[23] For Britain the figures are twenty-six and nine, United States twenty-eight and five, Germany thirteen and four, and France seventeen designs, of which eight became first-line equipment. While these are not exact comparisons, they do show that Italy designed substantially fewer tanks and accepted more of the designs that were produced than other countries. Her technology in armored fighting vehicles was in consequence well behind that of other countries, while she was ahead in policy. With the introduction (1939) of the new M 11/39, design began immediately on a cannon-armed turret to go on the chassis. Meanwhile the *Commissione Suprema di Difesa* attempted to deal in other ways with the problems of supplying equipment for mechanized war.

The first Italian tank in the field with a turret-mounted cannon was the L 6 light tank introduced in the spring of 1940.[24] Ansaldo had built a number of prototype light tanks on modified CV 35 (Carden-Loyd) chassis.

Figure 19. **Fiat Ansaldo M11/39 (1939) 11 Tons.** M-Medio (Medium). Riveted steel armor. Turret 1 3/16 inch frontal, 1 3/16 inch sides, 9/16 inch deck and floor, 1/4 inch V8 cyl. water-cooled diesel motor. Speed: road 21 mph, cross-country 9mph. Armament: 1 37mm cannon, 2 8mm machine guns. Crew: 3. Ammunition supply: 84 projectiles, 2808 rounds. Scene is Libya in World War II. Note towing cables. *Courtesy of the Historical Office of the Italian Army General Staff.*

Figure 20. Fiat Ansaldo M11/39 Tanks. Before battle in Libya, World War II. Two extra guide wheels are on the rear deck. *Courtesy of the Historical Office of the Italian Army General Staff.*

The main feature was a turret to alleviate the problem of fixed guns. The Italian army had shown little interest in these vehicles during their development and Ansaldo pursued the project with export sales in mind. But in 1940, when the army needed new tanks desperately, the *Commissione* adopted the only available design.

The new light tank (L 6) had a 20-mm cannon and a single machine gun mounted in the turret. These tanks replaced the CV 35s in the *celere* units. As such they were the only Italian tank used in Russia in 1941-43. The old CV 35s went to the armored divisions in Italy and to infantry-support tank units everywhere.

The medium tank with a cannon in the turret, the M 13/40, did not reach the army until late 1940. The production of all these vehicles now fell under the overall direction of the *Commissiarato Generale per la Fabbrica di Guerra.* Under Dallolio, and then after November 1939 under Generale Carlo Favagrossa, his replacement as head of *Fabbriguerra,* this agency allotted materials for tank production and set quotas. It determined that Fiat and Ansaldo could produce a maximum of 150 tanks a month, at full war capacity.[25] This meant that it would take about a month and a half to provide the tanks for one division. That figure combined the production of medium and light tanks, and the later production of proposed heavy tanks and self-propelled guns. At that rate of manufacture it would take a year to reequip the existing tank units, three armored divisions, three *celere* divisions, and three regiments of infantry tanks, without any combat losses. In a war where Italy lost one hundred tanks in a two-day battle, or nearly four hundred in a two-month campaign, the low production capacity of Italian industry doomed mechanized war by Italy from the beginning.

Maneuvers and Landings

The Italian armored divisions were active in training with the armored corps in Italy and in operations in Albania in 1939. These were the last maneuvers before the declaration of war a year later on 10 June 1940. The maneuvers paid particular attention to the training of *Littorio,* although the entire *Corpo d'Armata Corazzato* participated. The corps attacked south from the Po Valley into the Apennines, operating in mountain valleys for most of the maneuvers.

The corps General Staff and the individual commanders agreed on

Figure 21. **Fiat Ansaldo L 6/40.** (Disarmed) probably photographed at the Cavalry School in Pinerolo. *Courtesy of the Historical Office of the Italian Army General Staff.*

Figure 22. **Fiat Ansaldo L6/40 Tanks.** Being landed from ship, Libya World War II. About 44 of this type were used against Russia, 1942-43 by the 67th Battalion, Armored Bersagliere, forming part of the 3rd Division *Celere* (Swift or Fast Division). *Courtesy of the Historical Office of the Italian Army General Staff.*

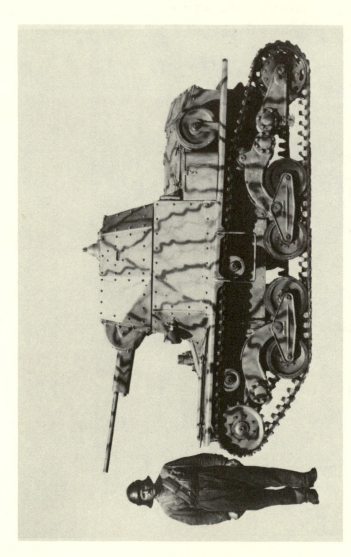

Figure 23. Fiat Ansaldo L6/40 (1940) 6.8 Tons. Riveted steel armor front, 1 3/16 inch rear and sides, 9/16 inch roof and floor, 1/4 inch both body and turret. 4 cyl. water-cooled gasoline motor. Speed: road 26mph, cross-country 10mph. Armament: 1 20mm cannon (or flame-thrower in some models), 1 8mm machine gun all models. Ammunition supply: 296 projectiles, 1560 rounds. Extra guide wheel on left-rear mudguard. *Courtesy of the Historical Office of the Italian Army General Staff.*

most of the problems discovered.[26] The tank battalions, the main striking force of the division, had inadequate power. They desperately needed new tanks and more tanks. Bitossi of the *Littorio* directed his officers to think in terms of the capabilities of the new vehicles rather than those they had to operate with. He also emphasized training, discipline, and the importance of cooperation between the tanks and the infantry. Colonnello Ugo De Lorenzis, commander of the armored regiment in the division, reiterated these points. He emphasized that all other countries were using tank-infantry teams and so the Italians should work on this also.

The maneuvers only reinforced the image of Italian lack of military preparedness that emerged from Spain and the requirements for new vehicles. But significantly, the 1939 maneuvers resulted in the most stringent criticism of vehicles and tactics of any interwar maneuvers. In many cases, the critics, like Bitossi, were Spanish veterans, who were now aware of how unprepared Italy was for the next war, not unprepared in comparison with other nations necessarily but unprepared in absolute terms.

* * * * *

It is difficult to compare Italian armored developments in 1939 and 1940 with those of other countries. All countries were unprepared for the scope of the war they were about to enter, and Italy, a nonbelligerent, was intellectually better prepared than many countries that were materially better equipped. The difference was that Italy was nearly at full capacity in tank development and production while her future enemies had an enormous undeveloped capacity for production.

Britain, France, and Germany were on a full war footing after September 1939 so that their efforts involved an urgency that Italy lacked. Despite this, Britain, for example, had only moved forward a little in the development of armored warfare. In the spring of 1939, the British Territorial Army, the main reserve component, had been doubled. These units mobilized at the beginning of the war and some divisions were quickly converted to armored divisions. However, many of the men were untrained, there were general equipment shortages throughout the army, and insufficient vehicles, so that the new divisions remained largely paper formations. But Britain did quickly and decisively move to convert all her remaining horsed cavalry units to other, more needed roles. France, with a large tank force, did little in the way of increasing or improving equipment or doctrine in the period before the German invasion. Germany, like Britain, was expanding its armored units in this period as fast as the supply of tanks would allow. The United States did convert some horsed cavalry units to the so-called horse-mechanized organization, with armored cars and motor transport for heavy equipment.

Each country was reacting to what it perceived its role to be in the next war. The important consideration would be not what each country had at this specific time, but its potential for increasing the number and quality of its armored and mechanized units.

In the eighteen months before its entry into the Second World War, Italy had tried to implement its policy of mechanization. The boldest and most important step was the adoption of Mussolini's automotive policy in an attempt to motorize Italian society. Mussolini and his ministers correctly understood that it would take a motorized society to support a motorized army. However, even that radical initiative would make only superficial changes in Italian society and not produce the profound changes necessary to revolutionize thinking to the point where Italy could be called a mechanized society. By that time motorized war had been replaced by mechanized war and Italy would require a higher level of mechanical sophistication.

Without even a motorized society to support the army, new vehicles and equipment for a small segment of the army would not be sufficient. The infantry could no longer walk, it must ride on the battlefields of North Africa, even with tank support. Italy's entire fighting force needed to be motorized and, eventually, mechanized. But Mussolini's automotive policy came too late. The Italians would be crippled by too few vehicles and inadequate supplies for mechanized war throughout the Second World War.

Notes

1. See chap. 7 for the role of the *Commissione Suprema di Difesa* in strategic planning.

2. Ministero delle Comunicazioni, *Ordinamento e Compiti della Commissione Suprema di Difesa* (Rome: Istituto Poligrafico dello Stato, 1940) lists members. *Almanacco Italiano, 1939* (Florence: Casa Editrice Marzocco, 1938), p. 335 lists the current holders of those offices.

3. Emilio Canevari, *Italia 1861-1943: Retroscena Della Disfatta* (Rome: Rivista Romana, 1965), vol. 1, p. 364.

4. Commissione Suprema di Difesa, Segretaria Generale, Verbali della XVI Sessione (6-11 February 1939) (Rome, 1939; typescript copy at St. Antony's College, Oxford). "E evidente la necessita di 'motorizzare la Nazione.' "

5. Verbali della XVI Sessione, p. 36.

6. Ministero della Guerra, Gabinetto, XVII Sessione della Commissione Suprema di Difesa (February 1940); Politica Automobilistica in Funzione Militare (argomento no. 6) Relazione di S.E. il Sottosegretario di Stato per la Guerra (typescript copy at St. Antony's College, Oxford).

7. "La politica automobilistica è elemento fondamentale di preparazione bellica."

8. Osservazioni e constatazioni fatte nella Guerra di Spagna, Ten. Col. Augusto d'Amico, 1 February 1939. Microfilm T-821, roll 384, frames 511-12, NA. This group of records belonged to Headquarters, *Armata Po*.

9. *Ibid.*

10. "La Volonta dell'attacco che si fa strada," paper by Bitossi, p. 13, Bitossi Papers.

11. Letter, Pariani to Generale Viscontini and Generale Soddu, 24 January 1939. Racc. 208, U.S.

12. Promemoria per S.E. Il Capo di Stato Maggiore. Subject: Trasformazione divisione celere e alleggerimento dei C.A. normali, 26 January 1939. Racc. 208, U.S.

13. Ispettorato delle Truppe Celeri; Studio per una nuova organizzazione delle truppe celeri, Agosto 1939. In special file for Avvocato Ceva. U.S. Also Trasformazione divisione celere in Divisione Corazzata, November 1939. Microfilm T-821, roll 384, frames 490-91, NA.

14. Letter, Comando del Corpo di Stato Maggiore, 18 July 1939. Subject: Ufficiali per la specialita carrista. Racc. 761, U.S.

15. Umberto Mascia, "Concetti di Tattica Tedesca e Raffronti con La Concezione Italiana a Francese," *Rassegna di Cultura Militare,* August-September 1939, pp. 793-804. Servizio Informazione Militare, *Gran Bretagna-I Reggimenti di Cavalleria Meccanizzata* (Rome, September 1939). Esame comparativo della costituzione organica delle G.U. corazzate presso i principali eserciti europei e dei criteri fondamentali del loro impiego-Colonnello Livio Negro, March 1939. Microfilm T-821, roll 384, frames 296-302, NA. Negro was the commander of the 32° Reggimento Fanteria Carrista, *Ariete* armored Division.

16. Letter, Ufficio Collaborazione S.E. al Gabinetto, 5 September 1939. Subject: Sottocommissione motorizzazione-Berlino guigno-luglio 1939. Racc. 208, U.S.

17. Letter, Ufficio Collaborazione S.E. al Gabinetto, 28 July 1939. Subject: Collaborazione I.U.-Sottocommissione automobilistica. Racc. 208, U.S.

18. Draft copies in Italian and German by Major Eugenio Midolla. Biographical information attached. In file FD 2058/44, Imperial War Museum, London.

19. "Le Grandi Unità Corazzate e La Lotta fra Carri," by Captain Gabriele Verri, *Ariete* Armored Division, August 1939. Microfilm T-821, roll 384, frames 360-74, NA. Carri Contro Carri, by Capitano Gabriele Verri, *Ariete* Armored Division, September 1939. Microfilm T-821, roll 384, frames 375-485.

20. *Memorie Storiche,* Divisione Corazzata *Centauro* 1939.

21. *Memorie Storiche,* Divisione Fanteria/Divisione Corazzata *Littorio* 1939.

22. Pafi, Falessi, and Fiore, *Corazzati Italiani,* 1939-45, pp. 85-86.

23. Chamberlain and Ellis, *Tanks,* each national chapter.

24. *Fronte Terra: Carri Armati 2, Carri Leggeri, parte terza, L. 6/40 sviluppo ed operazioni* (Rome: Edizioni Bizzarri, 1974).

25. Fabbriguerra, Segretaria, Notiziario no. 5, 31 May 1941. File FD 1940/44, Imperial War Museum, London.

26. Comando del Corpo d'Armata Corazzata, Ufficio Stato Maggiore Relazione sulle Grande Escercitazione Anno XVII. Microfilm T-821, roll 384, frames 438-41, NA.

9
New Ideas, Old Tanks

Mechanization had been the official policy of the Italian army for eighteen months when it entered the Second World War. In concrete terms, the Italian army had an armored corps, *Corpo d'Armata Corazzato,* consisting of two armored divisions, *Ariete* and *Littorio,* and two motorized divisions, *Trento* and *Trieste;* a separate armored division, *Centauro;* and three regiments of infantry-support tanks, 1st, 3rd and 4th, consisting of twelve battalions, one battalion for each of the remaining twelve corps in the army. The General Staff had developed this substantial mechanized force, second only to Germany, in the interwar years.

Even as Italy entered the war, the first indication of the impending failure of her military planning appeared. For twenty years the General Staff had planned for a war against Germany and Austria or against Yugoslavia, and the armored force had been created for use in the northern theater that such a war would involve. But Germany was now an ally and within a short time of the declaration of war Yugoslavia was defeated.

As a result, after short campaigns against France, Greece, and Yugoslavia, the army found itself in a protracted war in the Western Desert against the British. Because of the nature of the fighting, all the armored units of the Italian army were engaged there, rather than on the other active front, Russia. In this campaign the armored units suffered the fate of all the other Axis forces in North Africa: repeated defeats, occasional successes, and ultimate surrender.

The cause of this undistinguished record, after the successful development of a policy of mechanization, was the failure to adequately mechanize

the army, occasioned by the unmechanized nature of Italian society.
The Italian army did not mechanize a sufficient proportion of its army
and even those units that were mechanized suffered from inadequate
vehicles, lack of replacements for losses, and lack of supplies.

To provide the industrial base and the manpower for a mechanized
army required a mechanized society and Italy was not such a society. In
comparison with other industrial nations, it did not support the level of
automobile use and production to insure equality with them. In part this
resulted from poor natural resources and the need to import most of the
material needed for the construction and use of cars, trucks, and tractors.
Thus Italy could not produce the kind of army needed to fight a modern
war.

Italy Goes to War

Italy went to war on 10 June 1940. Mussolini decided to enter the war
in emulation of Hitler and his successful campaigns against Poland and
France. In taking this action Il Duce brought Italy into the Second World
War on the side of Germany against Britain and France. This aligned
Italy with a traditional enemy against two of her historic allies and trad-
ing partners, Britain and France, and eventually against a third, the
United States.

The most immediate effect of this change in traditional patterns of
alliance and supply was that Italy's military planning, based for twenty
years on certain assumptions, was now obsolete. Although the Western
allies had become the subject of more concern in the years since the
Ethiopian war, Italy had continued to base much of its planning and procurement on the possibility, or rather the probability, of war along its
Alpine frontiers. Instead Italy was now involved in a war in North Africa,
against Britain and its empire, defending the long Libyan-Egyptian border
and the entire border of Ethiopia, as well as the French Alpine frontier.

The Italian plan for operations in the opening stages of the war had
been limited in scope. The army would conduct defensive operations in
the Alps, in Albania, and in Libya. They would be ready for action against
Yugoslavia, but not initiate it. Only in Italian East Africa would the Italians
begin offensive operations and these would be against French and British
Somaliland, with only a counteroffensive planned against Kenya should
it be necessary. The first European offensive operation would be against

Corsica.[1] The limited operations were planned so as not to strain the army with its antiquated weapons and weak supply system.

A constant theme in reports from General Badoglio, Governor Balbo of Libya, and others was the lack of preparation and material. Yet Mussolini, when he declared war on France and Britain, directed offensive operations be taken against France in the Alps.[2] Soon thereafter, operations against Greece and Egypt began. By the end of 1940, Italian troops were in combat or had been in combat in France, Greece, East Africa, and Egypt. The overextended army won minor victories in French and British Somaliland. On the other fronts, if it had lost battles, with German aid it had won the wars. The armored divisions participated in these campaigns against France, Yugoslavia, and Greece.

The Italian Armored Division in 1940

The armored divisions at the beginning of the war were those created in the fall of 1938 and the spring of 1939. They had undergone little physical or doctrinal change as a result of the German experience in Poland. The only preparation that took place was the mobilization of the divisions to full war strength in May and June 1940.

The *Ariete* and *Littorio* divisions were stationed in the Po Valley, under the *Corpo d'Armata Corazzato*. Their mission would be to secure the Yugoslav border and defend the Po Valley. The *Centauro* remained in Albania, deployed along the Greek border.[3] All three divisions had the same organization and strength. The division headquarters commanded an armored regiment of three battalions, a *bersaglieri* regiment mounted on bicycles and motorcycles, and a motorized artillery regiment. The *Centauro* and *Littorio* were equipped primarily with CV 35 light tanks with a mixture of Fiat model 21 and 30 tanks in the medium-tank battalions; the *Ariete* had received the seventy M 11/39 medium tanks recently manufactured. These made up about a third of the assigned division strength.

The *Littorio* deployed west immediately after the declaration of war and attacked the French through the Piccolo San Bernardo Pass. The French easily stopped the CV 35 (now called L 3) light tanks,[4] but the Vichy armistice came before too many had been destroyed. The *Ariete* moved into reserve behind the front line during this campaign. The Alpine terrain allowed little use of the tanks except as infantry support. In this

SWITZERLAND

GERMANY

Verona
Divisione
Corazzata
"Ariete"

YUGOSLAVIA

Milan

Mantova
Corpo
d'Armata
Corazzata

Parma
Divisione
Corazzata
"Littorio"

FRANCE

*Divisione
Corazzata
"Centauro"
in Albania

Rome

N

Map 4. Location of Italian Armored Units, 1940

close terrain, with a limited maneuver role, heavy casualties were to be expected. The Italian army never penetrated far enough to allow any maneuver by the armored divisions beyond the Alps.

More maneuvering room was available in the next campaign, but the Italians were no more successful in their use of armor. The *Centauro* in Albania attacked Greece on 31 October 1940 and remained in that campaign until its end in April 1941. In the early stages, it had the ten- and twenty-year-old Model 21 and CV 35 tanks, although by this time only the CV 35s were used, as the Fiat model 21s had worn out. As the M 13 medium tank became available, units in Italy trained with the new tanks, then went to Albania to join the *Centauro* division. Arriving on 1 December 1940, the new tanks got their initiation in the battle of Klisura in January 1941.[5] The Greek artillery decimated the M 13s when they were used in a frontal assault.

Despite this setback, the *Centauro* fought through the rest of the campaign and also took part in the Yugoslavian campaign that summer. After the completion of the campaign, the division stayed in Albania until November 1942, when after the battle of El Alamein it moved to North Africa.

After the French campaign the *Ariete* remained in Italy until January 1941, when it deployed to North Africa, the first Italian armored division to do so. It participated in the campaigns there up to the battle of El Alamein. Equipped primarily with the M 13 medium tank, the *Ariete* had several successes against the British, but since the attacks often involved German tanks as well, most are regarded as German victories.

The M 11 tanks initially assigned to the *Ariete* had formed two independent battalions under the 4th *Reggimento Fanteria Carrista* and gone to North Africa in September 1940. These battalions, with their tanks, were lost in the first British counteroffensive there in November and December 1940. The M 11 battalions tried to defend the retreating Italian column in the battle of Beda Fomm, but were handicapped by their weak armament and supply difficulties. They were finally captured when the surviving tanks ran out of fuel. Committed to the defense of a retreating army soon after their arrival in the desert, the M 11 battalions never learned the tactics of the North African campaign. Nevertheless these units, trained to defend northern Italy against the Yugoslavs, made heroic stands at Beda Fomm as well as in earlier battles.

The *Littorio*, which had been reequipped with the M 13s as they became available in the spring of 1941, remained in Italy until the offensive against the Yugoslavs in the summer of 1941. Attacking through the Carso, the *Littorio* penetrated central Yugoslavia and linked up with the *Centauro*. After the defeat of the Yugoslavs (one of the main tasks for which the armored force had been developed) the *Littorio* returned to Italy for training and reequipment.

The *Littorio* attack on Yugoslavia was the single instance of Italian armor being used for the purpose around which twenty years of planning had centered. The Carso, focal point of Italian military fears in the inter-war period, became a sideshow in the Second World War. Even in this, the most successful of Italian armored operations in the Second World War, German successes overshadowed those of Italy. The Italian penetration of Yugoslavia followed the defeat of the main Yugoslav force by the Germans and largely involved the collection of demoralized prisoners who seldom fought their attackers. These divisions had little time to enjoy their victories before they moved to fight a more formidable enemy.

In January 1942 the *Littorio* sailed for North Africa, where it fought in the remaining battles before El Alamein in October 1942. With the arrival of the *Littorio,* the former *Corpo d'Armata Corazzata* had assembled in Africa. The *Ariete* and the two motorized divisions also participated in the North African campaign, although not usually as an armored corps. The corps headquarters personnel also fought in Africa, but again not as an armored corps. In the battle of El Alamein, the two Italian divisions were held back by the German commanders until the German divisions had been so heavily damaged that they were no longer effective. The Italian divisions then made a number of counterattacks against the advancing British but were able to do no better than the Germans.

In the retreat from El Alamein, the remnants of the *Ariete,* the *Littorio,* and the *Centauro* all fought in support of the various Italian infantry formations. They were slowly reduced to detachments and then amalgamated until the last, a *Centauro* combat team, surrendered in the general collapse of Axis resistance. All the vehicles and equipment had been lost. The Italian armored divisions had fought in an armored corps in the desert, although not in the corps that was created in November 1938. Nor did they fight the enemy they had been created to fight. Yet, given the very different conditions of the desert, the Italian armored divisions had done a very creditable job, always remembering the inadequate vehicles with which they had to fight. In the North African campaign Italy had finally achieved a mechanized army, although largely as a result of the destruction of the unmechanized elements of the Italian army in the campaign. Ultimately, this mechanized army lost because of the equipment, supply, manpower, and airpower superiority of the Allies.

In Italy the government attempted to recreate two of the divisions during the summer of 1943. The new *Ariete* became a cavalry armored division, using men from the unemployed cavalry regiments. The new *Centauro* became a legionary armored division, including several Fascist militia units that had not been used in an armored role previously. These two divisions were in part supplied with German equipment. Both were disbanded when the Germans occupied Rome. The *Ariete,* commanded by a son of the Cadorna who had been the *Capo di Stato Maggiore* in the First World War, made a heroic stand on the southern flank of Rome against the Germans when they attacked, but largely without tanks. Even after the lessons of the desert campaign and of the Russian front, the Italian government was barely able to form two new armored divisions using, to a large extent, German vehicles. Italy at this stage of the war could not even provide the manpower and equipment to recreate the limited armored force of the beginning of the war. Tank production, planned at 1,800 a year, had dropped to 667 in 1942 and to 350 in 1943 under Allied bombing and material shortages.[6]

The three *celeri* divisions had much less distinguished wartime careers. One remained in Italy, one occupied various parts of the Balkans, and the third fought in Russia. These divisions and various nondivisional tank companies in Italy and Russia received all the L 6 light tanks, of which about 300 were manufactured.

The record of the armored divisions in the Second World War has often been misread. In the one campaign for which they, and for that matter, the whole Italian army, had really prepared, that against Yugoslavia, the divisions were successful. In the other campaigns the Italians fought for losing causes. The Italian armored divisions were the only mechanized elements of a barely motorized army. They were lost fighting in support of units that were hopelessly out of date on a modern battlefield. It was not the failure of mechanization that doomed the armored divisions, but the political-industrial failure to create at least a motorized army. Italy had neither the industrial base nor the raw materials to be a major power in modern industrial war. Other countries with Italy's

lack of resources, Poland, even France, had collapsed in the first assault.
The only countries with fewer resources than Italy that remained in the
war were those that had the support of a major power. Italy had used
those same Western sources of supply in the First World War but Germany,
her current ally, could not provide equal assistance. This was the political-
industrial failure that prevented the mechanization of the army and led
to the defeat of the Italians.

Mechanization and Motorization

The Italian army accepted motorization in the First World War. Motor
vehicles replaced human or animal power in many uses. Then in the
1930s, after long debate, they realized the profound effect the motor
vehicle could have on the battlefield and adopted mechanization as a
policy. The tank and truck became basic weapons in a strategy of maneuver that transformed warfare. First used in the Italian corps in the Spanish
Civil War, mechanization became official policy in November 1938. Yet
the Italian army was not even motorized in the Second World War. It
lacked vehicles, trained personnel, and support facilities.

The Italian army had seventy-five divisions at the beginning of the
war.   These, in various states of mobilization, were ready by the end of
the year. Of these, three armored divisions and the two motorized divisions of the *Corpo d'Armata Corazzato* were mechanized. Twelve others,
called *autotrasportabili,* could be moved by motor vehicles. This meant
in practice that the artillery had motorized prime movers. Higher headquarters controlled the trucks intended to move these troops, but there
were not enough to move all twelve divisions at once. The remaining
divisions had horse-drawn artillery and there were not even trucks allotted
to transport the troops.

In 1940 the army had seven divisions capable of mechanized warfare
and fifteen capable of motorized warfare; the remaining fifty-three were
essentially nineteenth-century divisions, or certainly not beyond the First
World War, in tactical or strategic concept.

At the armistice in July 1943, after three years of war, the army had
eighty divisions, of which sixty-one were field divisions (the other nineteen were static defense units). Of these, two were armored, one motorized,
thirteen quasi-motorized (7,000 men and 350 vehicles), and three auto-
transportable. The army had increased its strength to sixteen field divi-

sions that were mechanized, four that were motorized, and forty-one that were neither.

Comparing the two sets of figures, the Italians only made a small increase in the total number of divisions capable of being used in modern war. In 1940 they had seven mechanized and fifteen motorized divisions, while in 1943 sixteen mechanized and four motorized divisions existed. Some of the mechanized formations may have actually been without vehicles, however. This was only a marginal increase, especially if compared to the Allies.

Both the United States and Britain had much better records. In 1940 the United States army had two armored divisions. The other six divisions in the active army were in the early stages of motorization (with the exception of the one cavalry division). In 1944, the ninety-division field army the United States had produced contained sixteen armored divisions and at least forty-three motorized divisions. It is difficult to make an exact determination about motorization of the United States divisions since transport was normally held by higher headquarters and assigned as needed. But certainly all those divisions that served in Europe were motorized in the sense of the Italian divisions.

It is more difficult to evaluate motorization in the British army. The British changed the roles of many divisions and disbanded or reorganized others. A similar increase certainly occurred. At the beginning of the war, Britain had two effective armored divisions, one in England and one in Egypt. During the war she formed a total of twelve, although by the time of the Normandy campaign only four remained. If we consider just the campaign in northwestern Europe, three of the twelve British divisions that participated in the entire campaign were armored and the rest were mechanized.

None of these examples can be directly related to the Italian experience. The United States and Britain, for example, had major forces in the Pacific, which could not be motorized, but both were able to mechanize a sufficient portion of their armies for the purpose at hand. The Italians were never able to do this, due as much to failure of truck production as tank production. Given the areas in which Italy was fighting, the Italian army should have been roughly a quarter armored divisions and the remainder at least motorized. That would have meant fifteen armored divisions rather than three.

Initially the Italian army had planned for a very limited defensive war along her Alpine frontier, in which a mechanized army would be of little use. It would have been a war of position with little room for maneuver against the static defense lines in the Alps. But after 1938, the new policy of *la guerra di rapido corso* and changing alliances showed that Italy could expect a war of maneuver, particularly in the desert. But Italy, not having a mechanized society, could not produce a mechanized army.

The Motorization of Italian Society

The ultimate support of army divisions is the society that produced them. How well that society itself was mechanized or motorized is a determining factor in the success of mechanization in any army. The ownership of cars or tractors is a quick way to judge that factor. Tractor ownership was limited in Italy. The small area of flat agricultural land reduced their usefulness, so Italy had only a restricted number in the interwar period; private cars and trucks made up the bulk of motor vehicles. Automotive production figures in a society, and especially the rate of increase, demonstrate industrial capacity. They do not indicate the true degree of mechanization, but these figures can give a sense of the impact of motor vehicles.

In 1939, the last year of peace, most of the countries of the world had motorized to some extent. A substantial portion of society owned motor vehicles for their personal use, and, in urban areas at least, a good portion of commercial motive power for street use was gasoline powered. This was motorization. But in some societies, those of the major industrial powers, the use of the motor vehicle was so extensive that it altered the life of every individual. The car changed their concept of time, speed, and distance. One could now do more in a day, reach distant towns, travel faster over familiar routes. And at some point in this process society became used to this, came to accept, and even expect it. That was when a society became mechanized.

On this point of making a deep and complete change in society's attitude, Mussolini's *politica automobilistica* failed. It attempted superficial changes but failed to understand the changes in attitude and knowledge throughout society that occurred when the motor vehicle became an essential. These changes produced the demand for motor vehicles, mechanics, and drivers that made a mechanized society. Simple doubling the number of vehicles would not produce this revolution.

To judge the mechanization of a society is difficult. The only hard statistic available is vehicles registered. Mussolini, in his *politica auto-mobilistica* speech, said Italy had three hundred thousand cars and to become motorized needed five to six hundred thousand.[7] Italy had roughly one car to each 130 people (although some sources indicate figures as high as one to 112 people).[8] Mussolini spoke of revising that to somewhere between one to 60 or one to 80 people.

But the other powers had ratios several times that of Italy. France, with the same population of forty-two million, already had 1.8 million cars.[9] This was a ratio of one vehicle to 23 people. Even if Italy could have made quick progress on its program, France would still have had three times as many cars. Britain, with a population of forty-eight million, had 1.5 million cars. Germany had 2 million cars and seventy-five million people. Britain thus had a ratio of one to 32 and Germany a ratio of one to 37. But the United States was a leader in mechanization. Out of 42 million vehicles in the world the U.S. had 30 million. For a population of 132 million, this was one car for each 4.4 people.

The figures show that Italy was well behind in the development of an automotive society. It was a gap that could not be made up by the program that Mussolini introduced. Given the basic facts of the Italian economy, especially relating to foreign exchange, it could not be made up without radical changes in political and economic policy. This meant that the process of mechanizing Italian society would be difficult.

As a result, Italian industry could not produce the vehicles necessary for mechanized war. In fact the *Commissiarato Generale per la Fabbrica di Guerra* established 150 as the maximum number of tanks per month that industry could provide.[10] Production would reach this figure in 1941 and remain there indefinitely. Annual production would be 1,800 tanks in a year. Italy never reached this figure because of the bombing of both Ansaldo and Fiat by the Allies. So total Italian production in the Second World War was approximately 2,800 tanks and self-propelled guns using tank chassis.

Italy suffered badly in comparison with other countries in these figures. In 1940, Britain and Germany were roughly equal in tank production.[11] Britain manufactured 1,399 tanks and Germany 1,460. The U.S. produced 331. This was a year when all countries were just beginning to mobilize production. Italy's production at full mobilization was 1,800. Britain reached its peak in 1942, after which American production was so plentiful that Britain could turn to other needs, such as cannon and self-propelled guns. Total British production in 1942 was 8,611. Germany, suffering under increasing bombing, reached her maximum of 9,661 tanks and 8,682 self-propelled guns in 1944.

The United States was the major country in production, just as it had been in ownership of motor vehicles before the war. In 1942, when Italy produced 667 tanks, the United States made 14,000 medium tanks alone. The next year production peaked at 29,497, after which lessening demand reduced the number of new tanks. Besides its own needs the United States supplied Britain, Canada, South Africa, India, and a number of lesser armored powers as well.

The slowness of Italian production also meant that its designs were qualitatively inferior. The designs of the M 11 and its successor, the M 13, were poorly powered and undergunned by the standards of 1941 and 1942. The design of these tanks used available engines and weapons; because of their long gestation period, 1936 to 1939, they fell behind contemporary standards. With the limited production new tanks could not be quickly produced. Germany, the only other possible source of supply, could barely meet its own requirements and only sent Italy a few tanks in 1943 after Italian production had virtually collapsed.[12]

Italy could not hope to have an effective mechanized army without either more production or an ally with production capacity of this type. Mechanized warfare used too many tanks too quickly. Britain lost 150 tanks a day on some occasions. The Italians and Germans lost nearly that each at El Alamein. But the British had the vast American arsenal to supply them, while the Italians only had their own meager production. It was here that the Italian armored units lost the battle, not because of their policy, doctrine, or morale.

* * * * *

Ferrea Mole, Ferreo Cuore

The defeat of the Italian army in the Second World War has obscured the record of achievement in military thought and policy that occurred in the interwar years. The General Staff attempted to create a modern army but failed. Responsibility for this failure has been the army's, since it was the army that failed most visibly. But in the modern world the failure of such an integral part of society cannot be isolated. The Italian defeat in a mechanized war did not result from the lack of intellectual mastery by the General Staff. Rather it resulted from the failure of the army as technical expert and military advocate, the failure of the government as overseer of national needs and planner and enforcer of national policy, and the failure of Italian industry as supplier of national needs.

The army, the most visible of these failures, had responsibility for what it did or failed to do. Through a combination of lack of initiative and lack of money it failed to do a number of things. In its planning, the army lacked imagination and willingness to deal with reality, with the worst possible eventuality. After 1936 the planners should have foreseen the possibility of war beyond the frontiers, against new and more powerful foes. They should have, at least, considered a major war against a European power in Africa and the problems of supply with Britain as an enemy.

No matter who the enemy might be, modern equipment and military preparedness would be important. There again the army failed to do things that it should have done. There was no military impetus for vehicle design. The army did not push industry to produce vehicles or to keep abreast of international developments. No officers took it upon themselves to advocate new designs or push industry for their requirements.

In mitigation of these failures, the army was asked to do a great deal with very little money and support. On the meager funding Italy could afford, the army conducted wars and pacification operations, universal military training, the support of a large political militia, and modernization of a radical nature. None of these was done well as a result. And in such a technical field as mechanization no funds meant no advance.

Additionally, the government made policy decisions that destroyed years of planning without supporting the changes necessary to adjust to new problems. After twenty years of defending the Alpine frontier, the army had difficulty in adjusting to traditional enemies becoming friends.

Despite these hindrances, the Italian army did make substantial achievements in the interwar period. Through continuous study and careful evaluation, the General Staff made several notable policy decisions. The most important, in the context of modern war, was to allow a policy of mechanization. From the decision to mechanize to the declaration of war the General Staff created the organization required for armored warfare.

This organization, the *Corpo d'Armata Corazzato,* with its two armored and two motorized divisions, formed a powerful striking force, theoretically superior to that of Britain or the United States. But the program of training for these troops suffered heavily from financial stringency. Training for a mobile war in the Western Desert on the limited battleground of northern Italy was difficult. Doing it with worn-out World War I tanks and little fuel was nearly impossible. It was not in military thought and execution that the mechanization of the army failed; rather it was in the Italian nation's failure to prepare an army adequate for its defense. In this Italy had two agents, the government and industry.

The government by its policies and financial support determined the type of army Italy would have. In the Fascist era, Mussolini's government did not reflect the direct wishes of the people in the sense of a democracy, but it did reflect the nature of society. Italy, with its limited resources and need for modernization in all aspects of society, did not have the money or the concern to emphasize military preparedness. The army was ill equipped and would be whether national policy had decreed mechanization, motorization, or a marching army. It was not a question of neglecting mechanization but of not being able to afford an army of the size they required, in addition to the other financial burdens the government undertook. The government made its biggest mistake here, in establishing policy.

The first policy failure was in aligning Italy with Germany. Germany could not provide the supplies and the Mediterranean security that Italy needed. Only Britain and her oceanic allies could keep Italy supplied. Italy could only hope to succeed on a limited battlefield, where she could bring the whole of her military might to bear on a narrow front. Overextension, financial and military, could not be counterbalanced by mechanization.

Even within the limited realm of defense policy the government failed to make the right choices. The one imaginative policy, *la politica automobilistica,* was limited and too late. Other policies, like *autarchia,* pursued goals that sounded important without regard for their effect on military preparedness. In a society without a great deal of flexibility, incorrect policies had a profound and long-lasting effect.

The final failure of the government was in dealing with industry. Without firm guidance Italian industry had little inclination to deal aggressively with the problems of mechanization. Because of its very nature, a mechanized army required an active and concerned industry. Despite the special government-industry relation that corporatism claimed to establish, the government failed to effectively direct industrial planning and produc-

tion. Industry for its part failed to initiate any action toward mechanization. In the philosophy of corporatism, the companies had public
responsibilities. No one exercised these responsibilities by proposing
tank designs or developing a realistic military production capacity. Most
firms seemed more interested in maintaining profitable civilian production than in contributing to national preparedness.

The lack of initiative, decisiveness, and determination in the army,
government, and industry meant that mechanization, or any other policy,
would have difficulty in reaching fruition. Taken together with the facts
of Italian society—lack of natural resources, lack of foreign exchange, and
lack of expertise—they meant the defeats that obscured the facts of military thought and policy. In an unmechanized society, lacking in resources
and background, any wavering or weakness in direction and determination
had a major effect. In Italy, the obstacles were insurmountable.

Nonetheless, in *La Dottrina Tattica nella Realizzazione dell'Anno
XVI* and in the creation of the *Corpo d'Armata Corazzato* the Italian
army demonstrated its intellectual awareness of mechanized warfare.
The General Staff, by careful thought, had reached the correct conclu-
sions about the next war. The combination of theoretical experience in
annual maneuvers and staff studies and practical experience in Ethiopia
and Spain had directed them to *la guerra di rapido corso,* modern mechanized war. Unfortunately, in modern war intellectual mastery of innovation in military thought and policy meant nothing without technological
support. And here, national policy, industrial development, and society
had let the army down. The *carristi,* despite their motto, *Ferrea Mole,
Ferreo Cuore,* had no adequate iron skins to go with their iron hearts.

Notes

1. Letter, Badoglio as Capo di Stato Maggiore Generale to Mussolini,
6 April 1940. Subject: Piano di guerra. Copy at St. Antony's College,
Oxford.

2. Letter, Badoglio as Capo di Stato Maggiore Generale to Mussolini,
1 June 1940. Subject: Situazione politica-militare.

3. Many sources cover Italian armor operations. I used Pafi, Falessi,
and Fiore, *Corazzati Italiani,* cross-checking with *L'Esercito e I Suoi
Corpi.*

4. Ugo De Lorenzis, *Dal Primo All'Ultimo Giorno* (Milan: Longanesi,

1971), chap. 3. De Lorenzis commanded the armored regiment of the *Littorio*.

5. Rinaldo Panetta, *Il Ponte di Klisura* (Milano: Mursia, 1975) is by a lieutenant who was there. De Lorenzis, author of *Giorno*, was the regimental commander. See chap. 1.

6. Benussi, *Carri Armati*, p. 14.

7. Italian figures are based on *L'Esercito e I Suoi Corpi*. Allied figures from Liddell Hart, *The Tanks*, vol. 2 and sundry other sources.

8. Verbali della XVI Sessione, p. 36.

9. Sedgwick, *Cars of the 1930's*, p. 220.

10. Car figures from Pugnani, *Motorizzazione Militare*, p. 242. Population from *Almanacco Italiano*, pp. 380-418.

11. Fabbriguerra, Segretaria, Notiziario No. 5. 31 May 1941. File FD 1940/44, Imperial War Museum, London.

12. Ogorkiewicz, *Armoured Forces*, in each national chapter.

Appendix 1
Organization of Italian Armored Forces, 1918–40

1918 (summer)	Reparto speciale di marcia carri d'assalto 1 Schneider tank, 3 Renault FT 17 tanks
1918 (November)	Batteria autonoma carri d'assalto 1 Fiat 2000, 3 Renault FT 17 tanks
1923 (23 January)	Reparto Carri Armati 100 Fiat 3000 (Model 21) tanks[2]
1925	Centro Formazione Carri Armati 100 Fiat 3000 tanks
1927 (1 October)	Reggimento Carri Armati five battalions of 20 tanks each 100 Fiat 3000 tanks
1930	Sezione sperimentale carri veloci 28 CV 29 (Carden Loyd) light tanks
1930 (July)	Sezione Carden Loyd (under Reggimento)[3] 48 CV 29 light tanks
1933 (December)	Reggimento Cavalleggeri Guide becomes training center for cavalry *carri veloci* units 3 battalions of 43 light tanks each 129 CV 33 light tanks
1934	Each cavalry regiment receives one squadron of 15 CV 33 light tanks 165 CV 33 light tanks
1934-1935	Three battalions formed and deployed to Ethiopia 143 CV 35 light tanks

1935	1° Reggimento Misto Motorizzato light tank platoon
	15 CV 35 light tanks
	motor machine-gun unit
	bersaglieri company
	artillery unit
1936 (May)	Reggimento Carri Armati expands
	5 battalons of 25 *carri di rottura* each
	125 Fiat Model 21 and 30 tanks
	19 battalions of 43 light tanks each
	817 CV 35 light tanks
1936 (1 June)	Brigata Motomeccanizzata
	5° Reggimento Bersaglieri
	XXXI Battaglione Carri Veloci
	43 CV 35 light tanks
	Gruppo Leggero Motorizzato (artillery)
1936 (August)	1° Reggimento Fanteria Carrista[4]
	4 battalions of varying composition
	2° Reggimento Fanteria Carrista
	4 battalions of varying composition
	3° Reggimento Fanteria Carrista
	6 battalions of varying composition
	4° Reggimento Fanteria Carrista
	6 battalions of varying composition
1937 (15 July)	1° Brigata Corazzata
	5° Reggimento Bersaglieri
	31° Reggimento Fanteria Carrista
	3 battalions of approximately 90 tanks total[5]
1937 (15 July)	2ª Brigata Corazzata[6]
	3° Reggimento Bersaglieri
	32° Reggimento Fanteria Carrista[7]
	3 battalions of approximately 90 tanks total
1937 (February)	Raggruppamento Carristi, Corpo di Truppa Volontaria
	2 battalions of 43 light tanks each
1938 (November)	Corpo d'Armata Corazzata[8]
	131ª Divisione Corazzata *Centauro*
	132ª Divisione Corazzata *Ariete*
	one regiment each of approximately 140 tanks
	101ª Divisione Motorizzata *Trieste*
	102ª Divisione Motorizzata *Trento*

1939	132^a Divisione Corazzata *Ariete*[9]
	8° Reggimento Bersaglieri
	32° Reggimento Fanteria Carrista
	3 battalions of approximately 140 tanks
	132° Reggimento Artiglieria Corazzata
1939	131^a Divisione Corazzata *Centauro*[10]
(20 April)	5° Reggimento Bersaglieri
	31° Reggimento Fanteria Carrista
	3 battalions of approximately 140 tanks
	131° Reggimento Artiglieria Corazzata
1939	132^a Divisione Corazzata *Littorio*[11]
(June)	12° Reggimento Bersaglieri
	33° Reggimento Fanteria Carrista
	3 battalions of approximately 140 tanks[12]
	133° Reggimento Artiglieria Corazzata

1940
(10 June)   Total strength of armored units in the Italian army on the
declaration of war

   1 armored corps
     2 armored divisions
     2 motorized infantry divisions

   1 separate armored division

   3 separate armored regiments each of 5 battalions

   2 separate battalions in Libya

   3 groups (battalions) of cavalry light tanks attached to
celere divisions

Notes

1. This chronological list is based on the best available information. It is designed to show the general development of armor in Italy and not to be a definitive list of units and their strengths. Number of vehicles in particular is extremely difficult to determine and all figures should be treated as best estimates.

2. At this time 105 Fiat 3000 tanks, 2 Fiat 2000 tanks, and 3 or more Renaults existed. The other vehicles may have been used for testing.

3. Unless otherwise noted, all units listed are separate organizations, under corps or army headquarters.

4. These regiments were produced by reorganization of the Reggimento

Carri Armati, which disbanded on formation of the 3º Reggimento Fanteria Carrista.

5. The strengths of the armor regiments in the brigades is difficult to determine. Nominally they had two battalions of Fiat Model 21/30 tanks (twenty-five each) and one of CV 35 light tanks (forty-three), for a rough total of ninety-three, but figures as low as twenty tanks total appear in some reports. This brigade was an expansion of the Brigata Motomeccanizzata.

6. The second brigade was a cadre unit, with only a staff active until the fall of 1938.

7. The 32º Reggimento was formed by reorganizing and redesignating the 2º Reggimento.

8. The corps headquarters was formed and a commander appointed in November, although only the two motorized divisions and the armored brigades existed at that time.

9. *Ariete* was formed by the expansion of the 2ª Brigata Corazzata.

10. *Centauro* was formed by the expansion of the 1ª Brigata Corazzata.

11. *Littorio* was formed by the conversion of the *Littorio* Infantry Division, a continuation of the army elements in the Corpo di Truppa Volontaria.

12. The exact strength of the armored regiments in 1939 and 1940 is difficult to determine. The advanced age of the Fiat Model 21/30 tanks meant the regiments often had three battalions of 43 CV 35 light tanks instead of 2 of Fiats and 1 or 2 of CV 35s. In that case there were 129 CV 35s in the battalions plus 10 in headquarters, for an approximate total of 140 tanks. *Centauro* had 4 battalions of CV 35s in June 1940, for roughly 180 tanks, but at the same time *Ariete* had only 2 battalions of CV 35s and two battalions converting to the new M 11/39, of which there were only 70 produced.

Appendix 2
Italian Tanks Used between the Wars

1917   Fiat 2000 heavy tank
        Weight—38,780 kilograms (40 tons)
        Speed—7.5 kilometers per hour (4.5 mph)
        Armament—1 65-mm cannon, 7 machine guns
        Number produced—2

1921   Fiat 3000 (Model 1921) light tank (used as a medium tank by
        the Italians, especially after the introduction of the CV 33
        light tank)
        Weight—5,500 kilograms (5.5 tons)
        Speed—18 kilometers per hour (13 mph)
        Armament—2 machine guns
        Number produced—5 preproduction; 100 production

1929   Carro Veloce 29 light tank (Carden Loyd machine-gun carrier)
        Weight—1,500 kilograms (1.7 tons)
        Speed—50 kilometers per hour (24 mph)
        Armament—1 machine gun
        Number produced—4 purchased from Britain; 24 built in Italy

1930   Fiat 3000B (Model 1930) light tank (Carro di rottura)
        Weight—5,900 kilograms (6 tons)
        Speed—21 kilometers per hour (15 mph)
        Armament—1 37-mm cannon
        Number produced—48

1933   Fiat Ansaldo Carro Veloce 33 light tank
        Weight—3,200 kilograms (3.1 tons)
        Speed—38 kilometers per hour (26 mph)
        Armament—1 machine gun
        Number produced—5 preproduction; 25 production

1935   Fiat Ansaldo Carro Veloce 35 light tank (modification of the
        CV 33)
        Weight—3,435 kilograms (3.2 tons)
        Speed—42 kilometers per hour (28 mph)
        Armament—2 machine guns
        Number produced—2500

1939   Fiat Ansaldo M 11/39 medium tank
        Weight—10,970 kilograms (11 tons)
        Speed—33.9 kilometers per hour (21 mph)
        Armament—1 37-mm cannon, 2 machine guns
        Number produced—3 preproduction; 70 production

1940   Fiat Ansaldo L 6/40 light tank
        Weight—6,700 kilograms (6.8 tons)
        Speed—42.3 kilometers per hour (26 mph)
        Armament—1 20-mm cannon, 1 machine gun
        Number produced—4 preproduction; 283 production (through
        1943)

NOTE

   There were eight individual experimental tanks constructed in the period 1936-38.
Three were developmental stages of the M 11/39 and four of the L 6/40. The remaining vehicle, a turreted version of the CV 35, was not proceeded with.

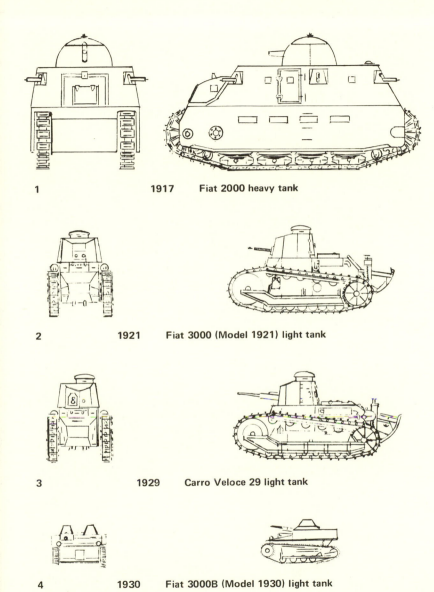

1   1917   **Fiat 2000 heavy tank**

2   1921   **Fiat 3000 (Model 1921) light tank**

3   1929   **Carro Veloce 29 light tank**

4   1930   **Fiat 3000B (Model 1930) light tank**

Figure 24. Line Drawings of Italian Army Tanks 1917-40. Prepared by John J. T. Sweet.

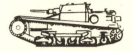

5   1933   Fiat Ansaldo Carro Veloce 33 light tank

 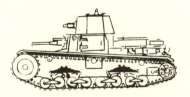

6   1935   Fiat Ansaldo Carro Veloce 35 light tank

 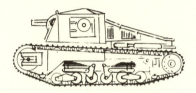

7   1939   Fiat Ansaldo M 11/39 medium tank

 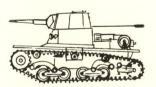

8   1940   Fiat Ansaldo L 6/40 light tank

Bibliography

I. Manuals and Published Military Documents

Ispettorato Truppe Celeri. *Addestramento ed Impiego dei Carri Veloci.* Rome: Istituto Poligrafico dello Stato, Libreria, 1936.

Ministero delle Comunicazioni. *Ordinamento e compiti della Commissione Suprema di Difesa.* Rome: Istituto Poligrafico dello Stato, Libreria, 1940.

Ministero della Guerra. *Direttive per L'Impiego delle Grandi Unità.* Rome: Istituto Poligrafico dello Stato, Libreria, 1935.

Ministero della Guerra. *La Dottrina Tattica nella Realizzazione dell'Anno XVI.* Rome, 1938.

Ministero della Guerra. *Norme per il Combattimento della Divisione.* Rome: Istituto Poligrafico dello Stato, Libreria, 1936.

Ministero della Guerra. *Norme per L'Impiego Tattico della Divisione. Edizione 1928.* Rome: Provveditorato Generale dello Stato, Libreria, 1928.

Ministero della Guerra. *Relazione Sull'Attivita Svolto per L'Esigenza A.O.* Rome: Istituto Poligrafico dello Stato, Libreria, 1936.

Ministero della Guerra. *Volontari dell'Esercito nella Guerra di Spagna.* Milan: Tipo Litografia Turati Lombardi e C., 1939.

Ministero della Guerra. Centro Studio Motorizzazione. *Caratteristiche Mezzi da Combattimento in Uso nel'Esercito Italiano.* Rome, 1943.

Ministero della Guerra. Gabinetto. *Norme per L'Impiego delle Unità Carriste.* Rome: Tipografia del Comando del Corpo di Stato Maggiore, 1936.

Ministero della Guerra. Ispettorato Generale Leva Sottufficiale e Truppa. *Istruzione per la Compilazione delle Memorie Storiche dei Corpi. Ed. 1939.* Rome: Istituto Poligrafico dello Stato, Libreria, 1939.

Ministero della Guerra. Comando del Corpo di Stato Maggiore. *Addestramento delle Unità Carri Armati, Mod. 1921-1930.* Rome: Istituto Poligrafico dello Stato, Libreria, 1931.

Ministero della Guerra. Comando del Corpo di Stato Maggiore. *Istruzione Provvisoria Sui Carri Armati Veloci.* Rome: Istituto Poligrafico dello Stato, Libreria, 1931.

Ministero della Guerra. Comando del Corpo di Stato Maggiore. Ufficio Addestramento. *Addaestramento Tratti dalle Grande Esercitazioni Sull'Appennino Tosco-Emiliano del 1934. Circolare N. 7500.* Rome, 1935.

Ministero della Guerra. Comando del Corpo di Stato Maggiore. Ufficio Addestramento. *Impiego delle Unità Carriste.* Rome: Istituto Poligrafico dello Stato, Libreria, 1938.

Ministero della Guerra. Comando del Corpo di Stato Maggiore. Ufficio Addestramento. *Impiego ed Addestramento Carri d'Assalto, Circolare 105000.* Rome: Tipografia del Comando del Corpo di Stato Maggiore, 1936.

Reggimento Cavalleggeri Guide, Centro Addestramento Carri Veloci. *Addestramento dei Carri Veloci.* Parma, 1934.

Regia Accademia Aeronautica. *Sommario di Arte Militare.* Prepared by LTC. Gian Giacomo Castagna. 2 vols. Leghorn: S. Belforte & Co., 1927.

Reparto Carri Armati. *Addestramento delle Unità Carriste, Parte Terza, Addestramento e Impiego Tattico (Stralcio di Regolmento Provvisoria).* Rome: Libreria dello Stato Maggiore, 1925.

Scuole Centrali Militari. *I Carri Armati, Traccia di Conferenza per i Corsi Informativi.* Civitavecchia: Premiato Stab. Tip. "Moderna" di Remo Coltellacci, 1924.

Servizio Informazione Militare. *Gran Bretagna-I Reggimenti di Cavalleria Meccanizzato.* Rome, 1936.

II. Contemporary Italian Books and Articles on Armor Policy, Doctrine, and Equipment, 1920-40

Almanacco delle Forze Armate 1927. Rome: Tipografia del Senato, 1927.

Barbato, Domenico. "Una Compagnia di Carri Armati nell'Attacco di un Battaglione di Fanteria." *Esercito e Nazione,* June 1930, pp. 533-40.

Bastico, Ettore. *L'Evoluzione dell'Arte della Guerra.* 3 vols. Florence: Carpigiani e Zipoli Editori, 1924-27.

Berardi, Paolo. "Della Brigata Corazzata o Divisione che dir si voglia." *Rivista di Fanteria,* anno 5, no. 5, May 1938, pp. 213-18.

del Mauro, Luigi. "Fanteria Carrista." *Nazione Militare,* August-September 1936, pp. 581-84.

Di Simone, Carlo. "Conviene Trasformare la Brigata Corazzata in Divisione Corazzata." *Rivista di Fanteria,* anno 5, no. 2, February 1938, pp. 79-88.

Enciclopedia Militare, s.v. 6 vols. Milan: Il Popolo d'Italia, 1927-33.

Gabrielli, Manlio. *I Carri Armati.* Rome: Tipografica delle Cartiere Centrali, 1923.

Mascia, Umberto. "Concetti di Tattica Tedesca e Raffronti con La Concezione Italiana e Francese." *Rassegna di Cultura Militare,* August-September, 1939, pp. 793-804.

Pelosio, G. Battista. "Sistemazione Difensiva Centro Carri Armati." *Esercito e Nazione,* January 1931, pp. 36-40.

Visconti Prasca, Sebastiano. *La Guerra Decisiva.* Milano: Arti Grafiche D. Grossi, 1934.

Pugnani, Angelo. *La Motorizzazione dell'Esercito e la Conquista dell'*

Quarra, Edoardo. "In tema di Grandi Unità Corazzate." *Revista di Fanteria,* anno 5, no. 1, January 1938, pp. 1-10.

Versi, Edoardo. *I Carri d'Assalto.* Parma: Tipografie Riunite Donati, 1927.

Visconti Prasca, Sebastiano. *La Guerra Decisiva.* Milano: Arti Grafiche D. Grossi, 1934.

Zoppi, Generale Ottavio. *I Celeri.* Bologna: Nicola Zanichelli Editore, 1933.

III. Italian Military and Economic History

Almanacco Italiano, 1939. Florence: Casa Editrice Marzocco, 1938.

Arena, Nino. *I Paracadutisti.* Modena: Stem Mucchi, 1972.

Beehler, Commander W. H. *The History of the Italian-Turkish War.* Annapolis, Md.: privately printed, 1913.

Benussi, Giulio. *Autocannoni, Autoblinde a Veicoli Speciali del Regio Esercito Italiane nella Prima Guerra Mondiale.* Milan: Integest, 1973.

Benussi, Giulio. *Carri Armati e Autoblindate del Regio Esercito Italiana, 1918-1943.* Milan: Integest, 1974.

Campini, Dino. *Nei Giardini Del Diavolo.* Milan: Longanesi, 1969.

Canevari, Emilio. *Italia 1861-1943: Retroscena Della Disfatta.* 2 vols. Rome: Rivista Romana, 1965.

Carri Armati: Carri Leggeri. Vol. 2 of *Fronte Terra*. Rome: Edizioni Bizzari, 1973.

Carri Armati in Servizio fra le Due Guerre. Rome: Edizioni Bizzarri, 1972.

Castronovo, Valerio. *Giovanni Agnelli*. Turin: Unione Tipografico-Editrice Torinese, 1971.

Catalano, F. *L'Economia Italiana di Guerra 1935-1943*. Florence: Istituto Nazionale per la Storia del Movimento di Liberazione, 1969.

Clough, Shepard B. *The Economic History of Modern Italy*. New York: Columbia University Press, 1964.

Conforti, Olao. *Guadalajara*. Milan: Mursia, 1967.

Coverdale, John F. *Italian Intervention in the Spanish Civil War*. Princeton, N.J.: Princeton University Press, 1976.

deBiase, Carlo. *L'Aquila d'Oro*. Milan: Edizioni del Borghese, 1970.

de Lorenzis, Ugo. *Dal Primo All'Ultimo Giorno*. Milan: Longanesi, 1971.

Falls, Cyril. *The Battle of Caporetto*. New York: Lippincott, 1966.

"Fiat," A Fifty Years' Record. Verona: Arnoldo Mondadori Editore, 1951.

Gazzo, Emanuele. *I Cento Anni dell'Ansaldo 1853-1953*. Genoa: Ansaldo, 1953.

Kalla-Bishop, P. M. *Italian Railroads*. New York: Drake, 1972.

Lami, Lucio. *Isbuschenskij: L'Ultima Carica*. Milan: Mursia, 1971.

Mack Smith, Denis. *Italy, A Modern History*. Ann Arbor: University of Michigan Press, 1959.

Mazzetti, Massimo. *La Politica Militare Italiana fra le Due Guerre Mondiali (1918-1940)*. Salerno: Edizioni Beta, 1974.

Morandi, Rodolfo. *Storia della Grande Industria in Italia*. 1931. Reprint. Turin: Einaudi, 1959.

Mosna, Ezio. *Storia Delle Truppe Alpine D'Italia*. Trento: Il Musio Storico Nazionale degli Alpini, n.d.

Pafi, Benedetto; Falessi, Cesare; and Fiore, Goffredo. *Corazzati Italiani 1939-1945*. Rome: D'Anna Editore, 1968.

Pugnani, Angelo. *Storia della Motorizzazione Militare Italiana*. Turin: Roggero e Tortia, 1951.

Puletti, Rodolfo. *Caricat*. Bologna: Edizioni Capitol, 1973.

Rochat, Giorgio. *Militari e Politici nella preparazione della Campagna d'Etiopia*. Milan: F. Angeli, 1971.

Roggiani, Fermo. *Storia Dei Bersaglieri d'Italia*. Milan: Cavallotti Editori, 1973.

Sarti, Roland. *Fascism and the Industrial Leadership in Italy*. Berkeley: University of California, 1971.

Smyth, Howard McGaw. "The Command of the Italian Armed Forces
    in World War II." *Military Affairs,* vol. 15, no. 1, Spring 1951.
Tosti, Amedeo. *Storia dell'Esercito Italiano.* n.p.: Istituto per Gli Studi
    di Politica Internazionale, 1936.
Ufficio Storico, Stato Maggiore dell'Esercito. *L'Esercito e I Suoi Corpi.*
    2 vols. Rome: Ministero della Difesa, 1971.
Ufficio Storico, Stato Maggiore dell'Esercito. *L'Esercito tra la 1ª e la 2ª
    Guerra Mondiale.* Rome: Ministero della Difesa, 1954.

IV. Other Secondary Sources

Addington, Larry. *The German General Staff and the Blitzkrieg Era.*
    New Brunswick, N.J.: Rutgers University Press, 1971.
Bryand, Arthur. *Jackets of Green.* London: Collins, 1972.
Chamberlain, Peter and Gander, Terry. *Anti-Tank Weapons.* London:
    MacDonalds and Jane's, 1974.
Chamberlain, Peter and Ellis, Chris. *Pictorial History of Tanks of the
    World 1915-1945.* Harrisburg, Pa.: Stackpole Books, 1972.
Gillie, Mildred Hanson. *Forging the Thunderbolt.* Harrisburg, Pa.:
    Military Service Publishing, 1947.
Higham, Robin. *Air Power.* New York: St. Martin's Press, 1972.
Higham, Robin. *Military Intellectuals in Britain, 1918-1939.* New Bruns-
    wick, N.J.: Rutgers University Press, 1966.
Liddell Hart, B.H. *Paris or the Future of War.* New York: Dutton, 1925.
Liddell Hart, B.H. *Strategy.* New York: Praeger, 1967.
Liddell Hart, B.H. *The Tanks.* 2 vols. London: Cassell, 1959.
Luvaas, Jay. *The Education of an Army.* Chicago: University of Chicago
    Press, 1964.
Macksey, Kenneth. *Armoured Crusader.* London: Hutchinson, 1967.
Nolte, Ernst. *Three Faces of Fascism.* New York: Mentor Books, 1969.
Ogorkiewicz, Richard. *Armoured Forces.* 1960. Reprint. New York:
    Arco, 1970.
Ropp, Theodore. *War in the Modern World.* New York: Collier, 1962.
Shepard, Michael. *Cars of the 1930's.* London: Batsford, 1970.
Thomas, Hugh. *The Spanish Civil War.* New York: Harper and Row, 1963.
Wright, John. *Libya.* New York: Praeger, 1969.
Younghusband, G. J. *The Queen's Commission.* London: John Murray,
    1891.
Zook, David H., Jr., and Higham, Robin. *A Short History of Warfare.*
    New York: Twayne Publishers, 1966.

Index

Index prepared by John J. Vander Velde, special projects librarian and editorial consultant, Kansas State University Library.

About the Author

John J. T. ("Tim") Sweet, a native of San Francisco, California, graduated from Berkeley high school in 1961. He then did undergraduate work at the University of California at Davis, where he came under the tutelage of Captain Sir Basil Liddell Hart and Professor Peter Paret, graduating in 1966. After another year in graduate school there, he was commissioned in the U.S. Army as a second lieutenant in military intelligence and eventually spent a year in Vietnam as an imagery interpretation section leader before returning to a similar post at Fort Bragg, North Carolina. In September 1970 he left the active army and joined the reserves. At the same time he enrolled in the MA program at San Jose State University, from which eventually emerged his first book, *Mounting the Threat* (1976) on the British campaign in Normandy. After receiving his MA, he enrolled in the doctoral program at Kansas State University, receiving his degree in 1976. On 12 March 1978 Major Sweet was killed in an air crash in Arizona while on active duty once again with the U.S. Army.